Nancy Astor

Nancy Astor

A BIOGRAPHY

Anthony Masters

McGRAW-HILL BOOK COMPANY

NEW YORK   ST. LOUIS   SAN FRANCISCO

First published in England, 1981,
by Weidenfeld and Nicolson,
91 Clapham High Street, London SW4

1 2 3 4 5 6 7 8 9 D O D O 8 7 6 5 4 3 2 1

LIBRARY OF CONGRESS CATALOGING IN PUBLICATION DATA

Masters, Anthony, 1940–
Nancy Astor, a biography
Biography: p.
Includes index.
1. Astor, Nancy Witcher Langhorne, Viscountess.
2. Great Britain—Nobility—Biography. 3. Politi-
cians—Great Britain—Biography. I. Title.
DA574.A8M37   1981   941.082'092'4 [B]   80-21615
ISBN 0-07-040784-3

To Johnnie

ACKNOWLEDGEMENTS

I would like to acknowledge with gratitude the permission of A.D. Peters to quote extracts from Christopher Sykes' *Nancy: the Life of Lady Astor*, to John Murray for extracts from *Tribal Feeling* by Michael Astor, to Jonathan Cape and the letters of T. E. Lawrence Trust for published and unpublished letters from T. E. Lawrence to Nancy Astor and Lionel Curtis, to Cassell for extracts from *Rose: My life in Service* by Rosina Harrison, to the Trustees of the late Nancy Astor for letters from the Astor archive at Reading University, to *John Bull* for Horatio Bottomley's article and to Louise Collis for extracts from *Nancy Astor* by Maurice Collis.

ILLUSTRATIONS

CARTOONS

CONTENTS

Prologue

'Drink is the ruin of the world.'

As the old lady castigated the surrounding company she held a Dubonnet in her hand! All the Cliveden guests who were about to imbibe enthusiastically before dinner hesitated. Did she mean what she said? Or was she joking? If she meant what she said, then why was she drinking herself? Or was the glass part of the joke? A mysterious joke. These and other uneasy questions flooded the minds of the guests as they stared rigidly at each other in the great country house library. Then the old lady's son appeared and reassuringly put their world of etiquette to rights. Calmly, collectedly, Lord Astor offered round the drinks.

Later, over dinner, the majority of the guests still wondered. Some thought Lord Astor's mother senile. Others thought her a tyrannical hypocrite. Some vaguely imagined that she was attempting a joke – that she was playing the role of a 'character'. A few, who knew Nancy Astor better, took the comment for what it was. She had meant it. And yet, in old age, she had started to drink alcohol. She drank in relatively small quantities – yet she drank. She also said 'Drink is the ruin of the world' – and meant it.

This inconsistency was typical of Nancy Astor. Throughout her life she spoke as she felt, no matter in whose company she was and regardless of diplomacy. Quite often she was gloriously and unconsciously inconsistent. But she didn't give a damn. .

Neither did she give a damn in her son's house, that sumptuous mansion where she had once been the political hostess of her generation. The table had echoed to the conversation of

1

statesmen, politicians, writers, the aristocracy and as many socialites as could get themselves invited. Her Christian Science friends had been silent watchers at the feast, unable to commit themselves safely to anyone but Mrs Nelson Eddy, her writings and their ramifications. Now, paying lip-service to her son William as Viscount and Master of Cliveden, Nancy Astor was no longer in charge. She lived in Eaton Square, a far cry from the Cliveden that her husband, Waldorf Astor, had inherited. She had become an irascible old lady, a shadow of her former self. Nevertheless, that shadow still retained something of Nancy Astor in her prime. There was still the echo of that vigorous, compulsive worker and talker whose heart, while in many places at once, often remained locked in her own subjective, rather idiosyncratic world.

Now she sat, a querulous, maddeningly eccentric disturbance at dinner. But she was also much loved, respected for her vivacity and the vibrance of her personality. She was respected too, for her social rights campaigns, despite their inconsistencies.

'You're drinking far too much.'

Nancy Astor directs her remark to an unknown young woman across the table who is lifting only her first glass of wine to her lips. Desperately the young woman affects not to hear. Mercifully, the old lady turns to somebody else, her grasshopper mind seizing on another topic. In her old age she is still beautiful. In her old age she is a personality. But despite this, she knows that she is no longer listened to. She has lost her influence and she is out of her time. Death and tragedy have stalked her life and now she is worn out, spinning her last years into a web of misery.

I

❧

The Virginian

Nancy Witcher Langhorne was born in Danville, Virginia, on the 19 May 1879. She was the seventh of a family of eleven, three of whom had died in infancy. Her father was Chiswell Dabney Langhorne and her mother was Nancy Witcher Keene. Nancy was born at a time when Chiswell (universally known as Chillie) was slowly hauling himself out of the mire into which the Civil War had thrown him. Originally from a well-to-do farming family, Chillie had lost almost everything during the war. Angus McDonnell, one of Nancy's closest friends, wrote:

> 'Mr Langhorne told me that when he got back to Lynchburg, after the war, there was nothing left of the old life; the countryside was decimated; there was practically no stock of any kind on the farms, neither horses, mules, cattle or sheep; they were using parched corn for coffee, if they could get it, and it was quite a while before the neighbourhood could get together enough money as a joint effort to buy a team and wagon to send to Illinois by road, to buy salt for the community.'

But Chillie was an entrepreneur of the old tradition. As he rather wildly told McDonnell, 'I had nothing but a wife, two children, a ragged seat to my pants and a barrel of whisky.'

With this foundation Chillie went into action. His main weapon was charisma, something that his daughter Nancy inherited from him. He was readily able to influence others and it was this that set him once more on the road to good fortune. Also, one last bastion of the Langhorne empire remained – a flour-mill in Lynchburg which a providential aunt had rescued

3

from the maelstrom. But this alone would not give Chillie's large family an income. So he progressed – and it was a startlingly quick progression – from a nightwatchman to a travelling salesman and from a salesman to a tobacco auctioneer. This occupation ideally suited Chillie's extrovert talents and he specialised in fairground patter which was so fast and so incomprehensible that he drew crowds for his jargon alone. The auctions were known as 'tobacco breaks' and there were a number of auctioneers, each of whom stood amidst a pile of tobacco on the warehouse floor.

Chillie, however, was far from content with this as a living and he supplemented his tobacco with other products. These were very diverse and included wheelbarrows, farm implements and various items of furniture. To add a touch of razzamatazz, Chillie hired a barrel organ and a Negro to grind it. Directly the tobacco had been auctioned, the barrel organ would begin to play and, with considerable panache, Chillie would draw the attention of his clients to other wares.

Nancy's mother was a very different personality. She was an extremely beautiful woman and according to her daughter's autobiographical draft '. . . her great charm was her gaiety and her goodness. I dare say goodness and gaiety were not found together any more often then than they are now.' She goes on to point out that 'one way and another she must have had quite a time with father.' Of Irish descent, Nancy's mother had met Chillie in Danville. The Keenes and the Langhornes were neighbours and she married Chillie when he was twenty-two and she was seventeen. Always dominant and often bad-tempered, Chillie represented all the usual traits of male chauvinism of the times. Although Nancy's mother was quick to answer back and had a cynical attitude to Chillie's charm, she was more forbearing than was good for her. She indulged Chillie's personality and allowed her own personality to be diminished. In her draft autobiography, Nancy makes an extraordinary comment about her seemingly loving mother. She writes: 'Mother never wanted any children. She had eleven, all unwanted, and not one of us has ever suffered the slightest frustration on that account. I was the seventh unwanted child.' Although there is no evidence to support the fact that I think Nancy subjective in this assessment, I feel she was. She was extremely frightened and even revolted by sexual intercourse, and it is possible that she wanted her mother to share her feelings.

Five of the Langhornes' eight surviving children were girls and three were boys. Lizzie was the eldest daughter and probably the least well-known. She eventually married quietly and took no part in New York social life. One of Nancy's sons, Michael Astor, writes in his book *Tribal Feeling*: 'She married before the Langhorne family had properly found its feet and as a result of this, as her younger sisters grew up, she came to feel that she had been deprived of partaking in the pleasure of a more exciting world than the one that the neighbourhood provided, a more cosmopolitan world in which her younger sisters were enjoying a wild success.'

Irene was the Langhornes' second daughter and became very celebrated. She eventually married Charles Dana Gibson. Gibson was an artist, famous for creating the 'Gibson girl'. This prototype was meant to represent all that was best in young American womanhood – a wasp waist, an elegant shape, a swan neck, a large bust and a look that combined pride with seduction. So, unlike the overshadowed Lizzie, Irene became the toast of New York. Nancy was the third daughter. She had positive, aquiline features which, according to Michael Astor 'conveyed a feeling of vitality and strength, also revealed an epicene quality that was not evident in any of her sisters.' Next came Phyllis and then Nora, who was the most romantic. She was to fall continuously in and out of love and at one point was in the embarrassing position of being engaged to two men at once – and quite unable to make up her mind about who she loved most.

The Langhorne boys lacked their sisters' sparkle. The older two, Keene and Harry, were intelligent, talented but idle and prone to bouts of drinking. This was no doubt the first of many trigger points to Nancy's life-time aversion to alcohol. The youngest son, Buck, was easy-going, unambitious and unassuming, later becoming a kindly country squire.

Chillie's career took a turn for the better in 1879 (the year of Nancy's birth) when he went into partnership with a man called Liggett. Together they began a trading company which soon became involved in the railway boom. Now the Southern slaves had been freed they were in no mood to work but Chillie had enough charm and guile to convince them that they were on to a good thing. Chillie and Liggett made bids for contracts and subcontracted the work out to young engineers who knew what they were doing. The workforce had to be marshalled and this is where Chillie was at his administrative best. The partnership succeeded with the first contract; investments were made in further equipment and other contracts in the engineering field were won.

In 1885 the partnership was dissolved and Chillie took the family away from Danville to Richmond, Virginia's state capital. This was a grave mistake for, unlike Danville, Richmond was full of railway contractors who were much more experienced than Chillie could ever be. Now he was such a little fish, Chillie was reduced to becoming a tobacco auctioneer again and the family was forced to move away from the middle-class district into which they had settled and set up residence in a much poorer quarter. Worse was to come, however, for the auctioneering could not possibly keep such a large family. In desperation arrangements were made for Chillie to stay in Richmond and continue to chance his arm, while the rest of the family moved to Albemarle County in Western Virginia, where they would lodge with a cousin. All their servants would have to be dismissed and the entire family was sunk in gloom. Then, just as they were moving out, Chillie met Colonel Douglas.

Because of his hard-talking, persuasive powers, Chillie managed to influence Colonel Douglas, a Northerner, who had bought the concession to build the Virginian railway. Douglas had not the faintest idea how to hire or acquire Negro labour. This was a subject that Chillie knew something about and it was perfectly logical that he should offer his administrative services to the Colonel in this project. With steely calm and ringing confidence, Chillie assured the naive Colonel Douglas that there was nothing he did not know about building and contracting railways. Impressed by this bombastic, garrulous man, the Colonel had a hunch that Chillie represented a special kind of Southern magic which would work. His hunch proved correct. Chillie made a success out of the contracting and as a result began to lay the foundations of his second fortune.

The family was able to remain in Richmond and a greater stability was achieved. Nancy was now six and the family had moved three times – from reasonably prosperous Main Street to downbeat Third Street and now to salubrious Grace Street. Although the turbulent early Richmond period was over in a comparatively short time, Nancy must have been influenced by the traumatic lifestyle of her parents. She must also have been influenced by the very different personalities of her parents. Her mother's high spirits and her cynical tolerance of her husband's domination and her father's tyrannical, self-indulgent yet loving nature. All the children, regardless of their sex, called him 'Sir' and on Sundays he would take them for walks, treating them as adults.

With the improvement in the family's finances came an improvement in their social standing. Richmond was primitive but 'County'. The streets were unpaved and gaslit, the telephone a rich man's toy and the only means of transport were streetcars and horse or mule-drawn carts. Church was important as a place to be 'seen' at and servants re-entered the lives of the Langhornes – not that they had long been absent.

Nancy was by no means a genteel child. Her two older sisters were growing up and therefore remote, and she was not particularly interested in playing a feminine role. Nancy preferred being a tomboy and she played baseball and Prisoner's Base in the large yard of their house in Grace Street. She enjoyed playing boys' games and Nancy was a fast runner. But despite these freedoms, Chillie still played his role of benevolent tyrant and the children went to considerable lengths to please him. But any remarks that offended would mean an instant spanking and a forced sojourn in bed. Chillie failed to explain his reasons for punishment and quite often the offender would not have the slightest idea what he or she had said to incur their father's wrath.

Chillie, himself a hardened gambler and man of the world, was highly conscious of protecting his children's morality. His methods, though, were crude and unperceptive. One day he took the children down to see a young horse. They stood in the sun by the stable door admiring it and Chillie asked them to choose a name. The sire had been called Prosper, so Nancy thought it proper that this should be the root of the name. She was delighted – and was also anticipating Chillie's delight. Guilelessly she exclaimed 'Why not call him Prostitute?' The result was devastating. Chillie ordered Nancy to her room and

7

when pressed for an explanation brusquely told her that 'Your mother will explain.' Morosely, and with some curiosity, Nancy went to her mother only to find that she seemed at a total loss, unable to explain anything at all to her. The mystery remained unsolved to Nancy for quite some time.

Horses were now a part of Chillie's life-style. So were other luxuries, like holidays and their attendant field sports. He was a countryman at heart and took pleasure in the qualities of the countryside. Chillie liked to live life to the full and everything he did was to extremes. This was another aspect of his character that Nancy was to inherit. Yet she was not always drawn to him and in later life she wrote abrasively: 'Father was very strict. His word was law. He would have complete obedience. There was no talking back . . . We took it out of Mother. Though we were fond of Father we were always delighted when he went away and we had her to ourselves.'

There were also other aspects of Chillie's character that considerably influenced Nancy. Without his ambition, for instance, the family would never have had Mirador – the country house which was to be the final symbol of stability to the Langhorne family. Mirador ushered in a golden age which all the children were to continually look back on with affection and nostalgia. Also without Chillie's religious leadership, it is unlikely that Nancy would have been so convinced that she needed a strong religious theme to her own life.

Before moving on to the idyll of Mirador it is worth analysing Chillie's religious traditions – for traditions they were rather than beliefs. Neither his business nor his personal life tended to be Christian in example but the traditional structure was rigidly upheld. Both he and his wife were Protestants and prayer and bible reading were daily routine in the Langhorne household. School also reflected religion in Nancy's life and in 1886 at the age of seven she went to a day school run by a Miss Julia Lee. Miss Lee was related to one of Nancy's heroes – a Confederate general – and was therefore equally hero-worshipped. Nancy remembered that Miss Lee was 'deeply religious. She never preached at us. It was something in the air all about her.' Miss Lee was a good teacher, and taught history, English literature and art particularly well. A fellow pupil, Mrs Barbara Trigg-

Brown writes about Nancy's schooldays, 'Nanny [the American corruption for Nancy] became a lover of words and for years after she left school she opened her dictionary every night and learned two new words.' Nancy realised that Miss Lee was a brilliant teacher: she taught her how to learn rather than what to learn.

Much to Chillie's pride, his second daughter, Irene, became a raving beauty at school and was even commented on in the newspapers. Chillie affected annoyance at this and even threatened to go to New York to shoot the editor of one of the newspapers. Certainly it was not quite respectable to have one's daughter photographed by the newspapers, but on the other hand it was very flattering. Fortunately, the rest of the family did not seem to be jealous of Irene. Nancy remembered that her sister remained modest and no doubt her brothers and sisters played a strong part in ensuring that her ego remained as deflated as possible. Indeed, when Irene returned from a series of balls about which the press had written flatteringly, the entire family fell on her saying, 'You may have looked beautiful at the party, but people ought to see the way you look now.' In the face of this attack Irene apparently remained imperturbed.

A strong influence on Nancy before the move to Mirador was the Confederacy. Despite the loss of the war everybody in Richmond was a keen Confederate and it was very fashionable to be called a Rebel. This label was a foil against the mannered complacency of everyday life. To be a Rebel was exciting, escapist and safe – for the Rebels had been defeated and had no reason to go on fighting. There were many reunions and old heroes were re-fêted. There were also a large number of parades and these were enthusiastically watched by the entire Langhorne family, with Nancy as its most entranced member. After all, the family's immediate history had been radically changed by the war. Chillie had volunteered for service at seventeen and throughout the rest of his life supported the Confederacy and, of course, that symbol of the Confederates, the State of Virginia. His first months of married life had been spent in the Confederate military camp at Danville and Nancy Langhorne had lived in a hospital tent. Later the young married couple were in Danville when the final Confederate government met. So the Civil War was part of the Langhorne spirit and vice versa.

Although Nancy may well have been a safe Rebel in Richmond, she was to have the courage to be a very self-destructive rebel in the future. With her inheritance of drive, authority, gaiety, religion and rebelliousness, Nancy was rapidly growing up to be a very formidable person indeed.

Mirador, which Chillie bought in 1892, was the final seal of success. The house was situated in Albemarle County, west of Charlottesville and near the Blue Ridge Mountains. Charlottesville itself was tiny – a mere railway halt – and the population was sparse. Many country houses, some like Mirador with farming estates, stood alone and isolated. The architecture was uniform – a pure classical style with red brick, white stucco pillars and pediment and a high front staircase. It had originally been built in 1825.

Shortly after moving to Mirador, Chillie added two wings either side, so conforming to the typical Virginian style of classical imitation. The house was used throughout the majority of the year, except for a few months in winter when the family moved back to Grace Street. They would, however, always return to Mirador for a traditional family Christmas.

Society in Virginia at this time was still virtually a two-class system. There were the white gentry and the freed Negro population. Admittedly there were also the poor whites (known as poor white trash) but these were regarded as socially lower than the blacks. In particular, the Virginians thought of themselves as very well-bred stock indeed, although less powerful than their English counterparts. They were, however, vastly superior to the Yankees who were dubbed materialists, money-grubbers and considered to be socially inferior. Although the loss of the Civil War had caused serious damage to the South and its former wealthy plantation life, its traditions continued.

All Chillie's servants were black and because of the expanding railroads were becoming increasingly travel conscious. For this reason Chillie had to use all his charm and guile to keep them with him. Indeed, on this basis, he hired an entire family to work at Mirador for an all-in sum of $200 a year. Chillie knew full well that unless he hired the entire family, he stood little chance of getting the one farm-hand he wanted – and of keeping him in one place.

The religious fervour and mercurial temperament of the blacks made a strong impression on Nancy. At this time she was adopting the usual bigoted views common to most Virginians. Basically conservative, the average Virginian was suspicious of foreigners. Also basically Protestant, the same Virginian was extremely prejudiced against Roman Catholics and Jews — something Nancy inherited. As for the blacks — the average Virginian was paternalistic and insufferably patronising. Nancy was to hold the family's servants in affection yet ever after she would parody their manner of speaking: sometimes she would also burst into prayer, imitating their tones. Nevertheless this hot-gospelling was another factor in Nancy's religious background.

One particularly well-remembered black servant was Liza Pratt. She was unable to read or write but she knew the Bible from beginning to end, although she often mixed up the characters. She did not believe in the Virgin Mother but was deeply committed to Jesus, however unacceptable his birth, and she would tell the children bible stories by the hour.

Nancy was used to the ways of her black servants and made allowances when they stole food and borrowed possessions. She knew that they would not steal money or jewellery. 'Food,' Nancy wrote, 'was considered a right. They said God made food for everybody.' Borrowing was another matter and it probably occurred because of release from slavery: in other words the servants considered it a 'right' to use the possessions of their employers as a symbol of liberation. For instance there was Sam, who used to wait at the Langhorne table. Sam was a sportsman and would borrow Chillie's gun on the quiet. Nancy protected him as best she could when he was off on his illicit shooting expeditions. One day, however, he arrived at the table wearing Chillie's gold cuff buttons. Lizzie asked Sam where he had acquired these and he replied that Miss Nancy had loaned them to him to go visiting. Immediately Nancy covered up for Sam, agreeing that she had indeed given him permission to wear them. Spontaneous acts of generosity like this were to become instinctive with Nancy as she became more mature and it would be impossible for her to rationalise them.

At Mirador, Southern hospitality was at its most archetypal. This was mainly because Chillie remembered his own temporary poverty so well. Whisky and mint juleps were the order of the day, although he stopped his children from drinking until they were twenty. After that they were strictly controlled – so much so that Keene and Harry would often go on long drinking jaunts to evade their father's autocracy. Chillie, meanwhile, did not stint himself and he gradually built up one of the finest wine cellars in Virginia. Nancy intelligently disapproved of her father's intolerant and possessive attitude to his sons. She realised that he was unable to control his possessiveness and indeed this was a fault that Nancy inherited from him.

A rich imitation of English County life, overlaid by some individual touches, could be found on the Mirador estate. Nancy became a keen and skilled horsewoman. She admitted herself that because of her personality she drove horses too hard and her sister Phyllis was the more subtle rider. Nevertheless her father encouraged aggressive riding and Nancy writes: 'I remember seeing my sister Phyllis breaking in a two-year-old, sixteen hands. The horse reared and swayed, but Father just said, "Damn it! Give him his head!" '

In their new-found luxury, the Langhornes were determined to excel. They rode to hounds, appeared successfully in the local show-rings, and entertained lavishly. Chillie and his friends – and indeed most Virginians at this period – were not renowned for their sobriety. In fact many of Nancy's obsessional prohibition views were a reaction against the experiences of her adolescence. For instance, one of the Langhorne relatives arrived at Mirador in a considerable state of intoxication. He sent a message to Chillie from the railway station that he would like to be picked up. But Chillie only replied with a string of oaths and a refusal. A little later, a drunken young man arrived, loudly proclaiming from the hall that he was going to kill himself. Nancy, still sitting at the table, told him to go ahead. But no shot was fired and he retired upstairs to sleep it off. Later he rejoined the house-party and was received as if nothing had happened. This was typical of the abrasively critical and yet always accepting atmosphere of Mirador.

The first person to influence Nancy outside the family was an English priest named Frederick Neve. An Oxford graduate and an ex-minister, Neve was thirty-three when he came to Virginia.

He became Archdeacon at St Paul's Church in a small town called Ivy, halfway between Greenwood and Charlottesville. Neve, however, had not come to Virginia to be a fashionable English priest. Instead he took the job for a certain reason: nearby, in the Blue Ridge Mountains, there lived a number of extremely poor and often violent hill-farmers. This was the community which interested Neve – both from the point of view of preaching to and caring for them. The hill-farmers' plight had considerably worsened since the Civil War; they received no medical aid and were ignored by the community. On a low stipend, Neve worked as a missionary to his spiritually and physically impoverished flock until he was over ninety years old. Riding on horseback over bad roads and dangerous, lawless territory, Neve's dedication was remarkable. Whatever the weather, he would ride over clay roads that were often thick with mud. At the end of these primitive wagon trails were the desperately poor hill-farmers. Neve tended the sick, gave advice and baptised the children.

When Nancy first met Neve she was immediately impressed, not only by his dedication but by the daily dangers he faced from his impulsive, violent and suspicious flock. Although caution deterred Neve from taking Nancy into the mountains, he took her visiting on pastoral work elsewhere. This was the first time she had seen the Church functioning as an outside, active force. Nancy wrote about Neve in her typically idiosyncratic fashion '. . . from the first I loved and respected him. Father used to say of me I didn't respect anything except goodness, and that is true. I have always liked and admired brilliance, but I loved goodness. The Archdeacon became one of my best friends. I wrote to him every month for forty years.'

Neve aroused Nancy's social conscience and she became involved in a home named The Sheltering Arms. Here the elderly and the crippled were taken in and cared for. Nancy became a regular visitor and found in the home a vast contrast to the kind of life she had previously been used to. Nancy commented: 'I don't think I had realised before how many poor and unwanted people there are in the world.'

Chillie was anxious that his daughters should marry well and become 'belles', i.e. fashionable beauties of the time. Lizzie was already married but the boys seemed unstable and decadent. Irene's engagement to Dana Gibson had been punctuated by disapproval from Chillie. Eventually, however, he agreed to the marriage and became friendly with Gibson. Nancy was a bridesmaid and her mother wrote dynastically in her scrapbook: 'Nanny Langhorne made her formal bow to society and by the right of every Langhorne immediately became a belle.' Despite being reconciled to Irene's marriage to Gibson, Chillie still looked to his other daughters to find themselves more acceptable suitors. The first of Nancy's admirers was very acceptable. St George Bryan came from an eminently respectable Virginian family. A graduate of Charlottesville University, he and Nancy became informally engaged for a year. However they both had volatile temperaments and would often fly into emotional rages with each other. Nancy wrote: 'He was eighteen and very goodlooking and I adored him. Our romance consisted mainly in our going for rides together. He whistled beautifully and would whistle me the latest tunes.' However the relationship foundered after two incidents. The first was when St George let down his own gallant name and refused to carry Nancy's petticoat when the elastic broke and the garment slid unceremoniously down her legs on the way to church. The second was when St George, with a little more panache, entered a steeplechase against his father's wishes. Disguised with a false beard he unfortunately had a fall at one of the fences and lay on the ground – unconscious and beardless. The petticoat episode forgotten, Nancy rushed to her fallen warrior and cradled his head. He was promptly sick in her lap.

Irene clocked up an alleged sixty-two proposals before marrying. Nancy claimed sixteen. But Chillie was not going to allow Nancy to vegetate in Virginia. At seventeen, he despatched her to New York so that she could attend a finishing school and learn the finer points of etiquette. The finishing school was called Miss Brown's Academy for Young Ladies and unlike Miss Lee's more modest but certainly more educational establishment, did not teach anything but the superficiality of society behaviour. This was a disastrous move, and the whole atmosphere of the school was alien to Nancy. Naturally she had been pleased to leave the parochialism of Virginia for New York, but she had also been very loath to leave the still exciting and mentally stimulating world of learning at Miss Jennie's. Nancy was right in worrying about leaving education behind so early and the mistake was to adversely affect the rest of her life.

Nancy found New York extremely exciting. She had a taste for glamour and her sister Irene's marriage to Dana Gibson made New York even more desirable. Dana was now famous and regularly published his work in *Life* magazine. The Gibson Girl had been created and Dana and Irene were growing in fashionable stature. As a result the times spent with Irene were, to Nancy, a pure joy. But she found Miss Brown's Academy for Young Ladies absolute hell.The problem was that the Academy was geared to the extremely rich New York girls whose world was very different to Nancy's aristocratic but parochial Virginia. Evenings were spent at dinner parties, or balls or at the Opera, where women competed against each other with clothes and jewels. In fact jewellery was in so much profusion that it was essential to find original methods of attachment. Mrs Frederick Vanderbilt, for instance, wore an enormous uncut sapphire or ruby just above her feet, suspended from her waist by a rope of pearls. In more conservative style, Mrs John Drexel would appear wearing her pearls in a wide band that crossed her bosom and travelled down her back like a Sam Browne belt.

Nancy's reaction to the jibes of the other girls was typical. She decided to play the Virginian country bumpkin. She wore tasteless clothes, and made good use of the difficult Virginian accent. She also told the most amazing stories about her parents, calmly stating that her mother took in washing and that her father was a drunkard. As a result, Nancy gained a reputation as an exciting but disreputable character. The girls were amazed by the frequent appearances in the school of Irene Gibson. This very rich, beautiful and fashionable woman would drop in to bear the Virginian savage away to her home or out riding.

Luckily for Nancy, her parents realised that she was becoming more and more depressed, so eventually they took her away from the venerable Miss Brown and returned her to Virginia. She was delighted to be back in Mirador during the idyllic summer days. Chillie, following the local custom, would take a nap after lunch. Unfortunately he would sleep in unexpected places and if mistakenly woken, would boil over into grim fury.

If this happened he would force the culprit to sit and fan him until he slept again.

The idyll was not to last. New York itself had attracted her and now, free of the shackles of Miss Brown's, she was able to involve herself in all the razzamatazz of that gilded and rackety city. It was not long until tragedy struck. It began, however, disguised as love. At a polo match, Nancy was immediately attracted to a spectacularly handsome young player. He rode a one-eyed pony and took a series of falls from which he emerged miraculously unscathed. They were eventually introduced and Nancy discovered that the young man's name was Robert Shaw and that he came from an old and distinguished Virginian family.

The attraction was mutual and in her autobiographical draft Nancy wilfully misremembers the circumstances surrounding her parents' attitude to the affair. She claims that 'In my own heart I was never sure' and

'It is strange, looking back on it, to see how through it all there ran uneasiness, a note of warning. It was not only I who was aware of it; Father was also. Something made him go to Mr Shaw and ask him candidly if there was any reason why Bob should not marry me. He was assured there was none, although both Bob's father and mother knew very well at the time that their son was an alcoholic.'

But all this massive self-justification was with hindsight. Nancy was certain enough in her own mind to refuse Chillie's advice against the marriage. Certainly there was no evidence to suggest that the Shaws regarded their son as an alcoholic. They knew him as rich, wild and dissipated – a not untypical product of rich New York at the time. But Chillie *was* worried – Bob Shaw had the reputation of being just a shade *too* wild. He did go to New York to question the Shaws but their opinion was that marriage was the ideal remedy to settle their son down.

Robert Shaw was not an alcoholic as such, but there was instability in his character and, in Mrs Shaw's family, there had been mental illness. Her father, a Swiss scientist, had had a nervous breakdown whilst working at Harvard University. Later her mother became insane. However, none of this came to light at the time and Nancy, partly in love with the New York which Shaw epitomised and partly restless at the thought of returning to the now dull sanctuary of Virginia, seemed determined to go ahead with the marriage. In October 1897 the ceremony took place at Mirador. Nancy was eighteen.

One of the reasons why the marriage was an instant failure (Nancy left her new husband on the second night of the honeymoon) was sex. Nancy had a strong aversion to the lustfulness of the sexual act. To her sexual intercourse was sacred, private and the means of producing children. But Robert Shaw was a highly-sexed man – and the lustiness of his love-making came as a very rude shock to her. Her son, Michael Astor, writes in *Tribal Feeling*:

'Robert Shaw was not an intellectual nor was he a particularly perceptive sort of man. He was good-looking, wealthy, agreeable, and, above all, easy going. He supposed he was marrying a typical Southern belle. He woke up from his reverie with the surprise of a man who had unsuspectingly got into bed with a wildcat. On the second night of their honeymoon his young bride left him and ran back to Mirador. Mr Langhorne tried to comfort his daughter, and allowed her to stay a few days, after which he sent her back telling her she had better go through with it.'

Dutifully, Nancy returned to Shaw. But she felt desperately homesick. This was predictable, for apart from the unpleasant sojourn at Miss Brown's she had not been away from her family before. She was only eighteen, sexually repressed and now not at all in love with her husband. She wrote: 'I felt much as I had done as a child marooned on the wrong side of the railway years before, when I prayed and a kindly bagman came and took me home.'

But the marriage was not easy to end and Chillie was unwilling to see Nancy leave her husband until she had really tried to improve the situation. So, reluctantly, she returned to Robert Shaw. He still drank heavily and still desired her in a way that she found repellent. She ran home again several times more until she unwillingly became pregnant. Nancy bore Robert Shaw a son. For a short time the baby, called Bobbie, took her mind off the constant misery but after a while it returned just as strongly as before. Nancy went to her father-in-law and told him she was unable to go on with the marriage. With considerable perception, he sent her home for six months, reassuring Nancy that he would reform his son's ebullient drinking and behaviour.

But he didn't. Six months later Nancy returned to find that her husband was still drinking – and he had another woman. Despite all this Chillie remained hopeful. He was fond of Shaw – in him he probably saw much of his own youth. In fact Chillie still gambled and drank, but, as far as Nancy was concerned, her father could be forgiven for much that her husband certainly could not. Her own sexual failure with Shaw was always in her mind, and it would not go away, however much she tried to erase the memory. In trying to save the marriage, Chillie bought the unhappy couple a very attractive country house near Mirador. He hoped this would assuage Nancy's homesickness, but it was a vain hope. In 1901 Nancy and Robert separated – this time for good.

The effects of the separation were far more traumatic to Nancy than to Shaw. Doggedly, Nancy refused to initiate divorce proceedings. Principally she found the renunciation of her marriage vows quite incompatible with her religious faith. Secondly she was unwilling to bring scandal to the Langhorne family. She clung to her resolution, despite strong advice from everybody to the contrary – including Archdeacon Neve. In the late autumn of 1902, however, the situation changed dramatically. The Shaw parents arrived at Mirador with grave news. Their unstable son, involved as he was with another woman, had not told her of his existing marriage to Nancy and had gone through some form of marriage service with her. If these facts ever became public there was no doubt that he would be tried and imprisoned for bigamy. Nancy's parents-in-law, of whom she was still fond, were clearly in a desperate position. Because of this, Nancy relented. But she still refused to listen to advice. To minimise the scandal, the Shaws suggested that she should sue on grounds of incompatibility of temperament. This she point-blank refused to do. She wrote 'I took a firm stand on the Bible. I would only have it on the grounds of adultery, and that was how, in the end, it was.' Luckily, the divorce was well-handled by the Langhorne family lawyers and went through smoothly and without scandal or publicity.

Chillie decided to send Nancy abroad so that she would stop dwelling on the catastrophe of her marriage. In February 1903 she left for Europe with her mother and Alice Babcock, a friend who was recovering from an unhappy love affair. It was not clear whether Chillie thought Alice was fitting sombre company for his divorced daughter or that he was killing two birds with one stone in trying to mend two broken hearts. Ironically, the trio were seen off at the quayside by Angus McDonnell, a younger son of the Earl of Antrim and a man who was to play an important part in Nancy's future life. McDonnell, an Irishman, had come to America to travel and to work as an engineer. He had already met Nancy very briefly in New York and was anxious to renew the acquaintance. He was at the quay for the purpose of seeing his own mother off on the boat. Lady Antrim had been told to look out for Nancy Shaw – who was recommended to her as a charming and lively travelling companion.

Angus McDonnell was the victim of one of Nancy's impetuously dramatic gestures, which invariably embarrassed their victims. McDonnell writes that Nancy presented the following image as she leant over the rail of the boat:

'the most attractive young woman you could wish to see, with laughing blue eyes, generally blonde colouring, and the neatest trimmest figure imaginable, looking gay and excited at the prospect of visiting Europe for the first time, carrying a large bunch of red roses that one of her "beaux'" had sent her to the boat. My mother introduced us, and much to my confusion and the delight of the passengers and those who had come to see them off, Nanny threw her roses to me saying she would look forward to seeing me on her return to Virginia in the early summer. Later, when I got to know her well, I realised the rose episode was typical of her: she always liked being the centre of the stage, even if it was a small one, and even if, in so being, she made others feel self-conscious. On this occasion, though I remember feeling miserably shy and foolish holding a great bunch of red roses, I also remember hoping that she would come home soon.'

The European tour did Nancy good. So did Alice Babcock. By pooling their misery they had a thoroughly enjoyable, if masochistic, time – condemning all men and ignoring them on the golf links. They travelled to Paris and then to England, which Nancy found surprisingly attractive. In England they met Mrs Astor, the wife of John Jacob Astor IV, who was a cousin of Nancy's future father-in-law. Mrs Astor found the two girls very appealing and asked if all three could stay with her for a month – extending the trip that was about to come to an end. Finally it was decided that Mrs Langhorne would return to care for Nancy's baby son, Bobbie, whilst Nancy and Alice would stay with Mrs Astor.

Although Nancy did not meet her future husband, Waldorf, during the course of this month it is still worth pausing, at this point, to consider the background of the Astors. Of Spanish descent their name had been Astorga. In the early eighteenth century, the family had emigrated to Germany where the name had been shortened to Astor. Unfortunately the Astors fell on hard times in Germany and by the latter part of the century the head of the family was a butcher in a village in Baden called Waldorf. Of his three sons the first went to London to become a manufacturer of musical instruments, the second went to America and the third, John Jacob Astor, went to London to work with his brother in the musical instrument business. He was sixteen. Later he created the American Fur Company and began a settlement on the Pacific coast called Astoria. From then on John Jacob expanded his affairs considerably. He bought a fleet of ships and took his furs to Europe, to China and to Russia, thus making a considerable fortune.

This first of the wealthy Astors then began buying land, realising that the then small port of New York was bound to become a large city. John Jacob Astor's wealth was inherited by his son, William Backhouse, who passed the family fortune onto the next generation – another John Jacob. The money was well invested in land and was not prone to uneasy fluctuation such as that of the Vanderbilts (ships and railways) or the Rockefellers (oil). The Astor wealth remained constant as New York grew. They were not a philanthropic family, nor democratic, nor did they have a social conscience. Neither were they very lively. Michael Astor writes: 'A heavy Germanic quality, inherited from the male line, coupled with a conscientious form of Lutheran orthodoxy, seemed to have deprived them of a sense of fun.'

William Waldorf Astor, John Jacob's son, was a typical product of the Astor dynasty. In New York he was a legendary success symbol and very much part of the self-made aristocracy of the Astor family. Educated by tutors, and an only child, he was 'finished' in Europe and took part in such gentlemanly sports as riding, fencing and boxing. William went to the Columbia Law School and at twenty-nine he entered public life, becoming a member of the New York State Assembly. In 1879, a year after marrying Mary Dahlgren Paul, he was elected a member of the New York Senate. In 1880 he decided to stand for the United States Congress and was later nominated, as a Republican, to stand for the rough, working class Seventh Congressional District. Immediately his class – and attitude – told against him and his opponent made great capital by accusing him of representing 'a landlord aristocracy'. William stated, somewhat weakly, 'I am very happy to be called a carpet bagger by my opponent. When I first went to the Assembly three years ago I remarked that I did not go in the interests of any class, but for the city's good. This is my position now. I have as great an interest in the Seventh Congressional District as I have in the part of the city in which I live.' But the landlord tag stuck and the poverty-stricken streets rejected Astor. Reaction from the press was predictable. The *New York Times* suggested he lost because 'of a personal canvas more suggestive of the electioneering methods of an old-fashioned English Borough than a Congressional District in an American city.' The *New York Tribune* was more tolerant and commented 'It is always dangerous for men of great wealth to expose themselves to the suffrage. The passion of envy is the most deeply planted and the most invidious in the human heart.' As a result William Waldorf Astor became deeply embittered. He took the rejection as outright humiliation and the publicity which surrounded it as personal degradation. His extreme reaction lasted for the rest of his life and he became paranoid about all forms of publicity.

In 1882 William became United States minister in Rome, although he was no longer politically ambitious. Instead, he turned his attention to the past and became a collector. He collected paintings, Roman marble, medieval armour, crossbows and Tudor prayer books. William Waldorf's acquisitions were certainly on a grand scale but were nothing compared to his purchase of the entire balustrade of the Villa Borghese. He later had it reassembled on the site of the jewel of his collection – Cliveden. Originally the English country house of the Duke of Westminster, this great mansion overlooked the Thames in Buckinghamshire. William Waldorf added to it impressively – with balustrades, statues and fountains. A mosaic floor was laid in the hall and a fresco showing the gods banqueting was painted on the ceiling of the dining room. Panelling was imported from a hunting lodge at Asnière which had originally belonged to Mme de Pompadour and an enormous fountain was built in the grounds, made entirely of Siena marble. One published description evokes the atmosphere of Cliveden well : 'Situated on high ground and bordered below by the Thames that threads its way through the woody slopes of this exquisite estate, like a silver riband linking the various shades of green, the ideal landscape thus presented lingers long in the memory.'

Privacy was William Waldorf's obsession. To this end he banned boating parties from landing on the banks anywhere near Cliveden and he closed the woodlands to picnickers. His wife, Mary, was very much in the background and wifed and mothered in a dutiful and colourless way. In fact they were both very colourless people indeed. Nevertheless Mary was reasonably popular with Queen Victoria's court set and she was eventually made Mistress of the Robes – an honorary but socially privileged position, which together with the Astors' particular brand of American aristocracy as well as their considerable wealth soon assured them wide-spread social acceptance.

In 1894 William Waldorf's wife, Mary, died, and his extreme loneliness and eccentricity date from that time. Having settled down in England and become a British subject, William bought himself a newspaper – a Liberal publication named the *Pall Mall Gazette*. He changed its political colour to Conservative and proclaimed it as a paper that was 'by gentlemen for gentlemen'. Waldorf employed an MP, Henry Cust, to edit the *Gazette* and he was soon installed in luxurious offices. Although William dominated Cust he also indulged him, together with other senior members of staff. Dinner parties were regularly held for them and Waldorf provided an orchestra and shaded light from dozens of light bulbs hidden in the centre of numerous roses.

William Waldorf was, of course, anxious to use the *Pall Mall Gazette* as a soapbox for his own reactionary views but luckily Cust (acceptable as a gentleman because he was the Earl of Brownlow's son) cunningly persuaded him to start a literary magazine in which to air his opinions. Called the *Pall Mall Magazine*, the first issue carried an essay by William on Madame Récamier. Later Wells, Kipling and Barrie were to be contributors. In 1911 Astor bought the *Observer* newspaper from Northcliffe and his empire was complete. Although still disillusioned by his experiences in New York, William felt that England had made him and now he had won back both the respect of others – and himself.

William Waldorf and Mary had three children – William Waldorf, John and Pauline. They grew up in a highly repressive atmosphere where the entire household was tailor-made to their father's whims and obsessions. Apart from little idiosyncrasies like painting all the family's coaches chocolate brown – the same colour as the Royal Family's coaches – William was obsessed with punctuality and scheduling. Certain periods were laid aside for walking, resting, driving, eating and sleeping. Woe betide any member of the family – or any house guest – who broke the regime. William's wrath would know no bounds and he would make the offender feel they had committed the deadliest possible sin.

Brought up in this atmosphere, the three children were severely repressed. Michael Astor (Waldorf Junior's son) writes that the children 'were brought up, instructed, but not educated in the ways of life.' William Waldorf rarely asked their opinions, expected them to be completely rigid in their views and at all times they had to be guarded in their replies. It was a suffocating atmosphere and the children emerged as restrained, dutiful adults although their sense of public service turned out to be far greater than their grandfather's.

When Queen Victoria died in 1901 and Edward VII ascended the throne, William was already socially close to the monarchy – a fact that pleased him very much indeed. William knew

Edward VII well but not well enough to ensure him a place at court. But if he was not to be welcomed into the deepest royal enclave, he could, at least, continue to enhance his image with material possessions. The next in line was Hever Castle – a neglected thirteenth-century castle in Kent which had once been inhabited by Anne Boleyn. Henry VIII had then taken over the building and given it as a present to his fourth wife, Anne of Cleves, at the time of their divorce. The castle then changed hands a considerable number of times until William Waldorf Astor bought it in 1903.

Immediately William began to restore Hever. He filled the building with treasures, the approximate cost being ten million dollars. A selective inventory is as follows:

1   Cardinal Richelieu's sedan chair.
2   Martin Luther's bible.
3   Anne Boleyn's bed-posts.
4   Queen Elizabeth I's toilet articles.
5   Flemish and Burgundian tapestries.
6   Paintings by Titian, Holbein, Clouet and Cranach.
7   Suits of armour as worn by Francis I and Henry II of Spain.
    And so on.

Outside, in the castle grounds, William diverted the River Eden so that it formed a sailing lake and, in keeping with his mania for privacy, he had the drawbridge repaired so that it could be taken up. The moat was filled and all guests were sent to bed in the Tudor houses in the village at night. The drawbridge was then raised and the Astor family were alone in their luxurious eyrie.

Gradually William was becoming more withdrawn – and more eccentric. He was determined to create a highly aesthetic environment. But this did not entirely satisfy him for he was aware that the English side of the family had no tradition – and no long line of aristocratic forbears. He also turned to self-indulgence of a harmless kind. William was both a gourmand and a gourmet and a typical pre-breakfast snack would be artichokes and prawns. Meals tended to be long drawn-out affairs and William liked to be read to during these by his daughter. Lucy Kavaler in her book *The Astors* describes William with some asperity: 'He sat there giving no expression of pleasure, an odd-looking figure in his stiff-fronted dress shirt, linen jacket, and rubber-soled tennis shoes.'

William Waldorf's idiosyncrasies were extremely trying. Shortly after buying Hever Castle, he asked members from the Psychical Research Society to watch for the unquiet spirit of Anne Boleyn during Christmas week. Unfortunately she did not grace them with her presence. On another occasion, when his daughter Pauline was making her début into society, he wrote to the Bachelors Club, asking for a list of fifty 'eligible' bachelors to invite to the party.

Most of William Waldorf's fortunes still rested in his Manhattan property. The American branch of the family had, with William's added investments, opened the Waldorf and the more exclusive Netherland Hotel in New York. To these was added the flagship – the Astor Hotel which, after opening in 1904, became famous for being the focus of cafe society. The ballroom was able to seat five thousand guests at one sitting and the hotel was typical of the Astor style.

But William Waldorf was far from being a happy man, despite being one of the richest in the world. At one point, his London home and estate office was so security ridden that if he heard any unexpected sound, he could push a spring and have every door in the house immediately and securely fastened. 'I die many deaths every day' he once admitted and there was no doubt that his sanity was at risk.

A year before Mary's death, *Harper's Bazaar* had written of William's migration in the following terms: 'Are we to argue from Mr Astor's apparent migration that the opportunity of the very rich lingers in England? . . . In England they take their millionaires more seriously than we do and are much readier to give them a chance and fit them out with a suitable rank and proper employment.' But this was not necessarily the case. When William was eventually given a peerage, not all public comment was favourable. 'There does not seem to be much enthusiasm displayed in English papers on the new peer's behalf' commented the *Literary Digest* bleakly. But enthusiasm was not part of William's personality either. No doubt he felt that the accolade of a peerage was a reward for his good works, but he had ensured its arrival beforehand by considerable donations such as $100,000 to Oxford University, $50,000 to Cambridge

University, $100,000 to the University of London, and $100,000 towards fighting the Boers. Later, during the First World War, William gave over $200,000 to the Red Cross, $135,000 to supporting officers' families, $24,000 towards Queen Mary's fund for women, $24,000 towards the *Daily Telegraph*'s fund for Army bonds and $125,000 towards the Prince of Wales' fund. So his peerage cannot have come as much of a surprise.

Ralph G. Martin in his biography of Lady Randolph Churchill wrote:

> 'Another friend of Randolph, among the richest men in the world, was former American Minister to Italy, William Waldorf Astor, impolitely known as "Wealthy Willie". Gossip writers coupled his name with Jennie's almost regularly throughout the years. After the death of Astor's wife and Jennie's husband, it was even reported that Astor and Jennie were engaged to marry. He was a big, blue-eyed, handsome man with a blond moustache, a rugged build, and an overpowering personality, aided and abetted by eighty million dollars. They called him "Walled-off Astor" because he had built high walls topped with glass around his 300 acre Cliveden Estate on the Thames, had barred his windows, and actually used the drawbridge at Hever Castle to keep people out. The real wall, though, was around his soul.'

Following Nancy's marriage to his son, on 3 May 1906, William Waldorf Astor spent his declining years fascinated by the genealogy of his family. He believed that the Astors were originally pure-bred Spanish and his grandson wrote: 'If he had a choice, if language had presented no barrier, I think he would have liked to have been a Spaniard, and certainly a grandee which in a sense he already was. In the old world there was no more backward country than Spain, no country so cut off from the feeling and fashion of the twentieth century. In politics and outlook he would have made the late Cardinal Segura, Bishop of Seville, the most reactionary prelate of his age, look like an evangelist.' Later, Michael Astor recalls a portrait of his grandfather hanging in a passage at Cliveden. 'My grandfather, staring out of the canvas, remained an awesome figure. I regarded the face of authority with misgiving.'

Michael Astor's misgiving was not ill-founded. William

Waldorf Astor's brand of authority was harsh, unimaginative and tyrannical. All this was based on his own loneliness and his three children were lucky to survive as balanced human beings, in view of their narrow and austere background.

Directly Nancy returned from Europe, Angus McDonnell took his opportunity. He was now working for the Southern Railway at Manansas and, when invited to Mirador, he dressed himself in what he described as his most respectable suit and hired a buggy to make the comparatively short journey. However, the roads between Manansas and Mirador were unmade and, in the summer, extremely dusty. He arrived at Mirador desperately thirsty and covered in dust, to witness a pastoral scene which stayed in his memory for the remainder of his life. The entire family were sitting on the lawn under the shade of a tree. They looked cool and happy in the insular way a family can. They were completely self-contained and McDonnell felt immediately excluded.

Then the spell was broken as Nancy rushed up to meet him. Amongst the Langhorne family present that weekend were Chillie and Mrs Langhorne, Nancy herself, her younger sister Norah, and the boys – Keene, Harry and Buck. The weekend was idyllic. Chillie took to him and invited McDonnell back – but it was Nancy that he was returning for. The basic problem, however, about Angus McDonnell's relationship with Nancy was that he put her on a pedestal and worshipped her from afar. He would dearly have liked to marry her but his self-abasement prevented this. Nancy instinctively wanted someone she could respect. Worship, although flattering, was not what she was looking for. In fact, at this stage, she was not even contemplating marriage. The Shaw interlude had been a considerable shock to her system – and she was still recovering. Besides, there was still the deterrent of sexual intercourse and, for the moment, she was happy to be back at Mirador or night-clubbing in New York under the safe chaperonage of sister Irene.

Writing in *Nancy Astor and her Friends*, Elizabeth Langhorne was abrasive about the relationship between Nancy and Angus McDonnell. 'One weekend appears to have conquered Angus for good and all. He fell hopelessly in love with Nanny. Unfortunately he made himself a doormat. She was not in love with him. Still sore from her failure in the serious business of marriage, she was not terribly disposed towards falling in love with anyone, much less, it appeared, with Angus. Nanny never spared anyone's feelings, and in this situation Angus's feelings were so conspicuous as to be hard to spare.'

Naturally Angus McDonnell remembered this period of his life in great detail: 'On looking back, I really don't remember any transitional stage between being a visitor, and moving in as one of the family and as such establishing myself in a room that I shared with Buck, and the old pointer Bob, and the desk in one corner which gave the room the title of "office". It seemed that the whole family was prepared to accept me on the recommendation of Nanny and her Mother.' But what Angus McDonnell failed to realise was the extent Chillie would go to in order to distract his daughter at this point in her life. He clearly saw Angus McDonnell as a very necessary distraction. McDonnell continues:

'Nancy and her father were of the same pattern, and it was clear to me from the first moment I saw her at Mirador that just as he, as a young man, had fought his way to prosperity, so she, having had a taste of what New York, Boston and Bar Harbour had to offer – and her first experience of England and Europe proving preferable to any of these – would not be content to remain long under the parental roof in Virginia, but was merely treating Mirador as a base headquarters for herself and her little boy from which to plan an invasion of Europe.'

Then the first of a series of tragedies that were to cast a dark shadow over Nancy's life occurred. Nancy was obviously very similar to Chillie in temperament, but she had a very great and constant love for her unassuming and tolerant mother. Nancy realised how much she had suffered during the family's changing fortunes and she also appreciated how difficult her father could be – and how long-suffering her mother had to be in face of his turbulent character.

A few weeks after Angus McDonnell had paid his first visit, Nancy went to a horse show at Lynchburg. She was not particularly anxious to go as she was still brooding over her broken marriage and was also heavily involved in bringing up her baby son, Bobbie, whom she loved deeply. But Chillie, who loved to see Nancy jumping, was very insistent. Reluctantly she gave in to keep the peace. Chillie went on ahead whilst Nancy, Keene and their mother followed by train. They had lunch on the train and everything seemed normal. Nancy Langhorne complained of a headache but apart from this, she appeared to be in perfectly good health. In fact Nancy and Keene diagnosed their mother's headache as a nervous one – and it was certainly true that she always dreaded watching Nancy jumping in case she fell.

Later that night Nancy Langhorne's headache seemed to have cleared and she looked particularly attractive. In fact so lovely did she look that even Chillie was driven to comment on it. She smiled back at him and her children. They were all due to go to a show but Keene and Nancy decided to go on ahead and it was agreed that their parents should follow. Nancy wrote: 'I remember kissing Mother and giving her a sort of playful push and telling her to hurry.'

But Nancy and Keene were not joined by their parents at the show. They thought this strange and at first assumed that there was some reasonable explanation. Soon Nancy was filled with a grim foreboding. She left the show and hurried straight home to seek the explanation. It was very simple. At the all-too-young age of fifty-five, her mother had suddenly died. The disaster was the final blow with which to end the tortuous year of 1903.

For months following her mother's death, Nancy grieved desperately. At the same time she tried to keep house for Chillie. But she was not a good housekeeper – nor was the family scene very settled. Angus McDonnell wrote:

'She (Mrs Langhorne) it was who used to pour oil on the troubled waters, and the family waters were often troubled. In the role of peacemaker Irene was the only other person who could take her mother's place, and when family rows looked like getting out of control Mr Langhorne would send for her. Nanny, after her mother's death, kept house rather sporadically for Mr Langhorne for the next two years, but it was not altogether a success. They were both forceful personalities, too much alike in character, except that when Mr Langhorne set himself a goal he proved a good judge of his own capacities, whereas it always seemed to me that Nanny set herself targets beyond her capacity, and she never seemed satisfied when she had got as far as her delightful appearance, her great charm, her nimble wits and her somewhat limited education could take her.'

Despite all this Nancy was determined to succeed in playing housekeeper to her unwilling father. No one wished to see her succeed – instead they wished to see her happy. Clearly she was extremely miserable, she hated domestic tasks and was desperately bored. So bored was she, in fact, that her temper became violent and one tempestuous scene followed another. Chillie was beginning to find life intolerable, although he realised how much his daughter was suffering. The double blow of her broken marriage and her mother's death had been too much for an already vulnerable nervous system. Nancy wrote, 'There was sorrow such as I had never known or imagined. The light went out of my life. I was ill for months, in a wretched, nameless fashion . . . The memory of those days is like a shadow on the heart still.'

Eventually Chillie took advantage of one of Nancy's rare visits away to employ a housekeeper. However, the storm broke directly Nancy returned. She immediately became hysterical, claimed that no one had the right to sit in her mother's chair except her, and ran upstairs to pack. With this intruder sitting at the head of the table, she raged, there was clearly no room for her. She would leave Mirador and never return. This went on for some time until the housekeeper left – and Nancy had her own way. She returned to apathetic and patchy housekeeping, much to the dismay of the household. A year passed and suddenly Chillie could no longer stand the situation. He told Nancy that she could not go on living in this way and neither could the rest of the family. She wrote naively: 'I think he had begun to realise that it was not right for anyone as young as I was to remain at home, sunk in gloom, prematurely of the opinion that my life was over and done with.' Chillie, of course, had realised this in the first few weeks of the tortuous Nancy regime but, because of her temperament, had found it impossible to advise her. Now he offered her a hunting season in England. Nancy was immediately excited by the prospect but held back, still thinking

THE VIRGINIAN

that her mother would not have wished her to leave her father on his own. But Chillie, mindful of continued slap-dash housekeeping, told Nancy it was exactly what her mother *would* have wanted. Eventually he succeeded in convincing his daughter, using all his powers of persuasion. He also guaranteed that he would come to England for Christmas and that Nancy and little Bobbie would travel with his nurse, Nancy's sister Phyllis, her children and their governess. Thus encouraged Nancy began to prepare for her trip. As she did so she felt suddenly alive. The shutters of depression had lifted and Nancy experienced an onrush of her old zest for living. She was young again – and curious.

2

❦

Life Begins Again

Once in England Nancy quickly assumed the ferocious, extrovert, eccentric role of the heavily dramatised American lady she had already played at the much despised Miss Brown's Academy for Young Ladies. Basically she was lacking confidence when she arrived and she was determined that this would not show through. Her sister Phyllis's marriage to Reginald Brooks was now heading towards divorce and Nancy was determined that they should both forget their problems. They began by staying at Fleming's Hotel in Half Moon Street, near Green Park. Because of Edward VII's influence Americans were 'in' for the court set but not so 'in' for the hunting set. There was a certain acceptability of Americans in general in England's aristocratic circles but they had to be of the 'right' type. No one was absolutely certain exactly what the 'right' type was but certainly Nancy did not fit instantly into this vague category.

Confrontations began when the Langhorne entourage moved to Market Harborough for the November hunting season. They rented a hunting box on the Bowden Road and proceeded to hunt with verve, at first with hired horses and later, on two horses bought for them by Chillie. At once Nancy's acting role came to the fore. On her first hunt she fell and replied angrily to her would-be rescuer 'Do you think I would be such an ass as to come out hunting if I couldn't mount from the ground?' But despite all this, Nancy Shaw as she still called herself, fell in love with the rolling English countryside and its wintry landscapes. The crisp air, the smell of woodsmoke, the frosted earth of the ploughed fields, the ringing turf under the horses' hooves

– all this was essential freedom after so many months of torment and misery.

In a very short time suitors began to emerge for this lovely young divorcee. There were those, of course, who suspected her of decadence and would have been delighted to have found it. But Nancy was becoming increasingly puritanical. She was a regular church-goer and totally abstained from alcohol, drinking vast quantities of tea and barley-water instead. She was also quick to fend off the most outspoken of her critics. Mrs Cunard, for instance, voiced the fears of many when she acidly said to Nancy 'I suppose that you have come over here to get one of our husbands.' To which Nancy replied 'If you knew the trouble I've had gettin' rid of mine, you'd know I don't want yours.' Nancy's direct approach won her many life-long friends, including Mrs Cunard. Her son, Victor Cunard, wrote affectionately of Nancy's stay at Market Harborough.

'Although it would be impossible for me to remember at first hand the impact this lovely stranger made on our neighbours round Market Harborough, she became the heroine of so many and such oft repeated stories that I feel I lived through those months as a grown-up, rather than a curious and slightly precocious child. She not only "went well" across country and scrupulously observed the complicated conventions of the hunting field, she was also an experienced rider who could be trusted not to ruin a fine horse. She was a good mixer – as the rather bold phrase went – and her conversation was never above people's heads but was so amusing that her presence would ensure the success of the dullest dinner party. Without her, some of those dinners, if my parents were to be believed, could be very dull indeed.

'Market Harborough had, no doubt, received hard riding and entertaining visitors before, but what made Mrs Shaw different from the common run, were her shining candour and almost Puritanical respectability. Except for the unusual frankness of some of her remarks, she furnished no pretext for the slightest breath of criticism.'

Victor Cunard neglects to point out how dominating Nancy was, how much she wanted her own way and how many temper tantrums would follow if she did not get it. She kept eligible suitors at arm's length – and gave those with 'dishonour-able intentions' a puritanical and contemptuous tongue-lashing. The trouble was that the ridicule was not just confined to the latter. The Cunard family considered that Nancy was inex-perienced and tender enough to require protection but this was an unnecessary, if noble, thought. She was more than able to look after herself. At the same time Nancy did *mean* to be a good person but she was also wilful and selfish. This was parti-cularly evident in her relationship with the ever-faithful Angus McDonnell whom she treated as a fond pet dog, and the rather colourless and sentimental Lord Revelstoke who courted her with ponderous tenacity.

Nancy met John Baring, Lord Revelstoke, whilst hunting. He was an appalling snob, a bore and an ardent sentimentalist; he was at the same time rather pathetic. Chillie took an instant dislike to him. Revelstoke was much richer than Chillie (he was a senior partner in Baring Brothers, the bankers), was very well bred and wanted to marry his daughter. But Nancy's reasons for falling in love (or imagining herself to fall in love) with this rather nebulous aristocrat were complex. After the excesses of Robert Shaw, Revelstoke exuded security, care and respect-ability. Nancy's little boy, Bobbie, despite the past associations, was her love-object. Bobbie's future would be entirely safe with Revelstoke. So, as a possible suitor, Lord Revelstoke was high on the list. Nancy, however, slowly came to realise what an appal-ling snob Revelstoke was. She also discovered that he was deeply attached to Lady Desborough and had been having – or was still having – an affair with her. Then, to add insult to injury, Revelstoke haughtily asked Nancy if she considered she was capable of meeting kings and queens and entertaining ambassadors. This patronising chauvinism utterly incensed her, as well as hurting her deeply, and it was from this moment that Nancy's love for Revelstoke began to die.

Yet the basic problem was Nancy's jealousy of Lady Des-borough. This was based on her own insecurity because of her broken marriage. In fact she had very little to be jealous of, for Lady Desborough was a popular court beauty and bestowed her favours on many other aristocrats besides Lord Revelstoke. In fact although he had once been Lady Desborough's lover he was now an old friend. He first met Ettie Grenfell, as she was then, in 1891 and one of his letters to her at an early stage of their relationship is typically humble:

2 June 1891

'My dear Mrs Grenfell,
I meant to ask you last night (but simply didn't dare) if you thought you would be passing this house about 5 o'clock. The reason I ask is that Margaret and Lady William are coming to play the organ, violin and piano, and as I know you like music I thought you might be persuaded to look in –
Your humble and very persistent admirer,

John Baring.'

Ettie had a number of lovers including George Wyndham and Evan Charteris. Later, using the code name of E, Revelstoke became more passionate:

'... E writes such a thankful letter of gratitude to her for having allowed him to spend such hours of absolute paradise. He tells me he has never felt the absolute sense of rest and happiness conveyed to him by the presence – the dear *dear* presence of his own beloved; or ever been more aware how entirely he loves her with his *whole* heart and soul. From what he tells me I can feel how grateful he is; and he adds that since he left he has thought over every happy minute, and recalled every expression in that beautiful heavenly face, with such a feeling of happiness and with *such* a yearning that it may be a very short time before he has the precious *heaven* of seeing his dear beloved again.'

Revelstoke accepted Ettie's other lovers and continued to profess his adoration for her in such missives as this (still in its third person code):

'... it was such heavenly rest laying my head on her shoulder and her dear cool hand on my forehead – I loved her *much* more than ever before – will you tell her please? and that I thought of her so much *all night*, and *so much so* in fact that I woke up perfectly well .... when I have my arms round her dear waist, supporting that poor *dear* little aching back, I feel that heaven has indeed been good in giving me the most perfect of women for my own angel girl ...'

This is vintage Revelstoke – and highly reminiscent of his later letters to Nancy.

Following the end of the hunting season, Nancy and Phyllis went on a motoring tour of France in April 1905. They then returned to England for a period until they sailed back to America in July. The relationship with Revelstoke continued during that period and there was no sign of a break or Nancy 'coming to her senses'. But once back in America there were indications of a distinct cooling on Nancy's part, whilst Lord Revelstoke became a prolific correspondent, writing her nine letters between 12 July and 6 August. After this flood he wrote another letter on 11 August, this time in reaction to Nancy's criticism of Revelstoke's dull dissertations on London high society. She also accused him of not defending her in face of a mutual friend's criticisms. Revelstoke's replies to Nancy's abrasive letters were highly obsequious and his hyperbole was unbearable. On 11 August 1905, he wrote to her from Aix-les-Bains. 'I appreciate and understand every word you say, Nancy dear. You are wonderful and golden, and you must know that my every wish must be to do what you tell me. I wrote you all those silly details about London not because I thought them of any interest but only because they concerned life to which you were close during the summer.'

Nancy's temperament did not take to such abasement. Indeed, during these encounters, she could be very cruel. She hated weakness, particularly as she had built (so far) effective barriers around her own. She wrote a still sharper letter back to the wretched Lord Revelstoke to which he predictably replied, although there was a shade more defensiveness in its tone. Nancy's letter still contained elements of jealousy – particularly as regards Lady Desborough. Revelstoke ends his letter by saying

'What possessed you to say you know I haven't missed you? How *little* you must know me really: I don't understand a great deal but I understand your angelic letter quite quite – Nancy, I'm very helpless here – What do you mean when you say "I don't know what I shall do – that's another story and not nearly such a nice one." What would you say of me? For

life is simple, I think, as far as the big things are concerned, &
I have no "*arrière pensée*", or other plans or possibilities. I
think from your letter of the 31st that you were sorry you'd
written the one of the 30th. I will not write again as you tell
me not to. But does that mean that you won't write to me?
I did so love telling you the 1,000 poor little things that
happen & I meant so well. What a pathetic failure I have
been.'

In a less wilful and impatient person, poor Revelstoke might
have touched a chord, even if it was only one of pure sentiment,
but Nancy was basically needing to have her cake and eat it. She
had been annoyed by an earlier letter from Angus McDonnell in
which he told her that hard work and distraction made his own
yearnings easier. There was also a further implication in the
letter which hinted that hard work and distraction would make
her life easier. This she bitterly resented. Also Nancy liked
people to be dependent on her (as Robert Shaw had not been)
and grew uneasy if she felt they were becoming in the least
independent. Contrarily, when they *were* dependent on Nancy,
she found the situation claustrophobic. This applied to Lord
Revelstoke. Nancy could not bear his doting dependence but any
hint of his friendship with Lady Desborough would cause her to
have an immediate seizure of jealousy – and dip her pen in
vitriol.

Nevertheless, the correspondence continued and Nancy maintained her paranoia concerning Revelstoke's suspected infidelity. Referring to Nancy as 'Emma', Revelstoke writes:

'You silly, there is no mystery at all – only "the impatience
of youth" as you say. There is no "dreadful reason" for this.
If it hadn't been for that horrible summer things would have
been very different. Nancy *doesn't* come after Russian loans,
or 8 Bish (Within) or Aix. How can you pretend to think so.
But you're ever *so* wrong, & got such an entirely false view,
in thinking that "Kings and Queens" did, you never believed
what I still think, which is the very very *grave* responsibility
of taking a young (quite young Emma) & planting her in the
middle of a busy life that can't be altered, for those Russian
loans and Bish Gt. & Everything else, would be there, &
cannot be given up, even for Emma & it's all my wish for her

to be golden. She *hates* them all I know, & always has: & I don't know how far her attraction and her dear self wd enable her to stand them. You silly dear, you have been wracking your dear little brain for "mysterious" & "dreadful reasons". I implored you long ago to look at something much more simple and obvious & straight forward. But you never would believe what I said, & stuffed yourself full of wild theories about impossible reasons.'

In December 1905 Nancy left America for England and another hunting season. The situation between her and Lord Revelstoke continued to be recriminatory on her side and placating on his. On the journey back to England Nancy was accompanied by Chillie, who no doubt increased her sense of injustice against Revelstoke, for Chillie's unreasonable dislike of him was as persistent as ever. If only her father could have been more objective, he could have assured Nancy that there was no campaign being run against her by Lady Desborough and although Revelstoke was a snob and a bore, he was only being honest by trying to warn her of the wearisome and irksome duties she would have to perform as a hostess if she did marry him. He was not implying that she was unfitted for the task.

Suddenly, Nancy's life radically changed and she lost some of her obsession about Revelstoke and his patronage – and Lady Desborough and her supposed scheming. For accompanying her on the voyage to England was a man who was to over-shadow all her other suitors. He was Waldorf Astor, son of the reclusive and eccentric William Waldorf Astor. Waldorf, by a strange coincidence, had been born on the same day as Nancy – 19 May 1879. As a small boy he had left America, and lived for a while in Rome where a series of tutors had versed him in English, French, Italian and Latin. At nine, he was plunged into the cold-bath and cane atmosphere of the obligatory English preparatory school. Michael Astor writes: 'The English boarding school at the end of the nineteenth century was a bleak institution, devised for the convenience of parents rather than of children. It was traditionally the first stage of a child becoming a man and being weaned from the comforts and attentions of home, the man-making process consisting of doses of cold baths, cricket, football, religion, the classics and the cane in proportions which varied only with the temperament of the head-master.' This treadmill broke or inhibited many thousands of children but in Waldorf Astor's case his past was too dutiful, his nature too conservative and his imagination too barren to come to much grief. He told Michael Astor that he found it embarrassing to arrive at a school where everyone regarded him as a foreigner – but this was the sum total of the effect.

Waldorf Astor was a high-achiever, both at games and work. He entered Eton where he became a member of the Sixth Form, Captain of his House, Treasurer of the Eton Society and Captain of Boats. He also won the Prince Consort's French prize and did a stint at editing the *Eton Chronicle*. Basically Waldorf had inherited his father's gravity and strong will without his eccentricity, domineering ways and terrifying idiosyncrasies. Waldorf, because of his background and maybe because of a sense of alienation from his adopted country, felt a strong sense of public duty and public conscience which had not been an obvious part of his father's personality.

He progressed from Eton to New College, Oxford, and Michael Astor writes: 'Eton moulded my father's character: serious, conscientious and modest. He came to trust in the legitimate standards of good behaviour. He acquired the tastes and values of those of his generation who were brought up to assume, as of right, responsibilities of their class in society.' This is a classic summary of Waldorf's personality; steady as a rock, with none of the more decadent strains of inter-bred English aristocracy.

At Oxford, however, problems arose. Waldorf was found to have strained his heart rowing and he was forced to give up the sport. To compensate, he took up fencing and polo, hunted, became Master of the Drag Hounds and spent a considerable time in the fashionable student club of the time – The Bullingdon. Strangely, his sense of duty appears to have deteriorated at this point and although his behaviour was impeccable, Waldorf eventually graduated with a fourth-class honours degree.

After coming down from Oxford, Waldorf toyed with the idea of going into politics but came to no firm decision. He wanted to marry but until he met the right person he lived the hunting, shooting, fishing life of the English country gentleman.

Waldorf founded a racing stable, studied bloodstock and even went so far as to apprentice himself to a veterinary surgeon so he could fully understand the horse's physical make-up. This was typical of his thoroughness, making his poor graduation even more inexplicable. Perhaps the lack of necessity of career, his inherited status and his idea of being an MP (considered 'part-time' politics by the aristocracy) made academic qualifications irrelevant.

Before Waldorf Astor met Nancy Shaw, he had one romantic affair that was to make Nancy as uneasy as she had been over Lord Revelstoke's relationship with Lady Desborough. The lady in question was Crown Princess Marie of Rumania, the daughter of Queen Victoria's second son, married to Prince Ferdinand of Hohenzollern-Sigmaringen, heir to the Rumanian throne. Waldorf's father had been friendly with the King and Queen of Rumania and had often taken his children to Bucharest. Princess Marie had been forced into an arranged marriage at eighteen and her husband was not in the least interested in her, being currently in love with another woman. Incarcerated in the pomp of the Rumanian court she found the Astors delightfully free and she was attracted to Waldorf in particular. As the years went by it became clear to both of them that this was a hopeless friendship, and could never become anything else than a romantic tryst. Nevertheless, Princess Marie was a strikingly self-sacrificing and warm-hearted woman, and despite her own arid predicament, was anxious at all times for Waldorf's happiness.

Then, in early 1905, the problems concerning Waldorf's health dramatically increased. Angina was diagnosed as well as a tendency towards tuberculosis. Waldorf was therefore forced to give up hunting, polo, and all other physically demanding sports. It was at this point that he met Nancy. She had originally refused Waldorf's request for a meeting because of the distance. But Waldorf had determination, patience and enough guile to concentrate on impressing Chillie with his stature and moral impeccability. In other words, Waldorf had determined he was going to marry Nancy and he went about it as if he was running a political campaign. Because of Waldorf's charm, his distinguished good looks and his persistence, he soon had Chillie where he wanted him. Then, with Chillie's blessing, Waldorf began work on Nancy. With surprising speed their relationship grew from mutual attraction to love. Waldorf found Nancy just the antidote he needed to the newly received shock of his own ill-health. She was lively, demanding yet strangely dependent, public spirited and ambitious. But Waldorf was also an antidote to Nancy's own insecurity. He was strong, resolute, and totally incorruptible. He was also conveniently undemanding and very tolerant. They were ideal partners.

Despite this new relationship, Nancy continued to persecute herself. She had two main neuroses. On one level there was Waldorf's relationship with Princess Marie. And on another level there was her still undimmed jealousy of Lady Desborough. She also still needed to dominate the wretched Revelstoke. Nancy was loath to let him go, although there was no question in her mind about the possibility of marrying him now. Revelstoke gave her various presents – a dog on her second trip to England and later, a Shetland pony for Bobbie. On learning of her love for Waldorf, Revelstoke wrote her an extremely sad letter, couched in his usual terms, making much use again of the word 'golden':

> 'I want so much to thank you for being so golden & under-standing: for I think you must have known how much I heard today which I did not know before: and as for me I like to think that you understood the reasons why I have been so unhappy. Much more deeply unhappy than I hope you will ever have any idea of. I only trust that you feel I have *some* excuse. I told you today & I mean from the very bottom of my heart every single word I said. Shall you be able to send me a little line here to tell me you know I did?'

Nancy's reaction to the letter was one of deepened security. She knew that Waldorf loved her, but it was equally good to know that Lord Revelstoke also cared for her so much. Now all the misery, isolation and feelings of inadequacy over the sexual part of her marriage were gradually receding into the past. No longer could she be deeply wounded by them. Nancy now had the gentle and understanding love of one man and the senti-mental love of another.

Nancy still felt an overpowering urge to keep Revelstoke under her thumb, and she was very annoyed therefore when he decided to spend Christmas with the Cavendish family rather than dance attendance on her. She sent him a sharp letter on the subject to which Revelstoke predictably replied:

'Your dear letter of Friday has reached me: I am grieved at your being [displeased] at my coming here: but you will be fair, I am sure. You always are. Remember I've constantly spent Xmas here for 10 years. I *didn't* last year, & hurt the old D[uke of Devonshire]'s feelings very much. This year he enquired particularly whether I was coming weeks before there was any idea of your coming over. I said I would. It is very probably the last time as he is getting very frail & has been a very old & good friend to me.

'It seems so desperately hard to do what is right. I never seem able to do so, or to please anyone. I am deeply unhappy – that's why I asked you if you realised but surely you do – what this means to me.'

As yet Nancy was not engaged to Waldorf and Revelstoke imagined that he was still marginally in the running. Through the early months of 1906 he showered her with letters and gifts and then, by correspondence, he proposed marriage. Nancy rejected him outright and Revelstoke wrote a letter back that was, for him, rather indignant. 'I found your letter when I got home last night, written I thought by a different Nancy to that one who talked to me on Monday – and you never telephoned.'

Revelstoke did not renew his proposal and the relationship drew to a close. Nancy was now far more preoccupied with her jealousy over Princess Marie than with keeping Revelstoke on a convenient lead. But there was nothing for Nancy to worry about. The relationship between Princess Marie and Waldorf Astor was purely romantic. In fact when Princess Marie learnt of his love for Nancy she assumed they were engaged and in a highly unorthodox manner for someone in her position she wrote a long and encouraging letter to Nancy. In referring to Waldorf, Princess Marie wrote: 'He has been through hard times because of a good deal of bad luck, ill health and disappointments, and so it is the greatest joy for his friends to think that such happiness is now soon in store for him . . . I hope you won't mind my having written and my repeating that I'm longing to know you.'

Nancy did not reply immediately to this admirably generous letter. Whether the letter raised Nancy's uneasy jealousy still further is very difficult to say, but on 27 February further distorted news reached Princess Marie to the effect that there *was* no official engagement and that Nancy had decided not to marry Waldorf after all. Immediately the Princess wrote a 1,200 word letter, urging Nancy to rethink her decision and giving details of Waldorf's earlier life and the trials and tribulations of his family background, ruined sporting career and current ill-health. A cable followed when there was still no response from Nancy and eventually, on 7 March, another letter. She wrote: 'I do so well understand all your hesitations. It's a big step to take and one that can't be decided hurriedly when one is not quite sure of one's own feelings. We had almost given up hope, and I could not reasonably hope that my letter would make such a difference, but if it helped ever so little you can imagine how happy it makes me as I would have done anything to try [?] Waldorf's happiness for him.'

Self-sacrificingly, Princess Marie was determined to do practically anything so that Waldorf's happiness was ensured and to this end she was determined that Nancy should marry him. However, she need not have worried. Nancy was equally determined to marry Waldorf and any rumours to the contrary were quite untrue. Indeed on 8 March 1906 Nancy cabled Chillie, telling him that she was now officially engaged. On the same day she wrote to Lord Revelstoke telling him of her final decision. The next day *The Times* carried the announcement. Revelstoke was heartbroken and yet still wished to go on seeing Nancy – although Nancy thought that any further meetings would be too painful and too disastrous. However they did meet shortly after the engagement. A letter followed this which bleakly stated at its conclusion: 'I have no plans for now or indeed for any time.' Revelstoke gave Nancy a wedding present of a diamond bow that had been modelled on an item amongst Louis xv's crown jewels. He had already received a locket from Nancy containing a few strands of her hair and on 2 May 1906 he wrote: 'My dearest Nancy, I met the little boy on the step bringing your note. God bless, always. I shall *never* forget – & shall never be able to tell you what I feel, except, *Bless* you, for ever and always, Yours J.'

Revelstoke continued to write for years after Nancy's marriage, which took place the day after this letter, on 3 May 1906. Since Nancy's engagement Revelstoke had gone from the pathetic to the tragic. It is true that a marriage between them would have been disastrous. It is also true that Revelstoke was very foolish. But Nancy dominated him completely, used him and often treated him like a pet dog on a lead. This was one of her greatest faults. Her insecure past had given her a tendency to cruelty and callousness that she was to use as a weapon for the rest of her life. Lord Revelstoke never married. He remained devoted to Nancy, finally proving that it was Nancy, and not Lady Desborough, for whom he had such deep feelings. Nancy must have realised this but Revelstoke's unrequited love merely acted as a confidence booster for her.

William Waldorf Senior found the marriage ceremony far too much for his reclusive nature and he took to his bed with gout. Another reason for taking to the sheets was that William realised that the London crowds might demonstrate outside the church, as Nancy was a divorcée. The Lennoxes, friends of the couple, had suggested a quiet country wedding and, as a final irony, Chillie, like William Waldorf, decided that he, too, had gout. But a few minutes before the ceremony the gout-ridden Astor decided that he would see his future daughter-in-law for a few minutes. Nancy wrote 'He seemed very much affected ... kissed me twice and remarked that my "gown" was becoming ... He's curious and not really human, but I think a great man.'

Nancy was married to Waldorf in considerable pomp and circumstance, the Bishop of London having given permission for a full Anglican ceremony because of the circumstances of her divorce. The wedding took place in All Souls' Church, Langham Place. They honeymooned in the Swiss Tyrol. Nancy was, for the first time for many years, ecstatically happy. She respected Waldorf and she knew she was safe with him. Now, living amidst one of the richest families in the world, she was determined to use her restless energy to good and powerful purpose.

William Waldorf's wedding present to the newly-married couple was Cliveden. The setting was magnificent, the house sitting on a hill overlooking the Thames between Windsor and

Maidenhead. The hill was partly natural and partly raised in terraces, built by George Villiers, Duke of Buckingham, who erected the first Cliveden in 1660. The house had a number of distinguished owners until it was burnt down in 1795. Rebuilt in 1824, Cliveden was again burnt down in 1849. Then in 1850, the Duke of Sutherland commissioned the Victorian architect, Charles Barry, to build a mansion in the Italian style. This he did with extraordinary and inspiring flamboyance. Magnificent lawns guard the approach and the central elevation of the house is 150 feet long, three storeys high with nine recessed windows across the front of each storey.

At this time Cliveden had a household staff of twenty-three but there were many more working on the estate. In fact the large staff felt as if they belonged to a special tribe and there was a village-like feeling to the servants' quarters as well as a sense of feudal community – with a Christmas ball each year and a regular cricket team. Nancy was at first overawed by Cliveden's size and then depressed by the gloomy, over-ornate furnishings and fittings that her father-in-law had installed. However, on handing over Cliveden to them, William Waldorf Astor idiosyncratically claimed that he would never set foot in the house again. He had removed himself to Hever and had turned the castle into a second fortress against the world.

William Waldorf's departure gave Nancy the opportunity to lighten the atmosphere by radically altering the interior. Nancy wrote: 'The keynote of the place when I took over was splendid gloom. Tapestries and ancient leather furniture filled most of the rooms. The place looked better when I had put in books and chintz curtains and covers and flowers.' Nancy went through Cliveden like an avenging whirlwind, crying out against what she considered was traditional Astor bad taste. She removed the curious jumble of stone wine-jars, Roman statues and sarcophagi from the main hall and the floor, originally of Italian mosaic stone, was replaced by parquet. William Waldorf's massive Italian ceiling, illustrating an Olympian banquet, was also removed – and replaced by Louis xv ceiling decoration. Flowers also began to burgeon all over Cliveden. Under William Waldorf's regime the fashion had been to place sweet peas and gypsophila in silver vases – an arid arrangement usually surrounded by framed photographs. Nancy had memories of

Mirador and how her mother's black maid used to pick flowers in the garden and mix them up in a large bowl, without the surrounding clutter of photographs and ornaments; reapplied to Cliveden, the house was soon alive with fragrance and colour.

Victor Cunard wrote of Nancy's personality during the early years at Cliveden:

'If Nancy Astor's understanding of childhood was nearly perfect, her approach to the problems of adolescence was less happy. She felt it her bounden duty to chastise, in and out of season, those weaknesses and uncertainties that beset young men and women as they begin to grow up; and she was never afraid to speak her mind. It was not surprising, therefore, that in the hope of avoiding galling, though often pertinent criticisms, even those who loved her dearly should, at about the age of 18, seek her company less assiduously. Though she might be conscious of this, she felt no resentment, and any disaster, illness or sorrow that befell someone she had known from childhood brought her immediately to the sufferer's side. The sight of pain or unhappiness, whatever their cause, drove all other considerations from her mind, and victims of circumstances or their own folly alike felt that they had a friend upon whom they could utterly rely.'

To own Cliveden was like running a small kingdom. The Cliveden estate was a perfect example of one of the great estates which existed in England before the First World War. Amongst the twenty indoor servants were eight maids, four scullery maids, a chamber groom, a chef, a butler, an odd-job man, a valet and three footmen. The footmen wore knee breeches, and powdered hair for more formal parties. Each man would dress, put a towel over his shirt, damp his head and sprinkle kitchen flour over his hair. The resultant feeling was rather like having a plaster cast round the head. Indeed, the entire process could not have been very good for the hair and seemed bound to encourage acute dandruff.

Outside, forty gardeners tended the fruit and vegetable farms as well as the park and gardens. There was a social club in a building on the estate for its workers with a billiard room and a hall with a stage. Each winter a staff fancy-dress ball was held there and each summer, on August bank holiday, there was a sports day including a tug-of-war that was refereed by Waldorf. The prizes were presented by Nancy. Cricket and football matches were played against other estates. Cliveden was an enclosed world of its own, but it was no longer a shuttered world as it had been when it belonged to Waldorf's father. Now Cliveden was one of the liveliest estates in the country.

In the summer of 1906 Nancy took Waldorf back to Mirador to meet Chillie and the rest of the family. Waldorf found that, to an outsider, Chillie entertained with an extraordinary blend of old world courtesy and total unconvention. Typical of Chillie's character was this letter (one of the few he wrote) that he sent Nancy on her return to England.

'My dear Nanny,

'I won't say how I have missed you for fear you may return (How is this for an Irish bull?). Really I am almost sorry I let you come to Mirador the parting was such a rench for me. We are getting on very well. Nora is trying her best at house-keeping & I am keeping busy. Catherine has just been phoned for to come home as her farther was dieing. To add to our depression it's been raining for two days. I read your little note & today also a nice letter from Waldorf which please thank him for. I sent the Ham Pickle and Apples to you at the boat & hope you & Waldorf may enjoy them. Take good care of your self & rest up or you will be old and ugly before your time. Don't let Bobbie forget me & be as nice to Waldorf as he is to you. Good by my dear. I didn't realise how I loved you till you left me. Send me your address & see Irene as soon as you can. Give Waldorf my best love & kiss Bobbie for me.

'Affectionately C. D. Langhorne.'

On the way back from America Nancy talked to some of the crew of the *Cedric*. This was the first time she had had such an encounter and she remembered it for the rest of her life; an inspiration when the time came for public meetings and for electioneering. Nancy was impressed by the way she could talk to 'ordinary seamen' and had her views corroborated by some-one from Brooklyn who conveniently passed by and apparently said: 'I would give my life to be able to do what that girl is doing down there.' However, this could well be one of Nancy's exaggerations for it really sounds too good to be true. No doubt she was thinking how pleased the Reverend Neve would have been over the episode.

Despite Waldorf's ill-health and her own hyperactivity and consequent bouts of exhaustion, Nancy decided that Cliveden should become a focus for elitist entertaining. She encouraged the staff to keep the lawns and the wood rides perfectly in trim, whilst the housekeeper slaved to give Nancy a detailed, daily report of the vegetables in season on the estate. She had a special policy in running Cliveden house-parties, largely based on the distinction of the guests. Apart from meal times, her guests' mornings and afternoons were largely their own, giving them time to write, or think, or compose – or secretly sleep away their exhaustion after a few hours of Nancy's frenetic company. Nancy was not a social climber – she had no need to be now she was an Astor. But she was ambitious and she wanted to turn Cliveden into a house where the most interesting and the most important people in the country came.

Nancy did not want to see Waldorf end his days as a wealthy invalid and Waldorf was as keen as she was that, despite his health, he should enter the House of Commons. At this time his political views were similar to many others in that he was at heart a Liberal but felt very strongly for the Conservative programme. Waldorf, however, was determined that he was not going merely to accept a safe Conservative seat. Naturally this was offered to him but he turned it down. He also realised that the party was principally after his money, and he was prepared to contribute, but not in such superficial circumstances. So Waldorf determined to cast around for a more marginal seat and a difficult contest. Meanwhile he would bide his time and study the field.

During this waiting period Waldorf created the Cliveden stud. From two mares he bred a number of racehorses that were eventually to constitute some of the best stock in the country. Nancy, however, did not enjoy racing particularly – nor the racing set. She had the responsibility of managing the weekend entertaining and, very soon, the guest list at Cliveden became extremely distinguished. Once he had discovered that there was good wine and good food to be had there, King Edward VII graced Nancy's dinner table. On that occasion Nancy was bored with the evening and annoyed to find that she was forced to speak to the Royal minions rather than to Edward himself. He brought with him his current favourite, Mrs Keppel, and Nancy was overshadowed. Even so Edward was captivated by Cliveden – so much so that he did not take his leave for hours. Later, Nancy met Edward elsewhere and much the same happened. Nancy indignantly wrote: 'One night King Edward came to dinner in a house where we were staying. They played cards till 1 am, and all that time I had to talk to a dull equerry. Three solid hours of dull talk. It was too much. No one spoke when Royalty was present until Royalty spoke, so on some occasions there were long and blighted moments.'

A legend grew up about a not particularly clever or amusing remark of Nancy's whilst Edward was at Cliveden, but its authenticity is doubtful. According to the anecdote, Edward had arrived at Cliveden and, far from ignoring Nancy, found her fascinating company, and sat with her for some time. The ladies of the court felt excluded and so they proposed a game of bridge to which the King concurred. He asked Nancy to partner him but she replied in the negative, stating that she had never played cards. She said 'Why, I don't even know the difference between a king and a knave." However, I prefer to believe the first version of the story; Nancy had been left in the wings and was forced to invest in legend to protect her confidence.

The once suspected Princess Marie often came to Cliveden and gradually Nancy began to accept her. One of Nancy's biographers, Maurice Collis, however, takes a superficial view of Nancy's antagonism to her.

'Lady Astor talks of her in an amusing way. She will tell you : "Marie of Rumania used to write to Waldorf every day at the time I first met him. I thought this too much on our honeymoon and I said I'd go home if it went on." Lady Astor's stories are never to be taken *au pied de la lettre*. She tells them for the fun in them; they are not meant to be pressed too far. Actually, she never took Marie of Rumania overseriously; she was far too clever for that. Though she had not much opinion of her, they became excellent friends.'

Nancy, however, was not as facile as this and had indeed taken Marie all too seriously.

Winston Churchill came to stay at Cliveden in May 1907, just a year after Nancy's marriage to Waldorf. Maurice Collis asked Nancy in her old age, what she thought of Churchill at thirty-three and she replied 'Not unlike what he is now, though he has mellowed. If seated next to a person he did not fancy, he would not utter a word. It is curious that he did not care for Americans at this date. Later they were so kind to him in the States when he was ill, that he became fond of them. His prejudices were very strong.'

Churchill's morose behaviour was quite likely due to the discomfort of Nancy's table arrangement – a discomfort she insisted on perpetuating despite her butler's pleas to the contrary. The Cliveden butler, Lee, complained that as the Cliveden luncheon and dinner parties grew larger, the more Nancy insisted in economy on seating.

'Her ladyship ... always thought that spreading out guests interfered with conversation, had now a further reason for keeping them close together; she wanted to fit in greater numbers. The table, with all its extra leaves, would hold in comfort a known maximum. But her ladyship would invite more than the number and tell me to pack them in. "Get those smaller chairs. Eighteen inches per person is ample." I used to protest: "Your ladyship is squashing your guests. They can't enjoy themselves. And what's more, the footmen and I cannot get between them to offer the dishes." I had noticed, too, that sometimes rather than try to help themselves, they would refuse dishes. I remember Mr Winston Churchill saying to me crossly when I tried to offer him the pudding: "Take the damned stuff off. I can't move." But her ladyship was not convinced. At last, however, I persuaded her to send me to Buckingham Palace to make enquiries. There I was told that each guest had two feet six inches. Her ladyship then gave in.'

One famous anecdote of Nancy's was the occasion when she had Asquith, Lord x and George Curzon amongst the guests at dinner. 'At the pudding course Lord x said to Curzon: "The Prime Minister's hand is resting on my wife's knee. What would you advise me to do?" Curzon gave the question his careful attention. "How long", he enquired judiciously, "has his hand been resting there?" "Since the soup," replied Lord x. "In that case," said Curzon, "let it rest." ' Once again she probably made this story up or highly exaggerated it but, because it is not personal, it is wittier. Curzon had just been made Viceroy of India and Nancy told Collis: 'He was always pompous, yet not always, for suddenly he could be like a boy. Though a big figure, he did not really know what was going on. His grievous disappointment near the end of his life, when the King summoned Baldwin instead of him to succeed Bonar Law as Prime Minister, was due to his being out of touch with realities.'

On 13 August 1907 Nancy gave birth to a son, William Waldorf, known as Billy. At this point, and much to Nancy's and Waldorf's horror, William Waldorf I decided to visit Cliveden – having said he would never set foot there again after leaving the house. Terrified that he would be furious over the drastic alterations she had made, Nancy hid in her room with the baby. But Waldorf did not seem in the least disconcerted and said to his son, 'The first joy of possession is to change everything and remould it nearer to the heart's desire.' Then he went upstairs to see Nancy and once again matters passed off very peacefully. He was very gentle with her, giving her a silver cup to commemorate the child's birth.

Hilaire Belloc was another regular visitor, particularly after the death of his wife. He brought his numerous children, but after a week's stay she suddenly seemed to find him tedious. This was not because of the children but because 'He had two manias – against the Jews and against the rich. I had to give him up in the end.' Maurice Collis believes that Nancy yearned for a sense of unworldliness in her male companions and Belloc did not measure up to this. Collis writes:

'She admired his brains and held his learning in respect, for she has always been modest in the presence of intellect, being very conscious that she was not intellectual or well read herself. But Belloc lacked the kind of plain sense she liked, and he had not the unworldliness which meant so much to her and which . . . was the bond between her and some men of great personal qualities, brilliance of mind and even genius, whom she was very fond of, as they were of her. She had a yearning, something very intense, a longing almost desperate,

for greatness and goodness; when she found these two qualities in a man, she was his friend. To get that close to Nancy
Astor was not easy.'

There were only four men in her life, apart from Waldorf,
who were to have that kind of relationship with her; Philip
Kerr, Julian Grenfell, George Bernard Shaw and T. E. Lawrence.
Meanwhile the Cliveden guest list continued to be star-
studded and Nancy was rapidly becoming a much favoured
political hostess, which is exactly what she had been aiming for.
In 1911 Lord Kitchener was a guest. He had a roving eye – not
for women but for *objets d'art*. Nancy told Collis:

'Kitchener was an extraordinary man, grave and austere, but
he had a weakness which was really comical. A well-known
collector of *objets d'art*, he had picked things up in Africa,
India, China. His method was simple and straightforward.
When he saw anything he fancied, he praised it and expected
the owner to give it to him. I knew this trait of his well, and
when I saw him eyeing my things, I just said flatly "I won't
give you anything." '

She disapproved completely of one of her other Cliveden
guests – Rudyard Kipling. 'I found him dour. He was very poor
company. He didn't seem able to take things lightly. And there
was something laughable about him, though I know I shouldn't
say it. He would sit on the sofa with his wife, an American, and
before answering a question ask her opinion. As one couldn't
get him away from her, it was impossible to do anything with
him.'

Nancy was absolutely calculating about acquiring success as
a hostess. She told Collis: 'There was lots to do at Cliveden.
My guests would go off and amuse themselves or talk to people
they wanted to, or read, ride, walk, explore the grounds or play
tennis. My rule was not to appear before lunch. I never interfered with them. That was how I got clever people like James
Arthur Balfour to stay.'

Other guests at Cliveden included James Barrie ('He got
spoiled and lost all his homely Scotch ways after being taken up
by the nobs.'), Lytton Strachey ('He was nervous, but excellent
company, so droll and lively.') and John Buchan ('The Scotch

are often that kind of snob.'). Henry James also came and left Nancy with the ambiguous but memorable phrase concerning 'the dauntless decency of the English'. Another famous guest was the portrait painter, John Singer Sargent. He was anxious to paint her and Nancy, now at the height of her new-found fame, was a willing sitter. Sargent would write her mock amorous letters which Nancy received in the spirit they were written. She was to have similar relationships with other men. Anyone who had the audacity to make real advances to her would have been immersed in all the ice her considerably frigid nature could muster. Sargent wrote in December 1907: 'I will clear a space around you, I will remove all that does not breathe to you of that passion which I have not been able to conceal and which by the means I will make you share or die, or know the reason why – Whereas I am so sorry I am engaged on Thursday; now I am catching a train. Yours sincerely John S. Sargent. PS I love writing to you – do let me write every day.'

The painting, after considerable changes had been made to its background, was completed by April 1909 and hung in the Royal Academy. For reasons of vanity, Sargent had turned Nancy into a tall and willowy beauty – whereas in fact she was very short. Despite her size though, Nancy was extremely beautiful and there seems little need for Sargent to have flattered her in this way.

Nancy then met the first of her 'unreals' – Julian Grenfell. He was the eldest son of Lord and Lady Desborough who owned a nearby house named Taplow Court. Lady Desborough, it will be remembered, was the woman Nancy considered had 'seduced' the wretched and now rejected Lord Revelstoke. Although there was no open feud between them, Nancy's unspoken rule was that no guest visiting Cliveden should have the audacity also to visit Taplow Court – the home of the temptress! Nancy's animosity to Lady Desborough was a publicly accepted fact and so there was another unspoken rule that guests of Lady Desborough should also avoid Cliveden. But after Nancy had lived in Cliveden for three years she had come to know Julian (who was nine years younger than she) and his brother Gerald (known as Billy), who was two years younger than Julian. Evelyn Waugh writing of Julian Grenfell in his biography of Ronald Knox summed him up in this way:

'Julian Grenfell in an exuberant, impersonal way, disliked everyone he did not know and loved all he knew constantly and tenderly. He was never a scholar like his brother Billy; he read too widely and too erratically for success in the Schools. A fine horseman and shot, a ferocious boxer, exulting in wild and natural things, he overtrained and overtaxed himself; moved by a passion to perfect his magnificent physique, he sometimes fell ill and moody. Born in the heart of the governing aristocracy to a mother who lived in a circle of devotees, he resented her occupations in the fashionable world and the endless, elegant house-parties in Taplow.'

Nancy attracted a number of people like Julian Grenfell. A restless personality herself, she was fascinating to those who were equally restless. Coming down from Oxford in 1910, Julian Grenfell joined the army, sailing to India in November. En route he wrote to Nancy and the following is an extract:

'Darling Nancy. Thank you awfully for your letter. I put you top easily for good-bye saying, or rather not-saying, which is so much better. You will go to heaven for keeping people cheery.

'Ld D, with his accustomed generosity, gave me "boot and saddle and horse and away", and I left England wanting for nothing. Never has anyone had such a good father. Terrible to say, I've got everything in the world I want, and a great deal that I don't want. It is delightful of you to want to give me a present – but the only thing I want is those three wasted years when you lived at Cliveden and we did not know you, fools that we were and blind.'

In 1915 Julian Grenfell wrote the war poem *Into Battle*. Both he and his brother were to be killed in the First World War and Nancy was to find their deaths an appalling loss. Billy, similar in temperament to his brother, wrote to Nancy as Sargent had – in a mock amorous way. He also delighted Nancy by his comment on poor Revelstoke. He wrote: 'Dear God, what a man! He has the mind of a haberdasher who reads the social column in the Daily Mail every morning before retailing secondhand trousers and "Modern Society" and Browning on Sunday afternoon.'

Billy was also anxious to heal the breach between his mother and Nancy. On 30 December 1910, he wrote: 'You know that you laughed me to scorn the other day when I told you that Lady D liked you. However it is *quite* true; she told me last night that she liked you very much and thought you an excellent friend for her children. I am so very glad aren't you? It will make everything a world simpler.' Unfortunately Billy misunderstood his mother, as a later letter points out: 'The Lady D. seems to regard you as an ideal friend for her children, but declines the honour herself. I wonder why? It can't be that old stone-cold John (Revelstoke).' Billy put the pressure on, however, and actually persuaded his parents to invite the Astors to dinner. Luckily they had another engagement and so mutual embarrassment was saved. Later Nancy took the children for tea at Taplow and, in the spring of 1911, Billy wrote: 'Is it true that you took your babies to tea at Taplow Court? The scene must have resembled one of those charming sacred pictures by Fra Bartolomeo representing the reunion of the Dove and the Cockatrice and their respective families.'

There was no doubt that Nancy Astor was an extraordinary hostess. If her guests appreciated her sense of humour then all would be well. But if they did not, they were damned. Nancy liked her sense of humour to be appreciated and she would be considerably put out if it was not. A typical example of her rather crass humour was when she made a fool of a new guest by introducing another guest as her husband. She insulted her 'husband' unmercifully, causing acute embarrassment to her victim. She would also break into the accents of one of her patronised but much loved Virginian negroes. Sometimes in mid conversation she would slap an enormous pair of celluloid teeth into her mouth, continuing her conversation quite impervious to her guests' horror, embarrassment or merriment. Charades were also regularly played after dinner, led by Nancy, although Waldorf was too inhibited to join in. The fun was fast and frantic and totally exhausted everyone, particularly Nancy.

In 1909 Mirador was suddenly fraught with disaster. Nora, the Langhornes' youngest daughter, proposed to marry a penniless young architect named Paul Phipps. She had met Phipps in England and fallen completely in love with him. Nancy backed the proposed marriage and wrote to Chillie enthusiastically, pointing out that Phipps was clear minded, clever, charming, and one of the nicest men she knew. Waldorf, writing to his sister-in-law, Irene, was fascinated as to how Chillie was going to react to the fact that Phipps had no money. Waldorf wrote 'Nora is in love! . . . A big secret – so big that nearly everyone is in it . . . This time it is *the real* article. Everything previous proves to have been spurious and of no account . . . We are all waiting breathlessly to hear what C.D.L. will do and say.'

They had some time to wait for C.D.L.'s reaction. The longer he delayed, Chillie reckoned, the more chance of a richer man coming along. Nora had had many suitors at Mirador and indeed so many were regularly sitting at the Langhorne table, that one night Chillie lost his temper and roared at his youngest daughter 'Damn it, Nora, I'm going to line up all these fellas in a row, and you can take your pick and be done with it.' This outburst concluded in Nora rushing hysterically to her room whilst the suitors remained, staring back inscrutably at Chillie. Nora was also considered to be extravagant which would not help if married to an impoverished husband. Chillie did nothing to cover up his daughter's weakness to the Phipps parents, who themselves behaved in a highly obsequious way. Mrs Phipps came to Cliveden to see the Astors, apologising for the fact that they had so little to offer Nora. Nancy, abrogating responsibility, wrote to Chillie asking him to come over and settle the matter. She told her father that she felt personally unable to take the responsibility, that Nora could not do anything until a decision was taken. But Chillie had no intention of deciding anything quickly and he still preferred to play the waiting game. For months the affair continued to drag on and there was no solution from either side of the Atlantic.

Meanwhile the worthy, dogged and humble Angus Mc-Donnell was still writing to Nancy, assuring her that he was not in the least in love with her – and breaking his heart because he was. In January 1909 he wrote:

'Now you say you have lots to talk to me about. Now really be honest. You know quite well that when you talk to me now you feel you have got to come down to my level which I don't resent in the least, because I guess the level is down in

57

the basement and undoubtedly yours has gone up and mine has gone down. However you are the best friend, man or woman, that I have ever had, or anyone else could ever have, and I love you and mother more than any one else in the world.'

Once again, although Nancy was intelligent enough to realise that McDonnell was still in love with her and to imagine the suffering that this must cause him, she was still happy to have him on a lead. McDonnell's undying, spaniel-like devotion gave Nancy a feeling of security as well as power. When he eventually married (without asking the advice of Nancy or Lady Antrim – an extraordinary idea which Angus McDonnell had agreed to because of his 'irresponsibility') Nancy furiously realised that she had lost her ewe lamb and sent him a hurtful and damaging cable. He had stepped out of line by stepping out of her power.

3

Politics and Power

In 1908 the Conservative party offered Waldorf his political chance at last and he was adopted by the Conservative Association of Plymouth. In 1909 the Astors bought a house there, an amazing confirmation of faith in an election which they had not so far won. Nevertheless they believed that they must become an essential part of the Plymouth constituency, and this would give them a strong advantage. The house the Astors bought was one of a distinguished row that faced the Hoe, overlooking the harbour. Also the coincidence of the association with America meant a great deal to both Waldorf and Nancy, since the Pilgrim Fathers had set sail on the *Mayflower* from the harbour at Sutton Pool.

Nancy, in her unpublished autobiography, had this to say of her first impressions of Plymouth: 'The moment I got there I had the strangest feeling of having come home. It was not like a new place to me. I felt that here was where I belonged. I remember sitting down and writing to Father to tell him all this. He wrote back saying there was nothing strange about it. One of the Langhornes was Member of Parliament for St Just in 1697, he told me, and a branch of the family had then been settled in Devonshire and Wales.'

As Nancy started to canvass with Waldorf she was reminded of her journeys with Mr Neve in his lumbering horse and buggy in the old days in Virginia. There was suddenly a sense of mission and purpose in her life that had been lacking during the last few years. During the campaign Nancy worked extremely hard, going from door to door with the same repeated state-

59

ment. 'I am Mrs Astor. My husband is standing for Parliament. Will you vote for him?'

Nancy loved her first journey into politics and became very keen on local affairs. She enjoyed going into people's houses and mixing with the 'common' people. Both she and Waldorf were given a good deal of advice about the best methods of campaigning, and it was suggested that Waldorf should buy a yacht as a status symbol. Luckily, both Astors rejected the idea.

Gradually they made progress, although a Conservative victory in Plymouth with its largely working-class population was not going to be easy. Luckily for Waldorf his wife's personality and charm was gradually overcoming resistance, but Waldorf was never to overcome his bad health, and the heavy electioneering took its toll. He contracted a bout of tuberculosis and his doctors insisted that he went to an open-air sanatorium in Scotland. Loyal, if desperately frustrated, Nancy accompanied him and they both slept out for many nights on a freezing balcony. The Astors then returned to Plymouth on polling day to find the election lost. Nevertheless the local people gave the young couple a tremendous welcome, even going to the extent of removing the horse from the shafts of their carriage – and hauling the Astors along by hand.

Waldorf had his second chance rather more quickly than he had imagined. There were two elections in 1910. Having lost the first, Waldorf then won the second. The first election was held in January – and the second in the following December. The reason for the second election was that the movement towards democracy which had been gathering strength since the first Reform Bill had taken on even more momentum after the Liberal victory in 1906 and the Labour Party had emerged as a force to be reckoned with. In January 1910 the major issue was whether Asquith's government should be backed over its ambition to abolish the more influential powers of the House of Lords – which had thrown out Lloyd George's People's Budget in 1909. Other burning issues included the gathering threat of Germany and the dismal prospect of Civil War in Ireland.

Nancy had known Margot Asquith for some time. In a way they were both thrown into the same predicament – two vivacious and intelligent women in a political man's world. Despite the fact that they had very different personalities and ideals, they had some qualities in common. Both women had courage, and both were ambitious. The famous story about Margot Asquith's railway carriage lectures underlines their common ability to dominate. Mrs Asquith made it her business to travel third class and to lecture her captive audience. She would rise briskly to announce: 'Now I am Mrs Asquith, and I expect you would like me to tell you something about my husband.' Like it or not, she was determined to tell them and any passenger who did not listen would be admonished.

Both Margot and Nancy shone in repartee (if not actual wit), but Nancy's conversation was more original than Margot's which tended towards diatribe. Typical of Margot's conversational style is her letter writing. In one particular letter she berates Nancy for what she considers her political naivety. Margot saw Nancy as a mere pupil and was neither sufficiently self-aware nor self-critical to realise that she was being outrageously patronising and insulting. But Nancy dared not express her opinion in case she harmed Waldorf's political career. Margot wrote:

'I wd like to have seen you and Waldorff but why didn't you ask Henry and me to see you once the whole year? Politics? I will say *one* thing to you [she was about to say many] (as a much older & far wider-ranged woman than you by education and inclination can ever be), You will never be leader in any society or have authority influence on a first-rate society if you xclude yr political opponents or have not the intellectual temper or social grandeur to be able to argue on big political points . . . You say like a child. "I know yr feelings about politics I hope you will *never* know mine"! You don't know my feelings nor do I know yours. You have never made a study of any political topic – never read a bill – never followed a debate closely . . . You are too young & crude to go into all this & why shd you? Instead of bothering to learn – take my advice don't think all that F E Smith and Ld Winterton say is the sermon on the mount. You add "Don't let's ever talk politics". My dear I *never* talk politics with my own sex for I've never met one now a days with the smallest political knowledge.'

Nancy must have been furious to know that she was classed

by Margot Asquith as a butterfly, since she was by no stretch of the imagination a suffragette. The letter continued in this semi-insulting and semi-patronising manner. Nancy did not answer, triumphing in Margot's unease and eventually placating note: 'Darling Nancy, I hope I wrote nothing in my long scrawl that hurts you – I was not the least vexed. You *never* offend me but as you've not written I feared I might have vexed you.'

Waldorf, meanwhile, was adding more influence to his political elbow. In search of a replacement editor for Harry Cust, and conscious of the fact that the *Pall Mall Gazette* was losing ground due to lack of forceful editorship, Waldorf's eye lit on James Garvin. Garvin was currently editor of the *Observer* and was locked in a policy battle with its owner, Lord North-cliffe. Waldorf knew that Garvin was a difficult but respected man. He also knew that Garvin was a brilliant editor, had brought circulation back to a previously ailing newspaper and would do the same for the *Gazette*. So, with the characteristic Astor approach, Waldorf decided that to buy the editor he would buy the *Observer*. This he did, beginning a close relationship with Garvin.

In 1912 Waldorf wrote a revealing letter to Garvin about his own philosophical and political ambitions. This statement is typical of his detachment: 'My own personal object and hope in life (including politics) is to be able to get certain things done, with, through or under the right people. I don't wish to spend time hunting for or shaping a career – my time and energy had much better be spent in getting things done . . . if the career follows and accompanies, by all means let it do so, but it would be a useless end to aim for if it had to come first! Therefore don't let's worry too much about an official career.'

The first major political grouping that Waldorf and Nancy became involved with was Milner's 'Kindergarten'. Lord Milner had been an administrator in South Africa, returning to England in 1903. His 'Kindergarten' was composed of young men whom Milner had either trained himself or who were believers in his Imperial ideas. As a result, Nancy met Philip Kerr who was to become her closest friend and spiritual adviser. Meanwhile, in the Conservative Party, splits were developing as a result of the recent defeats. The more reactionary members, i.e. those who did not wish to limit the power of the House of Lords and who were against the Home Rule for Ireland Bill, became isolated from the more progressive members. The progressives formed themselves into the Unionist Social Reform Committee, under the leadership of F. E. Smith, later to become Lord Birkenhead. Waldorf was amongst the most radical of this group as was Lord Henry Cavendish Bentinck. When Lloyd George's Health and Unemployment Insurance Bill passed its third reading, Astor and Bentinck voted with the government against their party. This was a matter of conscience for Waldorf; he had seen so much poverty and illness in Plymouth that there was no question as to where his loyalty lay. Following this political association, Lloyd George became friendly with the Astors, visited Cliveden and eventually invited Waldorf to become chairman of the State Medical Research Committee.

The Kindergarten group was not party political. They were 'liberal' in the then accepted sense of the word and all were concerned about the vulnerability of the British Empire. They believed that the Empire was about to crumble and therefore it was essential to strengthen both ties and unity. Dedicated to this cause, the Kindergarten were basically old-fashioned imperialists and their view on uniting English-speaking people was jingoistic. Typically, Nancy saw the scheme as missionary. The founder of the Kindergarten, Lord Milner, had himself left South Africa in 1905 and was merely passing on the basic philosophy and values of Cecil Rhodes.

Amongst the Kindergarten were Philip Kerr, Robert Brand (soon to marry Nancy's sister Phyllis and who was clearly in love with Nancy herself for some time), Geoffrey Dawson (later editor of *The Times*), Lionel Curtis, John Dove. Richard Feetham, Patrick Duncan, Lionel Hichens, Dougal Malcolm, Hugh Wyndham and Peter Perry. Their views were expressed through a magazine called *The Round Table* and the society itself was highly exclusive. Their monthly meetings, called Moots, were sometimes held at Cliveden although neither Waldorf nor Nancy qualified as full members. The Kindergarten was not concerned with the non-British inhabitants of the Empire. As far as they were concerned, racial problems in South Africa meant the conflict between the Boers and the British and the Kindergarten's aim was to try and encourage as many immigrants as possible into South Africa to ensure that the number of Dutch Afrikaaners were contained in a manageable minority. This, of course, they singularly failed to do. At the earliest stages of the group, Milner's main disciples, Curtis and Kerr, took to travelling around the Empire, making the necessary high-placed contacts to achieve the Kindergarten's aim. Nevertheless, however right-wing and reactionary this 'liberalism' sounds now, it attracted the Astors then. The Kindergarten credo lay in the absolute belief that Britain was the only country which was experienced enough to be able to keep an Empire and it was essential that the status quo was maintained.

At the same time the young men of the Kindergarten worshipped Nancy – which further attracted her to them. This is well illustrated in an essay Robert Brand wrote for Michael Astor in 1959:

'She wanted to get in touch with young people, who seemed to be interested in serious affairs and soon got hold of Philip Kerr and Lionel Curtis. For some reason I did not get to know her so soon. However, after a while she asked me to Cliveden and then to a weekend alone with her at Rest Harrow, Sandwich. I remember her saying to me at that visit: "Are you an Honourable? I see a letter addressed to you like that." I said, "Yes." She replied: "I am astounded. I thought you were absolutely middle class." . . . She certainly had a profound effect on the "Kindergarten" . . . We did not know it at once, but there was also an innate and irresistible force inside her, a sort of "power" engine, something that enabled her and indeed forced her to cut her way through life, something that compelled her to try to reform the world, and even to make the universe do what she wanted. She had many weapons available for the task; beauty, wit, an uncanny instinct both to hit upon one's weak or sore spot and sometimes to hit it hard and also to divine in a flash what one's inmost thoughts were. She had incomparable courage, great wealth at her command, which she used and which Waldorf was delighted she should use, and great generosity. She had money of her own, but as she used to say: "I didn't marry an Astor to spend my own money." Her reflective power was not so strong as her instinct. Reason was not a weapon she cared to use much, if at all, but she certainly had a very powerful intuition which worked like a flash. Her charm was such that we all fell easy victims. She liked our society because she was full of desire to do things in the world.'

This is an accurate summary of Nancy's personality and it is true to say that she liked people in groups because they represented to her 'doing' and 'power'. Unfortunately Nancy relied on her instinct and intuition too much, and she used reason too little. For instance, she continued to feel threatened by the young but increasingly influential Winston Churchill. Their mutual antipathy was to last the rest of their lives, but Churchill was not excluded from Cliveden for he was too great a rising star. One morning at breakfast Nancy snapped 'Winston, if I was married to you I'd put poison in your coffee.' To which Churchill adroitly returned, 'Nancy, if I was married to you, I'd drink it.'

Philip Kerr, like Nancy, was subject to bouts of neurotic exhaustion which were brought on by overwork. His work for the Kindergarten, his editorship of the *Round Table* and his more profound approach to race relations (studying the negro problem in America) had made him ill. In addition, a hyperactive imagination made him extremely restless and the other Kindergarten members became concerned about him. His religious struggles did not help his metabolism either. Both his father's and his mother's sides of the family were strong and devout Roman Catholics. At Oxford Philip Kerr toyed with the idea of becoming a priest. Then he fell in love with the daughter of an aristocratic English Protestant family and he realised with a grim shock that to be emotionally happy he would have to change his faith. Kerr felt morally unable to do this and he turned to Nancy for advice and comfort – which she gave in good measure. The romance continued until Kerr returned from travelling abroad to find his friend growing tired of the impasse. Predictably Kerr had a nervous breakdown and his doctor recommended a rest cure at St Moritz. Nancy and Waldorf, who were also exhausted, decided to join him. All three stayed in the same hotel and although there was no hint of any sexual relationship between Nancy and Philip Kerr, their spiritual relationship began to burgeon. In 1913 Philip Kerr went to India, partly to improve his health and partly to pursue his spiritual quest.

Philip Kerr's correspondence with Nancy was profound and 'seeking'. Both relied on each other in the search for 'truth' although Kerr, because of his stronger spiritual needs, took the lead and eventually became a kind of religious adviser to Nancy. The following extracts are typical of Philip Kerr's letters which were written to Nancy during his Indian journey:

'I like *Fortitude* (Hugh Walpole's latest novel). It's as you told me, quite one of the best of modern novels. It's so much stronger and clearer than Wells & Compton Mackenzie & there's freer poise about it & inspiration, & it shows life as it really is – an endless struggle against the lower forces in ourselves and round about all. I like two phrases in it too. One I wrote to you before "It isn't life which matters, but the courage that one brings to it" & the other "Art is listening – listening for the voice of God." That's quite true.'

The moralistic, puristic ideal of spiritual attainment and elevated peace of mind was shared by them both. Philip Kerr then read a copy of *The Brothers Karamazov* with marked passages that had particularly impressed Nancy. Sacred love was the theme and one such marked passage read as follows: 'In so far as you advance in love you will grow surer of the reality of God and of the immortality of the soul. If you attain to perfect self-forgetfulness in the love of your neighbour, then you will believe without doubt and no doubt can possibly enter your soul.'

Meanwhile Philip Kerr's Catholic faith was waning, despite a stay in a Catholic retreat before going to India. Unlike Nancy, whose religion was flexible, Kerr was confronted by the fact that he was either committing a deep sin by renouncing Catholicism, or was seeing a new way and therefore a new religion.

By now Nancy had borne four children. The eldest – Bobbie – was special to her. Although she loved the other three deeply, Bobbie, the product of that disastrous and inhibited marriage, was very dependent on her and she was devoted to him. He was now fourteen, her eldest Astor child, Bill, was five, Nancy Phyllis Louise (known as Wissie) was three and Francis David Langhorne (known as David) had just been born.

The year 1912 brought tragedy. William Waldorf Astor's

cousin, John Jacob Astor, sailed on the maiden voyage of the *Titanic*. When the *Titanic* struck an iceberg on the night of 15 April 1912, Astor was told of the collision before the general alarm was sounded. Eye-witness accounts claim he accepted the news with dignity and told his wife, Madeleine to 'Get into the lifeboat to please me.' She obeyed him and the lifeboat pulled away from the ship. He and his valet changed into full evening dress and shortly after the great ship plunged to the bottom of the sea. John Jacob Astor's body, with $2,500 in sodden dollar bills in his pocket, was later found floating in the sea.

Soon after this terrible event Nancy became involved in Christian Science. It began with her correspondence with Kerr whilst he was in India and gathered pace through her relationship with the obsessive Hilaire Belloc. Typical of Belloc's personality, style and distastefully jokey anti-semitism is this extract from a letter he wrote Nancy in 1911 whilst he was in Belgium, researching a book on the Battle of Waterloo.

'It was about half way between Waxre and Plancenoit, two villages of some fame, that I would have written to say that I should be delighted to come on that Wednesday to lunch, had I had pen, ink or paper; or it had been fine. But I was under worse conditions than Blücker and I just put it off. True I had (a) no army to conduct (b) no bruises from falling off a horse and (c) no old age – a vile disease. But on the other hand I was *aleph* [Hebrew] in the rain, *beth* [Hebrew] cold, and *gimel* [Hebrew] worried by mud. I put it off past Ligny and Quatre Bras. Then I did the lazy thing and telephoned.'

Belloc shared America and humour in common with Nancy. His wife was American and he knew that country well. As far as humour was concerned he was an enthusiastic subscriber to Nancy's style of practical joking and teasing. Belloc's religion, rediscovered Catholicism, was his main fervour. Then, quite by chance, Nancy tested him. Bill was taken ill and, for a time, it seemed possible that he might die. Nancy wrote to Belloc in her anguish and his reply made a very strong impression on her.

'The profound truth is all these things sound like platitudes or folly today because there is no common Faith in England. It is this: that all human life is subject to conditions of peril and sorrow which are intolerable unless, unless we get some hold upon why we are here and what we are doing. God made us : and the same force which created these awful necessities is the origin without which the love of children itself could not be. The strongest and most terrible thing on earth, though the children never know it, is the love of children. Meanwhile out of such perils the greatest good and happiness comes when by some providence they are averted, and you must not think it is a folly in me if I tell you that they are to be prayed down. In this family of mine the many and increasing perils have never had added to them such a trial as yours : therefore I will have all my little children pray for yours and that to Our Blessed Lady who never fails us unhappy children of her – at least so I have found it, always.'

Nancy wanted immediate answers to her prayers and not too long a search for religious truth. Impatient as ever, she seized on New Thought – which was both immediate and utterly vacuous. Nancy discovered this semi-religious movement in America on one of her periodic visits and even managed to interest Philip Kerr in it. Basically the philosophy of New Thought stated that if you concentrated all your mental faculties on something hard enough – you would get it. It was all very simple. Bob Brand, however, writes about New Thought in cynical style : 'The idea behind New Thought was that if you only thought about something hard enough, health or whatever it might be, you got it. I remember buying a New Thought pamphlet entitled "Dollars Want Me". The argument was that if you only thought about dollars hard enough they came rolling in from every direction.'

Mind over matter was an idea common to the ludicrous simplicity of New Thought and the profundity of Christian Science. In 1913, on another visit to the States, Nancy was encouraged by her sister Phyllis to read the renowned *Science and Health* by Mrs Mary Baker Eddy. Writing in *Tribal Feeling*, Michael Astor gives his explanation for his mother's growing acceptance of the movement :

'In the first place Christian Science is Protestant in character, nonconformist in essence, and accepts certain forms of miracles as being of everyday occurrence; an optimistic and unfettered view of life which always left my mother quite undaunted. Despite its name, its appeal is emotional rather than intellectual. Its horizons know no limits. It declares that man is capable of perfection and is in no way governed by conventions, or laws, or even by his own history. It is a religion which not only encourages the reading of the Bible but has issued a new interpretation of the Scriptures which has automatically widened the interpretation which its followers can place on Holy Writ. It also contains a strong dose of straight puritanical prejudice which was axiomatic to my parents' view of life. Its main thesis is that the true world is the world made by God, and the intolerable behaviour of man is the shadow rather than the substance of reality. It was this broad assumption that my mother accepted in her quest for religion. The answer, however, does not lie wholly in the tenets of the doctrine itself ... so much as my mother's interpretation of its theory. In terms of practical results it confirmed her in the feeling that she was right in her views, and it reconciled her conscience with her worldly position. The effect of this was a renewal of her vitality and strength.'

Nancy's belief in Christian Science stemmed from a miracle that she believed to have occurred. Christian Science claimed that miracles were everyday events, and Nancy was certain that she had been involved in one of them. I have already mentioned that Nancy was prone to bursts of great activity – and then to periods of 'illness'. This illness was nervous exhaustion and was a problem typical of such a hyperactive person. But in February 1914 a more serious form of illness was diagnosed – an internal abscess. Nancy underwent an operation and was told afterwards that a second operation was necessary. She wrote:

'This is not what God wants. It is not what He meant to happen. It can't be that God made sickness. It turns people into useless self-centred people who become a burden to themselves and to everyone else. I lay for hours there, puzzling it out with myself. I felt there was an answer to this riddle but I had no idea what the answer was. Then a wonderful thing happened. Whenever a soul is ready for enlightenment, and awaits it humbly, I believe that the answer is somewhere to hand; the teacher comes.'

The teacher was her sister Phyllis who told her more about Christian Science and its adherents. Nancy saw the light. 'She told me . . . there were people in America who believed as I did, that God never meant there to be sickness and suffering, and who could be cured by prayer. I was deeply impressed and in a way comforted, for it was a confirmation of something I had felt instinctively must be.'

After seeing a Christian Science practitioner and re-reading Mrs Eddy, Nancy underwent the second operation. She had the courage to refuse it, but Waldorf insisted. The operation was successful and so was her recovery, which Nancy decided to attribute to Christian Science. This was typical of her continuous manipulation of the belief to justify her own ends. By March 1914 Nancy was writing to her original spiritual mentor, Neve. He disapproved of her conversion and Belloc made light of it, peppering his letter with his usual anti-semitic drivel. 'So you have found a new religion! What a pity! Just as I have found . . .' and then he continues in fantasy Hebrew.

In April, Philip Kerr returned to England and Nancy was able to share, at last, her conversion and its implications with him. He was still very ill and a burst appendix was later diagnosed, followed by peritonitis. Nancy and Waldorf arranged for Kerr to be operated on at Sandwich Hospital. The operation was successful and to speed his recovery Nancy sent him Mrs Eddy. On 13 April Philip Kerr wrote to Nancy. He told her that he was 'flourishing' and that

'. . . it makes the day longer not having you to talk to and to see. I'm only just beginning to realise how much you've helped me – that morning before the operation and every hour since. My faith will grow all right, yours is so infectious. I've been reading S & H and understand it better each time. I've got Mother to begin reading it too. She's said nothing about it yet. I told her it had helped me to understand Our Lord's life and work like nothing else ever had. I don't miss you – only as I should miss a great pleasure – not aching or real loneliness – that's the wonder of it. We shall never be alone again.'

Another 'miracle' recovery and another convert. Nancy and Philip were now ecstatically happy and much insecurity and self-doubt was camouflaged by their new religion. Philip Kerr's conversion to Christian Science made a lasting bond between him and Nancy. There had already been considerable friendship but now this had become a deeply spiritual attachment. Nancy described this relationship as their 'secret way' and on the fly-leaf of a book she had given to Philip, Nancy inscribed:

'You and I have found the secret way,
No one shall hinder us or say us nay.
All the world may stare and never know
You and I are twined together so.'

There is no record of Waldorf's feelings on the subject but fortunately he was not a jealous man.

Philip Kerr became highly intolerant of his mother's continuing staunch Catholicism. Like many of Nancy's friends, he was very close to his mother and valued her good opinion of him. He wrote in a letter to Nancy, 'I sometimes think that my Mother is the most simple and honest-minded bigot I have ever met. She'll believe *anything* if it fits in with her preconceited [sic] world and suspects *everything* which doesn't. What a revelation it will be for her when it comes.' This from a former devout Catholic. Kerr's friends were amazed and some had a cynical reaction – such as Alice Roosevelt Longworth who replied at the news of his conversion: 'Perfectly simple, just a case of swapping Blessed Virgins in midstream.'

Nancy was soon to grow highly intolerant of Catholics, largely because of Philip Kerr's unyielding family. Michael Astor felt that Christian Science very much harmed his mother's perception and understanding of other people and he wrote:

'Her view of people remained, in one sense, like a child's. Some people were good and some were bad and the distinction had always to be drawn. Yet she kept encountering so much in life to disprove this notion. This was her dilemma; and the doctrine of Christian Science, which insisted that everyone was good, that failed utterly to take into account the complex nature of man which defies these simple moral ratings, encouraged her to hold on to her simple beliefs. It was, perhaps, these childish beliefs that kept her young and vigorous, a condition which she accepted as proof of the

71

efficiency of Christian Science teaching. But it was this over-simplified moralistic view of life which prevented her reaching any deep understanding of people, despite her natural intelligence and aptitudes.'

Philip Kerr's needs for spiritual attainment were much more objective and pure than Nancy's – but even so he was still capable of self delusion. Like Nancy, he now renounced all doctors and wrote on 23 April: 'You are quite right. It does make a difference being surrounded by Doctors and Nurses & RCs. It's almost if not actually impossible to practise C.S. [Christian Science] about your own body, and all night too, & a doctor comes twice a day & crows excitedly over the way its behaving & all one's relatives come in all day long & tell one to be careful & not do too much but remember what I've been through, etc.'

Wearing as this process was, it hardly justifies an argument for mind over matter. Yet there is no doubt that Nancy and Philip *were* on the road to better health. Her maid, Rose Harrison, later wrote: 'If good health is proof of a religion then my lady was a saint. There were only two occasions when she had anything really wrong with her, until her final illness.' But Rose was very disapproving of her mistress's religion. She was also extremely perceptive concerning Nancy herself:

'Christian Science suited her way of life. It had no dogma and could be twisted and bent to excuse her faults and actions. It made her smug and sometimes self-righteous. It was as though she had invited Our Lord to one of her parties, he had accepted and sat at her right hand. It encouraged her to hate groups of people, Roman Catholics – "Red Cherries" – as she called them, the Irish and anti-prohibitionists. Yet perversely, amongst her greatest friends were Hilaire Belloc, a bigoted Catholic and Jew-hater, and two godless socialists, Sean O'Casey and Bernard Shaw. The latter, with Lord Lothian (Philip Kerr) could without any doubt be called her two closest friends. Again Christian Science is only for the rich or the middle class. You can't get a practitioner on the National Health, nor do you find one of their Churches in a poor area. You buy your pardons. It cost the Astors plenty.'

A forthright view – but a superficial and over-simplified one. The search and the 'secret way' were serious matters to Nancy and Philip and they genuinely thought they had reached an earthly salvation. In the same letter of 23 April Philip wrote:

'Sin and pain are like lies, they cease to affect you directly you know they are lies. Only it's difficult to be *sure* in my heart at first that they are lies. But I'm getting nearer to it every day. I've had such a demonstration these last few days. D'you know old Moon says that the shock of the bursting of the appendix on Monday morning was the worst it is possible for anyone to have, that I was absolutely unfit for an operation in the morning & that I was probably half off my head. D'you think so? I seldom – no never – had a happier morning. Perfect love certainly casteth out pain as well as fear.'

Nancy now ensured that there was a Christian Science practitioner at most of her dinner parties. They seemed to have a doubtful role in the household – treated somewhere between guest and servant. Neither could they expect to remain in favour and many were dismissed, never to be seen again. Nancy now consistently believed that her own recovery from illness was a miracle and the fact that she had introduced the faith to Philip Kerr so successfully was proof of a second miracle. Because of this, Nancy subconsciously still used Christian Science to her own ends. As Michael Astor points out, the Christian Science practitioners at Nancy's dinner table were 'of course, trained optimists, and were left admiring her aspirations rather than her orthodoxy.' In fact her son had little faith in his mother's acceptance of Christian Science. He wrote: 'The members of the Christian Science Church with whom I have discussed this matter of her religion, whilst not losing hope for the future, hinted that my Mother never really understood what it was all about.'

The practice of Christian Science became a daily devotion to Nancy. Edwin Lee, her butler, remembered that she made it very clear that she no longer wanted to see any doctors. When, for instance, Nancy caught a cold she would stay in bed and read books on Christian Science. She seemed to recover quickly and this was almost certainly due to the conviction of her faith and her will-power. Rose Harrison said: 'Her ladyship tried to make me take up Christian Science and asked me to read the books. But I didn't. I'm a Protestant, and intend to remain so. In all the thirty years I have been with her, I have never seen anything that would convince me of its truth. I admit that she was never ill after she took it up. The only thing she ever had was a boil, and shingles not very bad, but then she is a very strong woman and Christian Science or not, she would have been well, I expect.'

It is true that Nancy had been more prone to psychosomatic illness than physical illness in the past, but it would be wrong to say that she was very strong physically. She may not have practised Christian Science adequately but she convinced herself she did – and that was the important factor. Her conviction gave her a psychological immunity – an immunity that worked.

What kind of effect did Nancy's practice of Christian Science have on her husband and children? Waldorf held out against the faith for nine years before eventually succumbing. But Nancy had her convert Philip, and was probably not so concerned that her husband resisted her evangelising over such a long period. The children did not escape so easily and they underwent an intensive religious indoctrination. Michael Astor reacted as follows:

'. . . when I was up at Oxford a friend of my father's suggested that I should read Sir Edmund Gosse's book *Father and Son*. He told me that our life at home was comparable to Gosse's early life as it is recorded in this work. Gosse wrote before the days of psychiatrists, before parents and teachers had evolved new theories for bringing up or breaking down their children, and he remembered and recorded his early childhood in astonishing detail and with a remarkable sense of detachment. His father, who was an intelligent man and a distinguished naturalist of his day, adhered to a blind religious faith in the pre-ordained nature of both the physical and the spiritual world, despite very considerable scientific evidence which he came to discover and which ran contrary to most of his religious belief. By conviction, or possibly by convenience, he also believed in the absolute right of parental authority. Young Gosse was made an acolyte to a crazy religion. Improvised prayers and the society of "saints" became his daily portion. His position as a child was embarrassing in the extreme. Quite clearly he would have been made to feel a fool amongst his friends, except that he was not allowed to have any friends.'

Nancy did not go to the extremes of Gosse – and the Astor children were allowed to have plenty of friends. But there is still the comparison, and the young Astors were forced to find ways of mental escape. They all took different routes. Michael, for instance, found that silence was essential for recuperative purposes. 'Life looked for in a permanently jazzed-up setting seemed like life going to waste. The throbbing syncopation drowned the melody. The music of sorrow and lament also had its harmonies and its meaning; and the breath of Puritanism, despite all the social trappings and the sounds of gaiety, blew like a cold north-east wind.'

But the social trappings were of great importance as Edwin Lee's description of day-to-day life with the Astors underlines.

'We would probably be at Cliveden for the week-end and on the Monday go to London, 4 St James's Square, or to Rest Harrow, Sandwich or to 3 Elliot Terrace, Plymouth. We also had a house in Scotland where the family used to go in August and September, but after a week-end at Cliveden we would generally return to London where Mr and Mrs Astor used to entertain on a very large scale. Dinners between 50 and 60 were very frequent and probably two or three balls for anything up to 500 or 600 would be given during the season and of course receptions were also held. I think the largest one I remember was for 1,000 guests. A fairly large staff was kept in both London and Cliveden but most of us used to travel between London and Cliveden. At that particular time we had a very fine French chef who was considered one of the best in the country and a very nice man to work with. He had five girls working with him. We also had a stillroom where all the bread and cakes were made. Baking was done at Cliveden twice a week. The Head Stillroom Maid used to travel always between London and Cliveden. One Under Stillroom Maid was kept in either place. There was a very large staff of gardeners and stablemen kept at Cliveden, between 40 and 50 gardeners and about 10 or 12 stablemen. All the lawns on the pleasure grounds were mowed by horses with leather boots strapped over their iron shoes. In the house at Cliveden there was a housekeeper, 6 housemaids, 6 laundry maids and always one or two left in the kitchen apart from the travelling staff, also an Odd Man to look after the boilers, carry coal, answer the telephone – a most useful man in every way.'

Nancy's domestic routine remained very puritanical. She was normally called at eight am with a tray of coffee and fruit. After this she spent the next thirty minutes reading the Bible and *Science and Health*. Then she would see the children, talk on the phone and lecture which members of the family were nearest to hand on her religion. Her commands rang out regally : 'Now keep still and listen to this, it will really help you. There's *nothing* like the life of St Paul, you must study it.' Sometimes she was in a more nostalgic mood and would address her children in the tones of an old Negro woman : 'Yessir, I'se gonna help you. Me and Mistah Jesus is gonna help you.'

Having prepared herself (and others) for the coming day, Nancy took a cold bath and did physical exercises. She would keep up a running conversation with her maid during this process and after breakfast she would start dealing with the servants. The day passed with much frantic activity but by evening, Nancy was still going strong on nervous energy. The evenings were taken up with mimes and charades as well as Nancy's impersonations. Michael Astor remembered some of them and wrote :

'There was the little Jewish businessman, and in order to do him justice she would hurry upstairs and a few moments later appear again wearing trousers, a tail coat, and a bowler hat crammed over her ears. This character had no name or any name. He was in business, any sort of business. He was excitable, affectionate, gigglish, a family man devoted to his wife and children; he was confidential, persuasive, but really suffered from terrible anxieties which at times rendered him hysterical. Then there was the horsey English lady who hunted in Leicestershire. The false teeth were enough to do her justice. This character went hard to hounds, swore a bit and suffered from no anxieties whatsoever. There was also the lady of infinitely good breeding and no brains, conventional and vague, who found Americans common. There was Margot Asquith, straight out of the bottle, by which I mean undiluted in essence, a true reporting from life. And there was the frightened mean old lady with no teeth in her head, her skin all wrinkled and her hair pulled down over her face, who looked shrewd and canny and who was deeply suspicious of her neighbours.'

Her work for Waldorf also continued ceaselessly. She took the Primrose League in hand, largely because she found it far too select a little band, dissipating itself in an orgy of genteel and ineffective tea parties. She re-arranged the programme and social content of the League, ensuring that the brew of upper class ladies was leavened with the involvement of working men's wives.

To achieve all this Nancy kept herself very fit, and played squash, tennis and regularly rode and hunted. She certainly needed a healthy body to maintain her exhausting style of life as Billy Grenfell, who adored her, makes all too clear. He writes:

'Nancy came down on Saturday bringing a moth-eaten wormy wordy little Tory called Maurice Woods . . . We had lunch in John's room which contained a hospitable fire. I was in the *most awful* state of wallop after five minutes, and had to take off my coat after fish, and my waistcoat between cutlets and roast fowl. Nancy spent half her time in calling attention to the course taken by the drops down my puffed visage, and divided the remainder about equally between noisy platitudes on the political situation and directions to Waldorf on the best way to force spinach down William's throat . . . Why are political discussions so b——y dull? I think it is because Liberals are never admitted to our house. So one only hears denunciation *ad nauseam*.'

Then, quite suddenly, this idyll of spiritual discovery and feverish living ended. The First World War broke out in August 1914 and with it came a reality of death and grief that even Nancy's abilities at self-deception could not dispel.

4

Death of the Golden Boys

The First World War deprived Nancy of two of her greatest
friends. It also brought out the very best of her personal
qualities. Both she and Waldorf centred their activities on
Plymouth, Waldorf putting up money for YMCA canteens, whilst
Nancy worked in the hospitals. Nancy remembered: 'I went to
my first military funeral. It was a man from Watford. His little
wife came, and stood stunned and sorrowful by the graveside.
I heard for the first time bugles play the Last Post. I think of
that woman still.' Waldorf was, of course, bitterly disappointed
that he was medically unfit to enlist. Nancy wrote: 'It was a
terrible grief to my husband that he could not join up and go
and fight. He was a young man, tall and handsome, to all outward appearances fit as a fiddle, for his heart condition gave him
a high colour. He went to Sir John Cowans and asked for the
most disagreeable job that was going. They made him a major
and gave him the job of trying to check army waste.'

In November 1914 the Astors offered Cliveden to the
Canadian army as a hospital. The house, however, was considered unsuitable and the decision was made to convert the
enormous covered tennis court and bowling alley. By February
1915, the conversion was complete and a hospital emerged that
could hold 110 patients. This was later enlarged to a building
that could hold over 600 patients. Cliveden itself was used as a
convalescent home and Nancy worked continuously both in the
house and in the hospital. For the first time her tremendous
energies were put to really good use.

Nancy's friends, Julian and Billy Grenfell, loved the war that
killed them. They had been 'trained' to serve their country by

79

their family and by their education at Eton and Oxford. Now, at last, their opportunity had come and they considered themselves very lucky indeed. An extract from Julian's poem, *Into Battle*, underlines this:

> And when the burning moment breaks,
> And all things else are out of mind,
> And Joy of Battle only takes
> Him by the throat – and makes him blind –
>
> Through joy and blindness he shall know,
> Not caring much to know, that still
> Nor lead nor steel shall reach him so
> That it be not the Destined Will.
>
> The thundering line of battle stands,
> And in the air Death moans and sings;
> And Day shall clasp him with strong hands,
> And Night shall fold him in soft wings.

The Grenfells' blind but courageous approach to war was also heavily romanticised. They were absolutely certain that God was on their side, that the enemy was satanically inspired and that heaven awaited the ennobled ranks of the dead.

These extracts from one of Julian's diaries show how much he enjoyed the war and its heady, barbaric excitement:

11 October 1914

'... It's all the best fun one ever dreamed of, and up to now it has only wanted a few shells and a little noise to supply the necessary element of excitement. The uncertainty of it is so good, like a picnic when you don't know where you're going to: and the rush and hustle of trying to settle things in the whole confusion, unpacking and packing up again, and dumping down men and horses in strange fields or houses or towns, and fighting to get food and water and beds for the men and oneself when one knows that probably another start will be made long before anything is got.'

Once they were in the trenches and death was imminent, Julian seemed even more intoxicated:

24 October 1914

'We had it pretty hot this last day or two in the *trenches*.

We take to it like ducks to water and dig much better trenches than the infantry ... I adore the fighting and the continual interest which compensates for every disadvantage ... I *adore* war. It is like a big picnic without the objectlessness of a picnic. I've never been so well or so happy. No one grumbles at one for being dirty.'

Julian's biographer, Nicholas Mosley, wrote: 'For the first time a generation brought up to be clean and bright and obedient could, without guilt, be fierce and babyish and vile. Such behaviour had been forbidden them when such attitudes might have been natural: the relief when it was allowed them later was overwhelming.'

Another of Julian's poems that expresses his passion for heavenly-inspired, justified bloodshed was written on the boat from England to South Africa but it was not completed and he screwed it up. Luckily a passenger picked up the fragment and preserved this for posterity:

> ... The ordered Past behind us lies –
> The past with ordered argosies
> Of memory's abiding treasure,
> Of pains and joys and driving pleasure.
> Passion, a burning fiery sword,
> Swooping, the Angel of the Lord,
> Has struck the soul with fire and rout,
> Has cut a flaming way about,
> Has struck, and cleansed, and wandered out,
> And lust, the son of Storm and Thunder,
> Has seized the empty souls for plunder:
> Lust, that Red Mimic, jagged light,
> Who deadens sense, and sears the sight ...

But despite all this passion, the Grenfells' courage must be emphasised. The First World War was one of the most debilitating of all wars, with its trenches, rats, hand-to-hand combat and high death-rate. The appallingly young age of the dead and the great odds against most combatants' survival was beginning to be grimly realised by a horrified country. Julian provides a graphic description of the conditions in his letter to Nancy of 21 November:

'My darling Nancy, Thank you awfully for your letter. How are you? I suppose you are frightfully busy now, working at hospitals and things? How is Waldorf? I have not seen John out here yet, but he is within five miles of us now. We have had the heck of a time for the last 3 weeks, doing infantry work with one man looking after about 10, and shells landing among them and killing a few every now & then. We have given these Huns a great walloping, when they apparently outnumbered us (at one time) by about 5-1. I have enjoyed it all tremendously – every minute of it: but it has been damnably cold. The worst trenches are the ones under heavy shell fire – most of them are. Then you simply crouch in the wet clay for 48 hours, and wait for the shells coming. You can hear them coming, and bet on whether they are going to land in the trench or outside it. The noise is the worst thing – it makes your head simply buzz by the end of the day. Their guns are horribly good.

'The other kind of trench is the one that is so close (30-60 yds) to the German trenches that they cannot shell you. That is the best fun. You snipe away at each other all day. Then they attack, quite slowly, in mass formation, and you just mow them down.

'But I wish we could get some cavalry work, and get in at the brutes with our swords and horses. I believe that will come.

'How is your lover Bill (a joking reference to Billy)? Please give him my best love, and tell him to come out here with a fur-lined coat, regardless of price. It is bloody cold – black frost and an inch of snow. Our poor horses stay out all night, with only one thin blanket; I can't make out why they are not dead. Just think of it.

'Nancy, you can't think of the soul in this war. (Presumably she had been lecturing him on Christian Science by post). It is absolutely at a discount. It is much better for us to leave it out altogether. Bless you. Julian. P.S. We get 48 hours on and 48 off, in a farm with the men in a barn. This is our 48 off.'

This letter illustrates the kind of relationship that Nancy had

with men of Julian Grenfell's personality: warm, direct, flirtatious and intelligent.

Then, in May 1915, Julian was hit in the head by the frag-
ments of a shell. At first the wound did not look very serious
and he wrote to his mother:

14 May 1915

'Darling Mother,

'Isn't it wonderful and glorious that at last after long
waiting the Cavalry have put it across the Boches on their flat
feet and have pulled the frying pan out of the fire for the
second time. Good old "iron ration"! We are practically
wiped out, but we charged and took the Hun trenches yesterday. I stopped a Jack Johnson with my head, and my skull is
slightly cracked. But I'm getting on splendidly. I did awfully
well. Today I go down to Wimereux, to hospital, shall you be
there? *All All* love.

Julian of the 'Ard 'Ead.
Longing to see you and *talk*! !
Bless you!'

Brain damage was diagnosed and after two operations paralysis
began to set in. For a while Julian rallied and exclaimed when
his sister, Monica, entered the room 'Here is the girl with sunshine in her hair, the sunshine lingering in her hair.' On 25 May
Julian said goodbye to his sister and asked his mother to 'Hold
my hand till I go.' Ettie claimed 'a shaft of sunlight came in at
the darkened window and fell across his feet.' Julian smiled at
his mother and murmured 'Phoebus Apollo'. He did not speak
again except to murmur his father's name. Then, on 26 May,
Ettie remembers 'at twenty minutes to four in the afternoon . . .
he moved his Mother's hand to his lips. At the moment that he
died, he opened his eyes a little with the most radiant smile that
they had ever seen on his face.'

Julian was buried in the Soldier's Cemetery in the hills above
Boulogne and Ettie covered his grave with wild flowers and oak
leaves. Ivo (Julian's brother) wrote from Eton: 'God bless Julian
for all his wonderful life on earth and for the joy he has been
to us all.' Henry James wrote to Ettie saying '. . . those extraordinarily living and breathing, ringing and singing, verses . . . I
seem always to have known your splendid son even though that

ravaged felicity hadn't come my way ... What great and terrible and unspeakable things! but out of which, round his sublime young image, a noble and exquisite legend will flower.'

Nancy was heart-broken at the news of Julian's death, remembering the gaiety of her relationship with him. She tried to imagine him when he was a child – in those days of burnished nostalgia on the Thames. She had seen a photograph of Julian and Billy trying to push Monica off a jetty into the river. There was laughter in their eyes – they were like young water gods as their reflections danced in the shimmering leaf-strewn surface of the river. Billy wrote to Nancy saying: 'Darling Nance. A million thanks for all your letters and for all your love. How could a man end his life better than in the full tide of strength and glory – Julian has soared the darkness of our night, and passed on to a wider life. I feel no shadow of grief for him, only thankfulness for his bright and brave example. We are just off to the trenches, looking like iron pirates, so no more now except all my love. Yours ever, Billy.'

By 30 July Billy was also dead, killed by machine-gun fire. He had written of Julian: 'I pray that one tenth of his gay spirit may descend on me.' His body was not recovered. The empty glory of the war continued, later enshrined by the piety of its war poets. Julian had written:

> Fighting in mud, we turn to Thee
> In these dread times of battle, Lord,
> To keep us safe, if so may be,
> From shrapnel, snipers, shell and sword.

Another poet, and a friend of the Grenfells, Patrick Shaw Stewart was more oblique when he wrote:

> I saw a man this morning
> Who did not wish to die:
> I ask, and cannot answer
> If otherwise wish I ...

Nancy confided to her memoir: 'After two years in that first war, we did not look at the casualty lists any more. There was nothing to look for. All our friends had gone.'

Nancy dwelt for years on the very last letter Julian had written her. He must have been well aware of the closeness of his death when he commanded Nancy 'Take care of yourself, my pretty, do your hair nicely, and do not overload yourself with charitable works in this ungrateful world.'

Nancy had tried to prevent Billy's death by attempting to manoeuvre him towards the General Staff but Billy refused. He wrote: 'It is too angelic of — to ever suggest taking me on his staff, but I don't really entertain the idea for a minute. The extra ADC is regarded with such deserved loathing and contempt here.' So the Grenfells slipped out of Nancy's net and plunged to their deaths. But she would always remember them as a symbol of youth and of sunlight – and of a time in her life that was now lost forever.

To assuage her grief Nancy sought commitment and she found this in her relationship with Colonel Newbourne, chief surgeon of her hospital. They worked together for many years and she grew extremely fond of him. Typically, Nancy was as possessive as ever and was openly antagonistic towards his wife. She claimed that she was not interested in the hospital or the men or anything else outside her limited woman's world. Indeed Nancy repeated a number of scurrilous anecdotes about the wretched Mrs Newbourne, including a particularly unpleasant one in which Nancy claims that she phoned whilst her husband and devoted nurse Nancy were busy in the operating theatre. She goes on to allege that Colonel Newbourne went to the phone, picked up the receiver, and said, 'Is that you Louise? Go to Hell!'

This is a cruel anecdote and it underlines how spiteful Nancy could still be, despite the all-absorbing work she was doing. She was still jealous about her male friends. Her relationships were asexual yet all were marred by Nancy's possessive attitude.

Nancy and Philip Kerr continued their correspondence in 1915 and gradually he slipped into the role of her spiritual counsellor. Nancy's work in the hospital was very much at odds with her faith. Nevertheless she was easily able to reconcile her conscience to the hospital work; it was important, it was the centre of things, it was a challenge. Meanwhile, the Christian Science movement itself was battling with its own conscience. Private conviction was stressed and mass hospitalisation ignored. Philip Kerr wrote to Nancy 'Anyhow C.S.ists are evidently all at sixes and sevens about the war. It's a great thing that they all trust to individual judgement & don't judge others. The general conclusion, I gather, is that if one has enough understanding of the truth one won't go, if one hasn't one will. Do you understand that?' She did – and was able to produce a naive and absurd example of Christian Science as a living miracle. She wrote that the Duke of Connaught was due to visit the hospital and there was a good deal of preparation going on in an attempt to make the place ready for him. Whilst this was going on, two sailor victims of the Battle of Jutland had given up the will to live. Nancy was told this by the doctor and she went immediately to see them. She asked where they came from and they told her they came from Yorkshire. 'No wonder you don't want to live if you come from Yorkshire,' Nancy claims she replied. One of the men then apparently raised himself up on one elbow and sternly admonished Nancy, saying that York- shire was the finest place in the world and he was determined to see it again. Nancy goes on to say that the man lived to return to his beloved homeland.

But the nervous strain was beginning to tell on Nancy and, despite her spiritual fantasies, irritability was beginning to creep in. The first victim was Hilaire Belloc with whom she was still corresponding in rather the same jocular vein as she had with the Grenfells. One letter he wrote angered Nancy considerably, despite the fact that he had made this point before in dozens of previous letters. Belloc wrote:

'Do you notice all around the really interesting signs of weakening towards this strain of the war? I don't think that's a fair way of putting it. It's rather symptoms all round of trying to persuade public opinion to climb down. It is in the very texture of half the press – think Harmsworth is working that way. It is most interesting to watch – but lamentable: if anything were left on earth worth caring for. For if the big monied interests compel England to give way it means a coalition against her in a very short time – and no one to fight for her in the future. People used to say when the fight was on against the swindlers and fools of Parliament that it didn't matter what the politicians stole or what bribes they took or how they lied, because the nation worried along all the same. They cared a little for the way our politics were becoming a bye-word in Europe, but for the effect at home they didn't care at all. Now I think it is beginning to come home.'

Nancy took all this personally, particularly as Waldorf's father had just passed him the ownership of the *Observer*. Nancy wrote Belloc a sharp note declaring their friendship was at an end. Penitently Belloc wrote back : 'No I did not mean and could not conceivably have meant this just criticism to apply to you. I have never written discourteously to a woman in my life. Do you think I would now so write to you who have shown me so much kindness in the past? . . .' Eventually Nancy forgave Belloc and their friendship and correspondence continued.

On 10 April 1916, Michael Astor was born and in the same year Waldorf's father was made a baron. Neither Nancy nor Waldorf were consulted and the first they heard of the title was when the press phoned Cliveden to gauge Waldorf's reaction and to ask him what title he was going to take. Immediately, Waldorf wrote a very bitter letter to his father, angrily opposing the idea. William Waldorf, not used to opposition, was equally annoyed and demanded to know if Nancy agreed with Waldorf. She said she did. Immediately William Waldorf cut his son out of his will, thus using the wealthy's ultimate sanction.

Meanwhile, the situation in Rumania, now occupied by the Germans, was emotively described by Queen Marie who had also just tragically lost her four-year-old son. She wrote:

'Thank you and Waldorf for your kind words of sympathy. Our trials at the moment are so beyond words that there is nothing to say. One can hardly believe that one is the same human creature as a few months ago. I have had to leave with many others, house and home. The Germans are fattening upon all that once was ours, even the little bit of country that still belongs to us may be torn from us soon, then we will be exiles. All these misfortunes are so fantastic that they hardly seem real. But nothing matters much after the death of my child. To have sat by his side for three mortal weeks fighting for his precious life and not being able to save him, that immense and unbearable sorrow has hardened me against other griefs. Tomorrow we shall perhaps have also to leave Jassy and then we can call nothing more our own. I am trying to teach heart and brain to accept the thought but it is such a preposterous one that it cannot be accomplished all at once. Certainly the Germans had their revenge against a king who tried nobly to do his duty towards his country. I am so pleased you are doing such splendid work. Love to Waldorf. Marie.'

In early December the coalition government broke down and in the ensuing battle for power Asquith resigned and Lloyd George became Prime Minister. Nancy wrote to Margot sympathising with her, although her sympathy was rather hypocritical. Naturally, Nancy did not lose the opportunity to suggest Christian Science as a method of encouraging Margot to turn to spiritual guidance in the crisis. But Margot was not impressed : 'The logical conclusion of Xtian Science is that you can fall out of the window & it is only fancy that you are killed – it takes a Xtian Scientist to believe what you write i.e. that nothing can hurt "our inner lives". The "God that is within us" who I have believed in – in spite of what the clergy say – has become a very shadowy conception to me in these days. It may be that I believed too much in honour & loyalty or too little in God.'

The change in the political pecking order gave Waldorf the opportunity he had been waiting for when Lloyd George made him his Parliamentary Private Secretary. Waldorf became a member of the Cabinet Intelligence Branch, known as the Garden Suburb because it operated from huts in the garden of 10 Downing Street. Philip Kerr was also a member as were many others from the original Kindergarten group such as W. G. Adams and S. T. Davies. To the Kindergarten's delight, the Dominion Prime Ministers and an Indian representative were also included in the Imperial War Cabinet. Waldorf achieved another ambition when he became Chairman of the Unionist Committee for Social Reform which produced a pamphlet entitled 'The Health of the People', advocating the creation of a Ministry of Health.

As Waldorf became more politically involved, so did Nancy. 1917 was the grimmest year of the First World War and Waldorf continued to worry that he was not actively involved in the fighting. Nancy wrote to Lord Milner asking if Waldorf could be posted to Headquarters in France, but Milner courteously refused the request saying that 'Waldorf is a great deal more use than he thinks. He would be a great loss if removed from the centre. In that poisonous atmosphere, & with all these hustlers, it really does make a difference to have a man of his character disinfecting the place."

Philip Kerr's position had meanwhile become vitally important and it was he who replaced Waldorf as Principal Private Secretary and accompanied Lloyd George on his various peace-seeking journeys. He also went with Lloyd George to Nancy's house at Sandwich which she had put at the disposal of the Prime Minister so that he could rest and hopefully recuperate from the strain of administering war. In January 1918 Kerr was part of the delegation that went to Switzerland in an abortive attempt to arrange peace. Kerr was discreet, however, and gave no hint to Nancy by word or letter that he was involved in such high dealings.

Philip Kerr also drafted the preamble to the informal conference that ended in the Fontainebleau Memorandum. It is this document which formed the basis for the Astors' political thinking between the wars. Part of it read :

'It is comparatively easy to patch up a peace which will last for thirty years (but) I cannot conceive any greater cause of future wars than that the German people, who have certainly proved themselves one of the most vigorous and powerful races in the world, should be surrounded by a number of small states, many of them consisting of people who have never previously set up a stable government for themselves, but each of them containing large masses of Germans clamouring for reunion with their native land ... If we are wise we shall offer to Germany a peace which . . . will be preferable for all sensible men to the alternative of Bolshevism . . . we will open to her the raw materials and markets of the world on equal terms with ourselves.'

On 29 August 1918 Nancy's youngest son was born – John Jacob, to be known as Jakie. In the same year a cemetery was created at Cliveden for those Canadians who had died in the hospital there, situated in a hollow in the woods; it was and still is a particularly beautiful place. Walking there before and after the Armistice, Nancy's thoughts must have often returned to the Grenfells who typified the thousands of young men who lost their lives in that most terrible of wars. The Autumn leaves carpeted the graves, turning them into anonymous brown mounds. There, amongst the gaunt trees, on a darkening October afternoon, Nancy sometimes imagined she could hear Julian's laughter or Billy's teasing. But the faint echoes of their spent young lives were soon lost in the silence of the night.

5

Nancy Astor MP

1 Take a seat, my dear!

The Bill proposing the right of women to vote became law in February 1918. On 23 October 1918 Sir Herbert Samuel moved that 'in the opinion of this House, it is desirable that a Bill be passed forthwith making women eligible as Members of Parliament.' This motion was carried by a majority of 275 to 25. Eventually this became law 22 days before the poll and there was a considerable flurry as women stood for candidature.

Christabel Pankhurst failed to be elected but another ex-suffragette succeeded. She was Countess Markiewicz who had stood for Dublin. Unfortunately the Countess was currently serving a spell in Holloway Prison and so was unable to make the journey to Westminster. As a member of the Sinn Fein (the politcal wing of the Irish Republican Army) she refused to take an oath of loyalty to the King and her election was invalidated. In March 1918 Miss Agnes McPhail took her place in the Canadian House of Commons but there was no woman in its English equivalent when parliament assembled.

Meanwhile Waldorf's constituency had been reshaped and he eventually became the MP for the eastern division – Sutton. Waldorf was elected in the 1918 General Election with a considerable majority. He was also still acting as Lloyd George's private secretary until the latter went to France in October 1918 as the First World War drew to a close. Waldorf then became Parliamentary Secretary to the Local Government Board and by 1919 he was rewarded by seeing the foundation of the ministry which he had long campaigned for – the Ministry of Health. Waldorf then joined the Ministry, becoming Parliamentary Secretary to Christopher Addison.

William Waldorf died in October 1919, without a reconciliation between him and his son. In 1916, this cantankerous and eccentric old man had agreed to become a viscount. This meant that his son would now be forced to enter the House of Lords – and forsake a career as a possible future Minister of Health. Waldorf tried to 'resign' his title but he was told that this was legally impossible. Legislation had to be initiated and ironically this would only be possible from the House of Commons. So Waldorf was faced with a situation where he had to rely on a friend to initiate the legislation required – or attempt to initiate it himself in the backwaters of the House of Lords. Almost immediately, rumours began to circulate, largely bred by the *Evening Standard*, to the effect that the new Viscountess, Lady Astor, was thinking of stepping into her husband's political shoes. Speculation ran rife, and even one of the Astor papers, the *Pall Mall Gazette*, agreed that Nancy might stand. The rumours broadened and suggested that Asquith might oppose her. But this was soon crushed by Asquith's denial.

On 24 October, the Conservative Association of the Sutton

Division of Plymouth formally asked Nancy to stand. She carefully considered the possibility over a period of some four days, whilst Waldorf stone-walled the press. He made it clear that this was his wife's decision – and his wife's decision alone. Finally, Nancy sent a telegram to the Association. She was willing to stand.

Philip Kerr drafted Lloyd George's endorsement, part of which ran: 'Now that women have been enfranchised I think it important there should be a certain number of women in parliament . . . There are a good many questions in regard to housing, child welfare, food, drink and prices in which it would be an immense advantage . . . to have a woman's view presented by a woman, and your sympathies were genuinely with the people long before you had any notion of becoming a candidate yourself, and even before women's suffrage became an accomplished fact.'

The letter now sounds both patronising and chauvinistic – but in the early twenties, it was considered revolutionary. Nancy thought she would wear 'something quiet' in the House providing, of course, she was elected. 'A coat and skirt', she told the company at one of Lloyd George's dinner parties. 'In the evening no evening dress. Only a "V" with a piece of chiffon. Of course, I should wear a few pearls.'

One of the greatest drawbacks that Nancy encountered at the beginning of her electioneering was her own views – and past statements – on prohibition. She knew that if she stood on the prohibition issue she would undoubtedly lose. So Nancy compromised – massively. She decided she would not advocate prohibition – but make a firm stand against drunkenness. Philip Kerr, however, considered that no such compromise should be made and in two strong letters he urged her to support prohibition. Nancy hid behind her secretary, a Miss Benningfield, a fellow Christian Scientist who was a close confidante and was known as 'Bunny'. Bunny was deputised by Nancy to tell Philip that he was not being helpful and so, suitably admonished, Philip sent back a contrite letter. 'Miss Benningfield rebukes me quite rightly, for my last letter. She said it was impersonal and unhelpful and full of opposition. I'm afraid it must have been, and if so, I'm very sorry for it . . . Anyhow I'm grateful to Miss Benningfield for telling me off, and I've told her by way of retaliation that she's just got to heal me off the wall or whatever it is you all complain of.'

Waldorf introduced Nancy at the beginning of her campaign and part of her first speech read: 'I've heard it said that a woman who has got children shouldn't go into the House of Commons. She ought to be at home looking after her children. That is true, but I feel someone ought to be looking after the more unfortunate children. My children are amongst the fortunate ones, and it is that that steels me to go to the House of Commons to fight the fight, not only of the men but of the women and children of England.' Another part of her speech read: 'If you want an MP who will be a repetition of the 600 other MPs don't vote for me. If you want a lawyer or a pacifist don't elect me. If you can't get a fighting man, take a fighting woman. If you want a Bolshevist or a follower of Mr Asquith, don't elect me. If you want a party hack don't elect me. Surely we have outgrown party ties; I have. The war has taught us that there is a greater thing than parties, and that is the State.' Nancy was unanimously adopted and as she continued to electioneer she began to develop a style of her own. Although Waldorf wrote many of her speeches, Nancy was inclined to wander away from these, which had the effect of making her argument erratic and sometimes illogical. Yet Nancy was at her best when she was empassioned or was in a mood for repartee. For instance, in answer to a member of the public asking her a question about police arresting women in the streets, Lady Astor replied: 'I must tell you something awfully funny that happened to me in London the other day. I saw an American sailor looking at the outside of the House of Commons. I said to him "Would you like to go in?" and he said "You're the sort of woman my mother warned me against". I went straight to Admiral Sim the other night, and said to him "Admiral, you have one perfectly upright young man in the American Navy".' When she was asked her chances of winning the election, she said they were rosy. 'And how do I judge they are rosy? Why, don't I know the women and children of Plymouth and can't I tell whether they are pleased with me or not?' She even criticised her own speeches. 'You will not expect long reasoned speeches from me, I hope, because if you expect 'em, you won't get 'em. I can't do it. It is not what I call my style.' But she made it clear she was going to be very forceful in the Commons. 'Twenty-four thousand men passed through the Cliveden Hospital. I was among them all day long, so if my manners are like a sergeant major's you'll know the reason why. I had to say to them – get to work you scallywags and heroes. They liked that.'

This is the way Nancy liked to project herself – as a 'character' with style. A press profile of her at the time warned its readers not to take her too lightly.

'Full credit may not be given to her deeper feelings by those who judge her superficially. Everyone knows her vivacity and sharp wit but with all her banter and superlatives she has a keen mind and a behind-the-scenes knowledge of politics. And if she rallies others, she will laugh at herself too, and has been heard, for instance, to tell the story of how one day at Cliveden, when showing a soldier her youthful portrait by Sargent, he said: "It must have been painted a long time ago, ma'm." '

Despite Nancy's compromises on prohibition, she was rather more reckless than would have been expected, considering how much was at stake and how easily she could become unpopular. When a newspaper announced she was a prohibitionist, she replied by sending this telegram to the chairman of the Plymouth Conservative Party : 'I have neither been asked to stand as a pussyfoot (prohibitionist) candidate nor have I any intention of doing so. It seems to me I detect the claws of some other sort of envious cat in this misleading suggestion.' But Nancy still had the courage to insist that she wanted to see the powers of the drink trade diminished and she even went so far as to tell the navy that if they wanted more rum, then there was no need to put a cross against her name.

Although the press were not as sensitive as they are today, Nancy courageously, if not particularly intelligently, spoke out against editorial policies. For instance, just after handing in her nomination papers at the Town Hall, she turned to a group of reporters and said 'I have nothing to say against the reporters. I believe they are acting decently. It is the editors who are responsible, and when I get to the House of Commons, as I intend to do, I will expose them all. They should publish facts and take this election seriously. They forget that I have principles and ideals. They are making my candidature funny, but they would make fun of the dead and would do anything for fivepence.'

Nancy's two opponents were W. T. Gay, the Labour candidate, and Isaac Foot, the Liberal candidate. Of Mr Gay, Nancy said: 'Mr Gay represents the shirking classes, I represent the working classes.' Typically individualistic, Nancy electioneered in a decorated carriage and pair. Her coachman, Churchward, wore an enormous rosette and stage-managed her canvassing. When he saw a sizeable crowd on a Plymouth street corner, he would stop the horses and Nancy would speak from her carriage. She campaigned with style and panache, although she was a little too brash, a little too pert. Nevertheless she had great novelty value, and was often able to turn heckling to her own advantage. But Nancy was aware of the dangers of showmanship and she promised her supporters 'I will behave at Westminster in the most dignified way and not pull members' legs more often than necessary.' To her hecklers, however, Nancy would shout 'Come along, who'll take me on? I'm ready for you!' A typical dialogue was as follows:

HECKLER: Go back to America.
NANCY: Get back to Lancashire.
HECKLER: I'm an Irishman.
NANCY: I knew it, an imported interrupter.
HECKLER: If I'd imported you, I'd drown myself in the sea.
NANCY: More likely in drink.
HECKLER: I'm a teetotaller.
NANCY: Well go and have a drink today. It might sweeten you.

Not exactly witty but courageous.

Sometimes, when her mood was right, Nancy could be both playful and gauche. One speech ended: 'And now, my dears, I'm going back to one of my beautiful palaces to sit down in my tiara and do nothing and when I roll out in my car I will splash you all with mud and look the other way.' Then she added: 'Today I heard a thing they are saying about me and must tell you. "We know Lady Astor. She comes among us all smiles and then goes back to her big house and calls her maid: 'Have my gloves cleaned, I've shaken hands with a Tommy.' " '

Nancy was adroit at averting unpleasant encounters – and was able to tease away some of her most difficult hecklers, as this piece of repartée indicates:

WOMAN HECKLER:	Why did you call me a virago once at a meeting?
NANCY:	I'll go down on my knees and apologise if I did.
W.H.:	Well you did.
NANCY:	Come, let's forgive each other. You forgive my sins and I'll forgive yours.
W.H.:	I have got none.
NANCY:	Got no sins! You are a lucky devil.

From the feminist point of view Nancy campaigned very crudely. She blamed men for the state of the world and claimed that this was only natural as they had been handling its affairs for so long. Once, when a large female audience asked why they had been crowded into a small room Nancy grandly replied that it was because 'the meeting was arranged by men.' Her humour was often geared to the kind of audience she had. For instance, to secure the sergeant's vote in a barracks where she was campaigning, Nancy asked 'Where are the drummer boys? The first time I came here I gave fifty of them toothbrushes. When I saw some of them the next time, I said: "You haven't used those toothbrushes. Look at your teeth!" They said: "Yes, we have. We polished our buttons with them." When I asked why they did this, they replied: "Because the sergeant looks at our buttons, but he doesn't look at our teeth." '

Meanwhile, the American press was covering Nancy's campaign with great enthusiasm and waxed lyrical over her style. 'This brilliant woman, dressed all in black, driving through the streets behind a dashing team of sorrels, with silk-hatted coachman, his whip and the bridles of the horses adorned with red, white and blue ribands.'

Nancy waited in considerable tension for the results of the poll. But she need not have worried for she won with a substantial majority with 14,495 votes. Gay ran her second with 9,292 and, as expected, Foot was well behind with 4,139.

Then, on 14 February 1919, her father died. Chillie was seventy-six and had not been in good health for some time. But despite the predictability of her father's death, Nancy was totally grief-stricken. She had been very close to Chillie and was very like him. There was a strong bond between these two domineering and idiosyncratic people and it was not a bond easily broken. Coming so soon after the death of the Grenfells, the blow would have been far more shattering if she had not been canvassing votes so furiously. As it was, she deadened the shock by plunging herself into her work. Her later and most over-riding superficial regret was that her father had not lived long enough to see her elected into parliament – a sight he would dearly have loved to see.

2 Cinderella and her Fairy Godmothers

Nancy was to be introduced into parliament by Lloyd George and Arthur Balfour. The ceremony was due to take place on

1 December 1919 and would occur at half-past three in the afternoon, just after question time. She arrived very plainly dressed in what was to be her parliamentary 'uniform' – a black dress with a white top, white cuffs and gloves – and a small black hat. She looked petite but confident and took her stand at the bar with Lloyd George on her right and Balfour on her left. The Speaker signalled to them and Lloyd George burst into a fast walk. He turned to find that he had left the others behind – and sheepishly returned. Laughter came from the members and Nancy finally bowed to the Speaker from a position half-way up the floor of the House of Commons. Lloyd George omitted to perform this duty and Nancy hissed at him 'George, you forgot to bow.' There was more laughter and comment. Then, the introduction continued more smoothly, and the flavour of vaudeville disappeared.

Years later, in the radio programme 'The Week in Westminster', Nancy remembered: 'I was introduced by Mr Balfour and Mr Lloyd George, men who had always been in favour of votes for women. But when I walked up the aisle of the House of Commons I felt that they were more nervous than I was, for I was deeply conscious of representing a cause, whereas I think they were a little nervous of having let down the House of Commons by escorting the Cause into it.'

Nancy had not rehearsed her maiden speech, relying on her usual charismatic instincts. Whilst she read the speech, Nancy thought about Chillie and his ebullient memory helped her confidence considerably. The following extracts from the speech are typical of Nancy's style – and obsession.

'I am perfectly aware that it needs courage to address the House on that vexed question. Drink. However, I dare do it . . . The Hon. Member has said that he and his friends were willing during the war to put up with drink control for the purpose of winning the war. It is not true. Ever since the Liquor Control Board started the Hon. Member and his friends have been kicking against it . . . I do ask Hon. Members not to misread the spirit of the times. Do not go round saying that you want England a country fit for heroes to live in, do not talk about it unless you mean to do it . . . I want you to think of the effect of these restrictions in terms of women and babies. Think of the thousands of children whose fathers had to put up with even more than these vexatious restrictions – who laid down their lives for you. Think of their fatherless children. Supposing they were your children or my children, would you want them to grow up with the Trade flourishing? I do not believe the House would. I do not want you to look on your Lady Member as a fanatic or a lunatic. I am simply trying to speak for hundreds of women and children throughout the country who cannot speak for themselves.'

Nancy always remembered a description of the English that Henry James had once used to her: 'the dauntless decency of the English'. Nancy wrote: 'That was how I was received by the Commons. Very few MPs were really pleased to see a woman in such a man's sanctum, but nothing could have been kinder than the way they treated me.'

Nancy had been given a private room and she was careful to remain in it. She would be able to attend to papers there and deal with her secretaries – just as future women MPs would. Tactfully, she kept out of the bar, the smoking-rooms and other male preserves. Because of this strangely humble anxiety to avoid overstepping the mark, Nancy hardly ever saw anything of the other members when she was not in the Commons.

Prohibition, Nancy declared whilst opening a bazaar, would not suit England. But this was a calculated statement, designed to remove from people's minds the idea that she was a bigot. Nevertheless the prohibition image stuck and her wax effigy in Madame Tussauds was carefully placed next to the American prohibitionist, Pussyfoot Johnson. Needless to say Nancy was not pleased.

Despite her generally good reception in the Commons, there were a few MPs who definitely resented her presence. One was Winston Churchill, who was now Secretary of State for War. He openly and pointedly ignored Nancy, and when she finally confronted him, Churchill told her '. . . I find a woman's intrusion into the House of Commons as embarrassing as if she burst into my bathroom when I had nothing with which to defend myself, not even a sponge.' Nancy fought back instantly with 'Winston, you're not handsome enough to have worries of that

3 The New Member

kind.' Their enmity was to continue unabated through the years.

But there was another MP who was more dangerous to Nancy than Churchill. Horatio Bottomley was not only an MP, but also the editor of the powerful weekly paper *John Bull*. Bottomley disliked Nancy for a number of reasons. Even on her first day in Parliament she had seriously annoyed him when, pontificating on in his usual pompous and slightly drunken way, Bottomley had been delivering an oration on the future charms of Premium Bonds. He had then been attacked by Austen Chamberlain, the Chancellor of the Exchequer. As Chamberlain completed his speech Nancy clapped her hands, although she was afterwards told that this was a breach of etiquette as response could only be vocal. Nevertheless Nancy was unabashed and loudly 'Hear Heared' Bonar Law when he, too, attacked Bottomley.

Nancy then voted against Bottomley and as a result the press gave him some bad publicity the next day, which was annoying to Bottomley as he was always anxious to have a good press. In addition, Nancy had seriously trespassed on Bottomley's territory; Nancy's successful campaign in naval Plymouth had been enhanced by the fact that she had substantially cared for wounded soldiers in the war. Bottomley, however, had also been known as the 'Soldier's Friend' and this was a nickname that he jealously guarded. At first Bottomley had to content himself with ineffective abuse but then, to his joy, the *Saturday Review* suddenly produced an intriguing item. It read: 'That astonishing *Who's Who* for 1920 has reached us ... We, however, have not got beyond the first letter of the alphabet as yet: for need we say we were arrested by the biography of Plymouth's heroine, the dashing, peerless peeress, Nancy Witcher, who is described as "the widow" of Mr Robert Gould Shaw at the time of her marriage with Mr Astor. We are loath to think that Nancy fibs: but is this a correct statement?'

This statement appeared just before Nancy made her maiden speech which concerned the Liquor Control Board. This Board had come into existence with the 1914 Defence of the Realm Act which gave a ruling on alcoholic content and restricted hours for the sale of drinks. Nancy had decided to use her maiden speech to reinforce what was known as the Carlisle experiment. This involved the state purchase and supply of all alcoholic beverages and was considered, by extremists, to be a precursor towards prohibition. Obviously Nancy was heavily advised against this unpopular cause but with her self-destructive courage she continued. Nevertheless logic played its part too for it would have been absurd for her to have sat silently through the debate, when her feelings were so well known in her own constituency. One very emotive part of her speech made a great impression on both the House and the press:

'I have as good a sense of humour as any other honourable member, but when I think of the ruin and desolation and the misery which drink brings into the houses of the working men as well as of the well-to-do [here she was no doubt thinking of her brothers' heavy drinking at Mirador] I find it a little difficult to be humorous. It was only the other day – I had been down to my constituency – that I was coming back from what they call the poorer parts of the town, and I stopped outside a public house where I saw a child about five years old waiting for its mother. Presently she reeled out. The child went forward to her, but it soon retreated, and the oaths and curses of that poor woman and the shrieks of that child as it fled from her – that is not an easy thing to forget, and that is what goes on when you have increased drunkenness among women.'

Bottomley, armed with the news of the 'omission' in *Who's Who*, was waiting his opportunity. This came after the debate on the Divorce Bill in April 1920, and Nancy fell neatly into his trap. The Bill's principal recommendation was that, apart from adultery, grounds for divorce should be allowed after three years if drunkenness, cruelty, insanity or life imprisonment could be proven. There were no allowances for incompatibility.

The resolution was opposed by an Ulsterman and lawyer, Ronald McNeill. To the House's considerable surprise Nancy opposed this resolution and supported McNeill. Part of her speech read :

'In the Christian world it is the spiritual aspect of marriage that the law attempts to protect, and it is the spiritual element that makes marriages happy. Most honourable members have said that. They all know it, and we women particularly know it. The spiritual idea of marriage, though started in the East, has been more highly developed in the West, and it is that that has elevated the Western women a little above their Eastern sisters. That is the difference between the East and the West. We must do nothing which will weaken it. Therefore I shall support the Amendment. I am not convinced that making divorce very easy really makes marriages more happy or makes happy marriage more possible.'

Although Nancy's speech was an able one it did not guarantee her popularity. Unfortunately, she then became involved in a petty and stupid episode with Sir William Joynson Hicks, an MP who had been away in India and who had now returned. Whilst he was away Nancy had taken his seat as her own but Sir William now wished to install himself in it again. Realising this, Nancy determined to steal a childish march on him. On 15 April 1920, she went down to the Chamber early in the morning to claim her seat. Sir William had been there first. In the early hours he had met the Speaker's Clerk and, unfortunately, Horatio Bottomley. Sir William had put his card on the seat and asked the Clerk and Bottomley to witness his presence. They both agreed, Bottomley with considerable delight. Not to be beaten, Nancy covered Sir William's card with a pink card which held her name and was also marked for a debate on Women Police.

Just after question time, Sir William, with due pomp and circumstance, rose to ask why the pink card had been slipped over his. T. P. O'Connor, the Father of the House, suggested that there was a question of chivalry involved as Nancy was Parliament's first Lady MP. He was shouted down, however, on grounds of sex equality and the Speaker, William Lowther, declared that 'I really do not think it is necessary to continue the "debate". The honourable member who initiated it has stated quite correctly what the rule is. It must be left to every honourable member to decide himself whether he will yield the place he is entitled to take on coming here at eight o'clock to anyone else. If he chooses he can do so; if he prefers to retain his seat, he is entitled to do so.' Only in the Commons could such momentum be made out of such triviality. Sir William gracefully made a few more comments, sat down and promptly tore up Nancy's pink ticket, ostentatiously throwing the pieces on the floor.

Later, both Sir William and Nancy were surrounded by the press as they left the Commons. Nancy, furious at her public humiliation stated that 'I shall give Sir William a good run for his money, and he will have to get up early in the morning to beat me.' She ignored the fact that he had just done that. However, she admitted to making a mistake about the pink ticket, claiming that 'I was in a hurry to attend the Committee on Policewomen.' Sir William merely contented himself with a few comments on the traditions of the House. Nancy would have dearly loved to have engaged in further games of musical chairs, but thankfully she was dissuaded by Waldorf. Nevertheless she was not left to stand, and MP Will Thorne offered her his own seat, proving that chivalry was not entirely dead in the House – or sex equality had not entirely arrived.

Bottomley, realising that Nancy was in a weak position, now seized his opportunity. With much trumpeting he rushed into print in *John Bull* with a headline that had also been carried on posters. This was both cunning and intentionally ambiguous. It read 'LADY ASTOR'S DIVORCE' and was clearly designed to whet the public appetite with its implication of Nancy divorcing Waldorf. The sub-title read more strongly 'A HYPOCRITE OF THE FIRST WATER — THE POOR AND THE RICH.' Horatio began his article with his own brand of hypocritical relish, and, as the piece almost destroyed Nancy's career, I reproduce the mischievous and sensational text in its entirety:

'I hope I am not lacking in regard for the amenities of the House of Commons, and, above all, in that sense of chivalry due to its only woman Member, Viscountess Astor; but during her election campaign she made it abundantly clear that in entering political life she neither sought nor desired any special favouritism on account of her sex – she was going into a men's House of Commons to be one of them; and she fully realised that once she discarded the mantle of a private lady and became a public woman, she would render herself liable to the same criticism as that with which every politician has to contend. That was why, having told her constituents that she was all against Prohibition – and that whenever anybody attempted to prohibit her from anything, she desired it all the more, and having during the Debate in the House of Commons on Local Option stated that she "hoped the time will come when the working man will go dry", and that the measure under consideration "would ultimately lead to Prohibition – the Press generally pilloried her for the obvious inconsistency. Personally, I set out the two declarations in parallel columns, and apparently one of my readers forwarded the paragraph to her Ladyship with a request for an explanation. I have before me the answer, dated 9 April, which he received. It is signed by C. G. Briggs, in his capacity as Secretary and Agent of the Plymouth Conservative and Unionist Association, and it says: "Many thanks for your cutting from some irresponsible paper, and the extract quoted therein does not in any way do justice to Lady Astor's declaration on that subject, neither at the election, nor in the House of Commons; nor yet should it be used to charge her with a change over of Pussyfootism. Her declaration re Prohibition, and denials to Pussyfootism, should be beyond question after the numerous repetitions that she has made on the subject. I am sorry that hostile Press and organisations so wilfully misapply her remarks." This somewhat cryptic communication having been sent to me, I ventured to address the following letter to Mr Briggs: "Mr Henderson, who recently sent you a cutting from *John Bull* of which I enclose a duplicate, has sent me your reply of the 9th inst. Will you please tell me in what way we have done Lady Astor any injustice?" That letter is dated the 19 April, but up to the present no reply has been vouchsafed. Probably Mr Briggs has come to the conclusion that the paper from which the cutting was taken was not so very "irresponsible" after all! I mention this incident, however, not only for the purpose of emphasising the fact that Lady Astor, MP, cannot claim to be immune from public criticism, but also as evidence, to use the mildest phrase applicable to the case, of inconsistency – if not of insincerity.

DIVORCE LAW REFORM

'And now I come to another matter – unfortunately with a personal touch to it – lending additional force to the same charge. On Wednesday, 14 April, a motion was submitted to the House of Commons in favour of giving legislative effect to the recommendations contained in the Majority Report of the Royal Commission on Divorce. This Report, it will be remembered, advised that in regard to divorce there should be sex equality and five new grounds for a decree – namely, desertion, cruelty, incurable insanity, habitual drunkenness, and the fact that sentence of death had been remitted. Lady Astor took part in the debate, and, in the course of her speech, used the following words: "In the Christian world it is the spiritual aspect of marriage that the law attempts to protect ... The spiritual idea of marriage, though started in the East, has been more highly developed in the West, and it is that which has lifted the Western women a little above their Eastern sisters. That is the difference between the East and the West. We must do nothing which will weaken it ... I am not convinced that making divorce very easy really makes marriage more happy, or makes happy marriages more possible ... *In America, where States have such easy divorce, I do not think that women have gained ... I beg the House, in thinking of this measure, to consider it from a large point of*

view, and not to dwell just on the miseries and inequalities . . .
Shall we help women and children and men by making
divorce easier? I think the world is too loose altogether.
What we need is tightening up." Here, then, is our Lady
Member's evangel. Marriage is essentially a spiritual institution, and the object of the law is to guard and preserve its
sanctity. That is where the superiority of the Western world
over the East comes in. There may be hard cases here and
there, but Christianity demands that such hard cases should
be endured; and America is actually cited as a warning
against the futility of easy divorce. Therefore let us, instead
of loosening our present marriage code, tighten it up. Of
course there is nothing particularly novel in that view. It was
propounded by other speakers in the course of the debate, and
is the conventional common-place sentiment of orthodox
religionists – just as Prohibition and Local Option are the
nostrums of the fanatical and narrow-minded "Social Re-
formers". Wherefore, as I say, in ordinary circumstances
Lady Astor's views on the great problem of marriage and
divorce would call for no more than a word of regret that she
brings no hope or comfort to the thousands of her suffering
sisters who are the victims of the present system. But now
comes the startling and appalling fact that every word I have
quoted must have been spoken "with her tongue in her
cheek", and was indeed rank hypocrisy. For who, hearing or
reading these words, would for a moment imagine that Lady
Astor had herself taken advantage of the "easiness of divorce"
prevailing in America? Turn your eye back to the words I
have italicised – "In America, where States have such easy
divorce, I do not think that women have gained". And yet
such is the fact.

THE MARRIAGE CERTIFICATE

'I have before me a copy of her Ladyship's present marriage
certificate. It is dated 3 May 1906, and records the marriage
at All Souls' Church, in the Parish of Saint Mary-le-bone, of
Waldorf Astor, Bachelor and Gentleman, of 28, Cavendish
Square, with Nancy Witcher Langhorne Shaw, "single and
unmarried – the marriage of the said Nancy Witcher Langhorne Shaw with Robert Gould Shaw, 2d. having been duly

dissolved on the 3rd day of February, 1903, upon her Petition." Where, and why, and how do you think this divorce was obtained? Would you be surprised to hear it was in the State of Virginia – where marriage laws are admittedly more lax than in almost any other place on the face of the earth? And, remembering her Ladyship's protest in the House of Commons against introducing any new grounds for severing the marriage tie, will you be surprised when I tell you that the cause cited in her original petition was simply that of desertion – although, as I shall show you in a moment, by arrangement between her and her husband, further "statutory reasons" – that is, according to the law of Virginia – were at a later stage introduced? And, in what circumstances, do you think, the decree was obtained? I will tell you. It was when the Court was empty – neither Lady Astor nor her husband, nor his Counsel being present – the whole thing being rushed through in a few moments, amidst such secrecy and mystery as led to considerable comment at the time. Let me reproduce the report which appeared in the *New York Herald* – "*The Times* of America" – on 5 February, 1903:

' "Charlottesville, Virginia, Wednesday. – Secrecy which has attended the proceedings of the divorce suit of Mrs N. W. L. Shaw against R. G. Shaw, of Boston, was maintained when the decree was entered to-day, and Mrs Shaw was granted custody of the child. When there was no one in the Court House except the Court's officials and Mr Daniel Harmon, representative for Mrs Shaw, the Plaintiff, the matter was submitted, and the decree of divorce awarded. Mr Herrick, Attorney for Robert Gould, was not present, nor was Mrs Shaw. The latter, accompanied by her mother, Mrs Chiswell D. Langhorne, and her youngest sister, sailed Wednesday for Europe. At the beginning of the divorce proceedings, the single allegation upon which Mrs Shaw relied WAS desertion, and it remained the only contention until after a conference in New York, in January, between the legal representatives of each family. Then divorce was sought on statutory grounds. All the circumstances point to willingness on the part of both parties to separation. Mr Shaw went to Europe 'to make things easy'. No evidence of a demand for alimony is to be found in the papers in the case, and if one was made, and finally acceded to, it was in the nature of a private arrangement outside of Court."

'I say without any hesitation whatever, that this was a collusive divorce – such as would certainly not be possible in this country – and that every practicable step was taken to hush it up. And this is the "honourable and noble lady", an American by birth and a Peeress by marriage, who comes to the British House of Commons and dares to sermonise upon the spiritual aspect of the marriage tie and to protest against the slightest slackening of our laws of divorce! And listen to how she emphasised this attitude when speaking in the House: "Women's voice," she said, "ought to have a special value on the subject, because nothing else concerns them quite so intimately. *In my experience*, women want to preserve the dignity of marriage . . . There are always tragic cases, but laws are made for the majority, and the minority very often has to suffer." I am no moralist and no purist. If Lady Astor's first marriage was an unhappy one, I congratulate her upon having got rid of her husband – but I want to see similar facilities, with due limitations, for unhappily married persons in this country – not only in the exalted spheres in which she moves, but equally in the humblest walks of life. But I do detest cant. That is what *John Bull* has always been up against, and what it is up against in this particular case. Nor am I in any sense an enemy of female representation in Parliament – although I confess I would prefer plain, British-born Mrs Smith to the most Noble Viscountess of American birth. After all, Lady Astor was the protagonist of a greater experiment – and she has dismally failed.

A HYPOCRITE OF THE FIRST WATER

'I hate being rude to a woman, but my public duty compels me to denounce Lady Astor as a hypocrite of the first water – and, I think, in view of this revelation, her constituents and the House of Commons will endorse my view. Just reflect; one of the objects of the proposal before the House was to make desertion a cause for divorce – and desertion in a very true sense, extending over a long period. And although this was the very ground upon which Lady Astor instituted her own suit, not a syllable escaped her lips on the subject. On the contrary, with eyes upturned to Heaven – and in unctuous tones – she declaimed against tampering with the sanctity of the marriage vow upon this or any other of the grounds suggested. I wonder what could have been her inmost feelings as she stood there before the British House of Commons, hugging the fond but vain delusion that her own marriage antecedents were a long-forgotten secret! How she must have revelled in fooling her hearers – the Prime Minister in his most mischievous mood, is not in it with her! It is a sad reflection that our first woman Member of Parliament should have inaugurated the new order of things in such discreditable circumstances, and I am afraid that the cause of Parliamentary equality between the sexes will be irretrievably damaged. And here let me quote this phrase from one of her Ladyship's speeches during the Plymouth election: "I know my election will be a test, and that according to how I behave myself in the House of Commons will future women candidates be judged." That was surely, a most unhappy utterance – which has speedily come home with the force of a boomerang. Well, what is to be done? The House of Commons is the most humane and tolerant assembly in the world, but it has a strong objection to being fooled. In more than one respect, Lady Astor has already flouted its best traditions, though the facts I now reveal will come as a final shock to members of all Parties. The next move is with her Ladyship. It is due both to herself and the House that she should volunteer some explanation. Failing her doing so, every one of her fellow-members will be placed in a position of considerable embarrassment, whilst her constituents will naturally demand an immediate effort on her part of vindication. I therefore call upon her Ladyship to avail herself, without delay, of the privilege which the House of Commons always extends in such circumstances to a Member, and to tender a personal explanation.

A WORD WITH 'BURKE'

'But there is yet another point to be cleared up. On

reference to *Burke's Peerage, Who's Who, Whitaker's Peerage*, and other standard books of reference, I find Lady Astor in each case described as "the widow of the late Robert Gould Shaw" – the following being typical of the particulars – of course since the compilation of these volumes Lady Astor's present husband has succeeded to the title.

' "Astor, Hon. Waldorf, MP (C) Plymouth, since 1911, Parliamentary Secretary to the Local Government Board since 1919: owner of the *Observer*, eldest son of 1st Viscount Astor: born 19 May 1879: MARRIED 1906 NANCY WITCHER daughter of Chiswell Dabney Langhorne, Mirador, Greenwood, Virginia and WIDOW OF ROBERT GOULD SHAW."

'Now everyone knows that the information on which these particulars were based was of necessity supplied by Lady Astor herself or on her behalf, and of course accepted in good faith by the publications in question. *Yet it is the fact that Mr Robert Gould Shaw is still alive in New York* and is a member of the Brook Club, in that city. What right, therefore, has Lady Astor to describe herself in these semi-official volumes as a "widow"? No doubt, after this revelation the entries will be duly corrected in the next editions. And there for the moment, I leave the subject. My task has been a painful and a delicate one, but it has been forced upon me by Lady Astor herself – and it may interest her to know that every Member of the House whom I have consulted – and I have consulted many before writing this article – has approved of my action. My only regret is that, with the single exception of the *National News*, no other journal has dared even to hint at what I have now very reluctantly disclosed. There will, of course, be some who will blame me. But it is the role of this journal to draw aside the veil in whatever form it cloaks hypocrisy in public life.

THE POOR AND THE RICH

'And I confess I feel very strongly on this particular matter. Week after week, month after month I have brought before me cases of cruel and heartrending hardship due to the operation of the existing Divorce Laws, and I have always used my voice and pen in favour of humanising them. Indeed, when previously in Parliament I myself introduced a Bill somewhat on the lines of the recommendation of the Royal Commission; and but for a public engagement in Shropshire when the matter recently came before the House, I should have been there to support the motion already referred to. Certainly I should have gone into the Division Lobby in favour of it. As it was, an adverse vote was recorded, and I cannot help feeling that many Members must have been influenced by the specious pleading of the only Lady Member of the House – who did not fail to emphasise the fact that the question was one mainly affecting the happiness of women and children, and otherwise to play upon the sentiment and sympathies of her hearers. Now we know that her earnest pleading and emotion were camouflage; and I have reason to know that many Members who listened to, and were influenced by them, and who have since become aware to some extent of the things I have revealed, are full of indignation. Whether they will stand by me now that I have turned the searchlight of Truth upon Plymouth's member, I cannot say; nor do I care. I have done my duty – not, as I have already explained, in the role of moralist – to which I make no claims – but as one jealous of the honour of Parliament, and, at the same time, deeply interested in the removal of the great social tyranny of which Lady Astor herself has in days past been the victim, although she denies to others the liberty she found so easy and convenient.'

Naturally Bottomley hoped that the Astors would sue him and therefore more scandal could be dredged up. But Nancy and Waldorf were not prepared to sue under any circumstances because they knew the entry in *Who's Who* to be false and because their public reputations would suffer badly if they were dragged through a court of law.

Luckily Nancy's still considerable popularity won the day for her publicly, and when Nancy appeared in the House for the first time after the article's publication, she was greeted with applause. Bottomley, however, was greeted with hostility. In fact Nancy was extremely depressed by Bottomley's campaign, but she ensured that her public image gave the impression that she did not care a damn. To boost her failing confidence Nancy leant heavily on her correspondence with Philip Kerr and on the unyielding strength of Waldorf during this period.

Later, in the summer of 1920, she decided, very unwisely, to answer Bottomley's allegations. She chose to justify herself at a Unionist Association meeting of her constituency on 9 July. Her constituents were more tactful than Nancy for they begged her not to continue. But, as usual, she was determined. Nancy began by saying:

'I have waited for this meeting to deal with charges which, if true, would affect my position as your representative. You would have been entitled to ask whether the charges were true. I assume that you have not done so because you trusted me and may have guessed the motive behind them. If you assumed that there was no justification for the attack, you were right. But however unpleasant it is to deal with the period of great unhappiness I went through seventeen years ago, I prefer to tell you all about it.'

She then went on to answer all Bottomley's charges and dealt frankly with the problems of the divorce. Unfortunately Nancy glossed and muddled her way through the technical details of the divorce which, although this brought no criticism from the faithful in Plymouth, did give Bottomley another opportunity. Nancy concluded her speech histrionically 'This is the history of these painful occurrences. I have told you fully of the sorrows of my early life. I knew that when I set out from Plymouth I would encounter foul weather and be tossed by storms.'

On 17 July, Bottomley published an article repeating all his charges, pouring scorn on her justifications. He stated that Nancy knew she had a weak case and that was why she had taken so long in replying to his accusations. As with Sir William Joynson Hicks, Nancy would have been happy to continue the battle. Thankfully Philip Kerr realised the dangers of this policy and wrote to Nancy saying, 'Well your speech seems to have gone off very well, judging by *The Times*: I'm sure you've done the right thing, though it can't have been pleasant!' Then Kerr delivered the real message: 'Don't refer to the subject again! I don't suppose you will want to.' She did, but luckily Nancy took the advice, despite the fact that Horatio Bottomley continued to campaign against the Astors until he himself fell from grace when he was arrested for fraud and given a seven-year prison sentence. In prison he was as colourful and bombastic as he had been in the Commons or in Fleet Street. One famous anecdote is always told of Bottomley's sojourn as a guest of His Majesty. Apparently a prison visitor came across the disgraced MP and magazine proprietor gloomily sewing mailbags. Remarking on the obvious, the visitor said, 'Ah, Bottomley – sewing I see.' But Bottomley did not agree and gave but a single reply. 'Reaping,' he returned.

Nancy Astor was a very hard-working MP. She attended the House frequently and her popularity rating remained high in Plymouth. She became a spokeswoman for the Royal Navy, for the unemployed and she continued to campaign for a force of

4 Lady Astor

women police. She also supported the cause of women in the Civil Service. But, once again, emancipation was not Nancy's primary concern. Social reform was her métier such as the campaign against venereal disease, the suppression of brothel-keeping and prostitution, and the protection of the young from indecent assault. Continuously, Nancy made enemies, largely because she was outspoken, tactless and sometimes muddled. But she was a hard-worker, a liberal reformer and her worst excesses were moderated by advice from Waldorf and Philip Kerr.

Normally Nancy was quick-witted enough to hold her own in most exchanges but she was severely put in her place by Sir Auckland Geddes when she teased him at a dinner party just before he left to become British Ambassador in Washington. Nancy asked him: 'Sir Auckland, I am told that anatomy is one of your subjects. Well then, answer me this. Why is it that my eyes being beautiful, my nose good, my mouth the right shape, my hair lovely – so people say – and yet I am not a pretty woman?' Back came the bleak reply from Sir Auckland: 'Because they don't fit,' he said.

Nancy continued to receive considerable support from America, and as a result, she wrote to the *Evening Journal* in Virginia saying: 'I am overwhelmed by the way Virginia is backing me up. I had no notion that anyone outside Plymouth would really care. I don't like the limelight, but I do like the friendship of my friends. The joke is, I am the most ordinary person you ever met.' In fact Nancy enjoyed the limelight very much indeed and would have been mortally offended if anyone thought her ordinary.

An excellent summary of Nancy's personality was given by the Hon. Mrs Alfred Lyttelton, a leading feminist. She described Nancy as 'A woman of many gifts, who can be mordant, even a little cruel in her laughter, but never so by intention, for above everything else she has a heart. No one is old, dull or dim to her. I have seen her change the whole atmosphere of a hospital ward in a few minutes. She can, and often has done it, sit for long stretches by the sick and dying.'

The drink question still engaged Nancy's mind obsessively. After a meeting in Wolverhampton Nancy told the press: 'Whether they take it well or not, I can't leave the drink question alone. At home they say to me – where are you off to this evening? My reply is – I'm off on the drink. I have been asked by the House – why don't you leave that drink alone? You'll be so popular if you do. I said – I could no more drop it than drop a baby.'

Then a curious, almost mystic and certainly terrifying event occurred in Nancy's life which undoubtedly illustrated her strong personality and courage. She was standing in the doorway of her Plymouth house when a man approached her and, alarmingly, told her: 'I intend before the week ends to return to prison on your account.' Nancy immediately asked him if he was threatening to kill her. He told Nancy that he was. Using all her powers of persuasion Nancy began to talk to her would-be assassin. A few minutes later the man left, soothed and calmed by Nancy at her reassuring best.

However, his departure brought no relief to Nancy who was now tense and curious, and she was desperate to discover more about the man. Without even thinking of contacting the police, Nancy followed him. Eventually he saw her – and took flight. Nancy said, 'I gathered up my skirts, ran after him and caught him in the yard of a mews. "What is your name?" I said. "I will not tell my name," he answered. Maniac killer or not I was beginning to feel sorry for him,' Nancy continued. 'There was nobody in the yard. I thought – if he wants to kill me, now is his chance. But when he looked at me, he became dismayed, and took to his heels again. Again I followed. He now ran into a public house. I do not go into public houses but did on this occasion. He bolted out through the back door. I continued the pursuit.'

Chased by the indefatigable Nancy (squash and tennis had made her very fit), the man was eventually stopped by a policeman. Nancy arrived and demanded the man's name. Humbly he gave it to her and, to the policeman's surprise, Nancy appeared quite satisfied. The policeman then asked her if she was making any charges, and Nancy replied: 'No, but you should keep an eye on him.' Nancy then calmly returned home. This incident is absolutely typical of Nancy's courage and tenacity. But it is also typical of her need for adventure and her restless desire to pursue any path that was exciting and challenging whatever the dangers.

Nancy had not been to America since Chillie's funeral and she suddenly had a longing to return. She knew she would receive a tremendous welcome. The enmity of the discredited Bottomley still lingered as an unpleasant and threatening memory. Nancy wished to feel secure and be needed – and she knew Virginia would provide this. She had been invited to a Women's Pan-American Conference and this would give her a respectable reason for absenting herself from the House of Commons for seven weeks.

Nancy and Waldorf set sail on 13 April and arrived in New York on 18 April 1922. Waldorf confided to his diary, 'I feel like the agent, secretary, manager, booster and adviser of a prima donna, cabinet minister and circus all in one. The press are trying to make us into a circus, while just at this moment one realises the importance and effect of anything N. may say as an MP – the supposed confidante of the Prime Minister – and absolutely in the public eye.'

The pace was fast and Waldorf wrote:

'One can only say that the Southern papers are even more enthusiastic than the Northern ones. I sigh daily – nay, hourly – for our secretariat from St James's Square, who know my ways. What with helping with speeches, dealing with the press, watching the papers, tackling endless correspondence, answering cable invitations from every part of the States and Canada, altering dates of meetings, telephoning, fixing cross-country journeys etc. etc. it's like being in a maelstrom and in a monsoon in a thunderstorm.

'Yesterday I asked Geddes (Sir Auckland Geddes, now British Ambassador) how the relations between the USA and the UK were. He said that almost for the first time in their history there was no centre of trouble. He was wrong. The more we travel and meet people, the more do we realise the amount of bad feelings Mrs Asquith has created. She apparently indulged in crude criticism, and they also feel that she insulted their intelligence by the stuff she talked.'

The Astors were very much in the wake of Margot Asquith's disastrous lecture tour. She had spent most of her time telling the Americans how absurd they were not to join the American-founded League. This was bad enough but to pile on the agony Margot was massively ignorant of the structure of American society and informed a large audience in Canada that Abraham Lincoln was their President. Nancy had been aware of Margot Asquith's demolition of Anglo-American relations before she left England and another reason for her trip was to counteract the appalling impression Margot had made.

In America, Waldorf had an even more difficult time preparing Nancy's speeches. He wrote: 'Unfortunately on most occasions, particularly when we are rushed, N. insists on trying each different method of preparation, of changing her system of notes and of swapping her train of thoughts. The task of helping her on these occasions would turn a nigger's curly locks into the straight wisps of an albino.'

Using a private railway car loaned by a friend, Nancy and Waldorf travelled from point to point, attending meetings, conferences and social occasions. Then, at last, they arrived in Virginia. Nancy's reception was as warm as she could have hoped and Waldorf recorded joyfully in his diary that the reception the Astors were given was stupendous. The train arrived at 7.10 am and without eating or washing Nancy and Waldorf tumbled out onto the platform, to be immediately surrounded by a swarm of photographers and reporters, all anxious to know the Astors' first impressions of Richmond. In the great marble hall of the station were long lines of children, with crowds of adults behind. When Nancy and Waldorf appeared, now bathed and showered, a band struck up 'Dixie' and then 'Back to Old Virginia'. People literally sobbed and cheered and the schoolchildren threw flowers.

En route to Nancy's birthplace, Danville, Waldorf wrote that privacy was impossible ' – particularly with a honey-pot butterfly like N. who flits from rosebud to rosebud or alternatively as a honeyed rose attracting all sorts of bees, butterflies, etc. Today we had a stateroom but no privacy. Our fellow travellers are kindness itself but don't realise one needs quiet at times. I woke up from a doze to find 2 men expounding to me their views on life.' Waldorf was beginning to find the tour extremely exhausting but Nancy, with her indefatigable nervous energy, loved every minute of it. She had not felt so secure and happy for years.

At Danville, Waldorf wrote that they 'motored to the hotel where we had decided to stay as all N's relations were quarrelling as to who should put us up. We never made a wiser decision. N. estimated before reaching Danville that she had 60 cousins in Danville. She may have had that number a year ago but like rabbits they have since then bred much and often. Litters of them invaded our room at the hotel – all talked at once – all wanted us to modify our itinerary and programme in some different way.'

Danville initiated a number of official ceremonies beginning in the Town Council Chamber where Nancy and Waldorf were presented with some golden keys, although quite which doors they unlocked (if any) was unclear. They then moved to the site of Nancy's birthplace, acompanied by bands, choirs and massed groups of schoolchildren. The mayor presented a silver loving-cup to Nancy and made a highly-coloured speech in which he referred to Nancy as a 'dove of war and an eagle of peace'.

Next morning the Astors continued their tour of Virginia and eventually they reached Mirador. There Nancy briefly met her spiritual mentor, Archdeacon Neve, again but conversation of any depth was made impossible by the well drilled and relentless hospitality. The Astors then left Mirador and travelled to Chicago where Nancy's anti-Catholicism suddenly marred the trip. At one reception she infuriated American Catholics by the firm and totally inaccurate statement that America had been founded by Protestants in the Protestant Faith. She also considerably annoyed the famous anti-British newspaper proprietor Randolph Hearst. At yet another reception Nancy stated that she was against bonuses being paid to those men who had enlisted during the war. She said 'A great rich country like the US cannot do too much for the disabled soldier, but for the fit and strong, give them work, not charity.' As a result of this controversial speech, Hearst furiously thundered into print pointing out that 'A patriotic American might properly find a few things to complain about his own statesmen. The subservice of his Government to those international bankers who are the fiscal agents of England; in the snobbish humility of his diplomatic agents and in the domineering, dictatorial, ungracious, ungrateful attitude of England we so lately saved from destruction.' Philip Kerr wrote swiftly, dissuading Nancy from the reply that she was considering making. 'Don't attack Hearst or Hylan as persons. It is the impersonal evil, hatred, animosity, greed, political manipulation, which is handling them and from which some day, they like everybody else will wake up, that you want to rebuke and destroy, with good.'

The Astors then toured Canada and returned to New York on 20 May. On the 22nd Nancy gave a final speech to the League for Political Education. Nancy was anxious that America should join the League of Nations – an association they had firmly decided against. 'You need not call it the League of Nations,' Nancy told them. 'You can call it anything you like. You can give it a new name every week. But for God's sake give it a chance.' She then went on to point out that, at a time when there were severe problems in China, the United States Government had called on Great Britain, through the League, to protect American oil interests in Iraq. But they refused to actually join the League committee of enquiry into the persecution of the Christian population in the Far East. Nancy said: 'Now I ask you, which is the most important in the end – oil concessions or bleeding humanity?'

The next day the Astors were due to depart on the *Aquitania*. The tour had been the highlight of Nancy's career – a homecoming which had been beautifully stage-managed. Waldorf's weary diary jottings exactly describe the final, frantic farewell.

'Final visits of friends.
Final words with reporters.
Final press photos.
Ship sailed at 12 noon.
After lunch I slept till dinner.
After dinner I slept till breakfast next day.'

On 26 May 1922 the *New York Telegraph* wrote:

'Lady Astor has sailed away. It is no exaggeration that she has left a grateful memory. We did not take her very seriously up to the time of her arrival a few weeks ago; that is to say, we did not look upon her as a really great person. But she took us seriously and in discussing us and our affairs, always with the limits of good taste and courtesy, she revealed those qualities that have made her Great Britain's foremost woman. Her gifts are remarkable; her faculty for saying the right thing at the right time amounts to genius.'

The Catholic community and Randolph Hearst did not, of course, share these feelings. But despite this, there was no doubt that the tour had been a great success and good Anglo-American relations were now restored. Also, Nancy felt whole again, ready to resume her political and social career in England with a new confidence.

A hopeful Nancy at the beginning of her ill-fated marriage to Robert Shaw.

Langhorne family servants at Mirador, the romantic country house in Virginia.

Nancy joins the aristocracy. She is wearing the $75,000 tiara given to her as a wedding present by her father-in-law, William Waldorf Astor.

A composite picture of Ettie, Julian and Billy Grenfell, made after the deaths of Julian and Billy, who were Nancy's 'Golden Boys'.

ABOVE: Margot Asquith in
1911. Margot and Nancy were
too similar in personality to
have anything other than a
very abrasive friendship.

ABOVE RIGHT: The man who
irritated and yet flattered
Nancy by his worship - Lord
Revelstoke (from *Vanity Fair*,
August 1898).

Two of Nancy's most intimate
friends - George Bernard Shaw
and his wife in 1934.

Nancy with her children in 1919. *Left to right*: Phyllis, John Jacob, Nancy, Robert Shaw, Michael, David and William Waldorf.

Nancy speaking after her election in November 1919. *Left to right*: Viscount Astor; Mr W. T. Gay, Labour candidate; Nancy Astor; Mr Isaac Foot (holding hat), Liberal candidate.

Cliveden, the Astor country seat and home of the so-called 'Cliveden Set',
photographed in 1931.

The Queen of Rumania visits Nancy in 1927. *Left to right*: Viscount Astor;
Don Alfonso Infante of Spain; the Infanta Beatrice, sister of Queen Marie;
Queen Marie; Nancy Astor.

ABOVE LEFT: Nancy's constant enemy, Horatio Bottomley, editor of *John Bull*, photographed in 1921.

ABOVE RIGHT: T. E. Lawrence. Obsessed by his own problems and isolation, Lawrence of Arabia struck up a soul-baring friendship with Nancy.

Nancy and George Bernard Shaw on their idealistic trip to Moscow. They saw Communism through rose-tinted glasses.

Nancy in typical extrovert campaigning form during the general election of 1931.

Nancy and her beloved friend Lord Lothian after he received his Honorary Degree at Oxford in June 1939.

Nancy holds court as she reads extracts from *The Social History of England*. This book was presented to her by other women Members of Parliament after she had served as an MP for 25 years.

6

Demon Drink

Nancy's concern with inhibiting the sale of alcohol almost ended in her electoral defeat. In 1922 a General Election seemed very likely, largely because Lloyd George had lost much of his popularity. When Nancy lodged a private member's bill demanding further drink legislation, many of her constituents and a large section of the Conservative Party completely lost patience with her. At the end of July one Tory group decided to set up a rival candidate, Dr Wansey Bayly, to run for Plymouth. Bayly was a dangerous rival because he was an able speaker and, like Nancy, had charisma, but he did not have her guile. Rumour claimed that the drinks industry was behind Bayly's nomination but he quickly renounced this publicly as totally untrue. Just when Bayly's credibility was riding high he made the mistake of publishing in *John Bull* a personal attack on Nancy's reactionary sociology. Had Bayly chosen any other paper, his attack might well have succeeded but *John Bull's* credibility was just about as low as its imprisoned owner.

During the early part of the election campaign, however, the Astors also made a disastrous mistake that could have had dire consequences, had not Bayly failed to capitalise on it effectively. Dr Bayly's wife had written in a scientific journal an article which argued that sexual infidelity in the man was less serious than in the wife because paternity, in the latter case, could always be called into question.

The Conservative Association immediately produced a pamphlet, ridiculing the original *John Bull* article and firmly stating that, as a result of Mrs Bayly's view, a vote for her husband was a vote for sexual permissiveness. Immediately an enraged Bayly issued a writ for libel against Nancy and Waldorf, and the offending pamphlet was hurriedly withdrawn. Delightedly, Bayly referred to this calumny against himself throughout the election campaign, until, by persistent stupidity, he ruined his advantage. He proceeded to issue writs against a dozen people or so who might have read or spread the libel. This was clearly absurd; the press found Bayly ridiculous and his popularity waned. Much encouraged, Nancy returned to the hustings stating somewhat loosely, that 'The Brewers paid Horatio Bottomley to destroy my reputation. But I've still got my reputation and Bottomley is in gaol.'

Finally Nancy won – but with a reduced majority. She returned 13,924 votes, the colourful Labour candidate, Captain Brennan 10,831 and the tactless Dr Bayly 4,643. With the election results came the ending of the Coalition Government as well as Lloyd George's domination, and the Liberal Party, because of internal dissent, also lost momentum.

Despite her reduced majority, Nancy was determined to press on with her drinks bill although it was a much more modest piece of legislation than she would have wished. The proposed bill merely advocated the prevention of sales of intoxicating liquor to young persons. This satisfied Nancy's moral stance in the sense that she was at least doing *something* against 'Demon Drink' but it was also far less than she wanted. The architect of the bill was Waldorf and it was he who persuaded Nancy to take a low-key approach. Waldorf believed that politics is the art of the possible and he was continually anxious not to damage Nancy's political career – which anyway had a self-destructive mechanism of its own.

Nancy's moderate bill was, however, dogged by a Left Wing Independent extremist called Edwin Scrymgeour who was determined to achieve total and complete prohibition in England. Any association with such a derided ally would have been disaster to Nancy and unfortunately, simply because of her anti-drink views, comparisons were made. On 16 February 1923, Nancy's brain-child entitled Intoxicating Liquor (Sale to Persons under Eighteen) Bill found third place amongst the ballot for private members' bills, but the Scrymgeour all-out abolition bill appeared in seventh place and further substantiated the link. Nancy's bill received a long debate on the Second Reading, and was four days in the Committee stage. There followed a further debate on the bill's third reading. Thanks to Waldorf's careful scripting, Nancy was able to answer effectively much of the criticism that threatened to demolish the bill. She answered one argument in the Commons, for instance, by stating: 'Then it is said why not deal with spirits only and leave beer out? If alcohol is bad in its scientific effect it is obviously equally bad in whatever form you take it. People often feel that you can safely drink more beer than spirits because there is less alcohol, but the result is exactly the same. If there was not alcohol in beer it would be all right for adolescents. But there is alcohol in beer.' Eventually the bill was passed by 157 votes to 10 and Nancy, as parliament's first woman MP, had succeeded in steering a private member's bill through parliament.

Nancy was not to rest on her laurels for long. In the summer of 1923 she published a short book of her speeches entitled *My Two Countries*. On 14 July the book was strongly attacked by *New Statesman* reviewer Desmond MacCarthy. An Asquith admirer, MacCarthy hated Nancy. She had exploited Asquith's unpopularity. In a scathing review of *My Two Countries*, Mac-Carthy wrote: 'Each speech is a straight talk full of lofty sentiment . . . This is Lady Astor's theme. I doubt her postulates, and her eloquence is spoilt for me by remembering that having divorced her husband on the vaguest grounds she spoke as eloquently against relaxing the harshness of our divorce laws.' The review was anonymous, MacCarthy signing the article as Affable Hawk. The next week Affable Hawk appeared to repent marginally, perhaps fearing the influential wrath of the Astors.

On 21 July 1923, MacCarthy wrote this letter to the *New Statesman*:

'Sir – On reading last week's "Current Literature" in print I noticed a phrase which went further in its implications than I intended, and was most unfair to Lady Astor. The sentence, as it stood, suggested that she had not what would be generally considered good reasons for seeking divorce from her first husband. On such a point I had, of course, no right and no intention to express an opinion. My point was that, having taken advantage of the well-known facility of the American Divorce courts herself, she had afterwards done her best to prevent men and women in this country having even approximate facilities, a proceeding which those who think our divorce law stands in need of reform find it impossible to forgive. Yours, etc. Affable Hawk.'

Waldorf's solicitors then wrote to the Editor of the *New Statesman*, Clifford Sharp, pointing out that they had repeated the libel perpetrated by Bottomley in *John Bull*. Sharp published the letter in the next issue of the *New Statesman*, re-asserting the libel. The Astor solicitors then wrote again, insisting that Nancy had never attempted to be divorced in America on easier terms than in England. Sharp duly published the solicitors' letter in the *New Statesman* adding the comment: 'We are bound to draw attention to the fact that Messrs Lewis and Lewis have quite abandoned the tone which they saw fit to adopt in their previous letter – printed here on July 28. We have not, of course, and never had any objection whatever to publishing clients' versions of the facts – leaving it to our readers to form their own opinions on the matter – Ed. N.S.' Once again, Nancy's 'Vanity whitewashing' in *Who's Who* had caught her out. Neither was she in any better position to sue than she had been in the past. The Astors now needed a miracle to save their credibility – and the miracle came.

An American lawyer and acquaintance of Waldorf decided to investigate the case in America. The result of his investigation was incontestable evidence that Nancy was absolutely right when she insisted she had not tried to gain an easy divorce in America. J. R. Hughes, himself a divorce reform advocate, wrote forcefully to the *New Statesman* and his letter was published on 6 October. No editorial comment accompanied its publication, neither did Sharp or MacCarthy apologise. Nevertheless, the Astors claimed a muted victory.

In 1924 Nancy made a charitable donation of £10,000 to Plymouth for workers' houses and all rents from the houses were to go to new building. Generous though this act was, however, Nancy's action must have been coloured by her reduced majority and the need to be indispensable to the people of Plymouth. But Nancy's other acts of charity were less political and she often gave money to beggars and tramps who would make a point of putting Cliveden down on their vagrancy

routes as an important port of call. One extraordinary account
of an act of charity carried out by Nancy is typical of her
domineering nature and reminiscent of the way she pursued her
potential assassin in Plymouth. Nancy's son, David, remembered
the incident vividly:

'One day when we were all out riding at Cliveden we came
on a woman tramp on the road a short distance outside the
park gates. She had a remarkable face with clear cut features,
an impressive air of dignity, like a very duchess of the road.
Mother drew rein at once, struck by her appearance, and
asked her where she was going. The woman maintained an
absolute reserve, replying in some laconic monosyllable.
Mother could get nothing out of her; she gave no information
about her means of livelihood nor whether she was in want
of anything. Her farouche independence delighted Mother,
[in fact it probably annoyed her] who suddenly said, "Come
and live at Cliveden. I'll give you a cottage and a nice job."
The woman put the offer aside with indifference. "You're
afraid to come!" said Mother. "I dare you to come." The
woman averted her hawk-like face and without further word
passed on down the road. Mother remained watching from
her horse. When the woman came to Cliveden park gates she
stopped a moment and then turned in at the gate. Mother was
overjoyed. The woman's name was Mrs King. She was given
a cottage and light work. She remained at Cliveden for thirty
years. We got very fond of her.'

The British government found Nancy particularly useful in
dealing with the wives of American ambassadors. Her relaxed
attitude was well received as was her originality of approach.
For instance, Nancy, giving a lunch to welcome a Mrs Kellogg,
wife of a new Ambassador, said:

'I am getting an old hand at welcoming ambassadresses and
ambassadors. They come and go, but I seem to go on forever.
I want to warn Mrs Kellogg about one thing, and that is the
climate. Someone said to me today that the climate was all
right but the weather was bad. I have never seen an American
ambassadress or ambassador here who did not immediately
say "I don't know how we are going to face this English

weather." But I have never known one of them go away
without saying "I don't know how I am going to face the
climate at home." '

At Cliveden the Astor dinner table was becoming more
sophisticated and its guest list more distinguished. Nancy presided over these glittering occasions in the sure and certain
knowledge that she was still in the prime of her career – despite
the continuous attacks of her enemies. One of the most evoca-
tive descriptions of Cliveden life at this time comes from Walter
Elliot, a favoured guest and Conservative parliamentary
colleague:

'I do not know which was more pleasant; to appear at tea-
time in winter when the tea was set in the centre hall before
the big fire, or in summer, when it was laid out with infinite
detail, under a pavilion roof at the end of the broad terrace.
Tea, did I say? It was more like a Bedouin encampment.
There was a table for tea, a table for cakes, a table for
children, a table for grown-ups, a table for more grown-ups,
and generally a nomadic group coming and going somewhere
in the neighbourhood of Nancy herself. Cushions, paper,
people, were mixed in a noble disarray. Nancy presided over
the whole affair like a blend between Juno at the siege of
Troy, and one of the leading Valkyries caracoling over an
appropriate battlefield.

'Somehow or other the party evolved, arranged itself,
separated, and came together again, re-arrayed for dinner. It
might contain anybody – Henry Ford, the Queen of Rumania,
Mr Charles Mellon, Jim Thomas, Philip Lothian, Bernard
Shaw, Tom Jones, Dame Edith Lyttelton, Arthur Balfour, a
general, a scientist, a Christian Scientist, relations, protégés,
American Senators, whether sober or not (this was the only
category to which such licence was extended), people of High
Society, people of no society, and, if you were lucky indeed,
one or more of the other Langhorne sisters, the only beings on
earth whom Nancy really regarded as equals. Phyllis Brand
(with her entrancing baby black-eyed daughter Virginia)
would appear, sometimes with, sometimes without her husband, Bob Brand of Lazard Brothers, whom Nancy always
greeted as a Jew, actual or honorary.'

Michael Astor remembered Cliveden as a series of sounds:

'The background music varied with the seasons. In summer it would be the motor-mowers on the lawn below the terraces and the swifts whistling through the air and fluttering into the eaves above the nursery windows. In winter it was the crackle of the log fire in the hall which burnt day and night, and the sound of the cowls on the roof which revolved and clanked in the wind. On a still day the chime of the clock tower could be heard far away in the woods or from the other side of the river. At night the chime was turned off and it was only turned on again at eight in the morning. But each department on the place had its own particular sounds. There was Mr Harrison, the nightwatchman, going on his rounds from the cellars to the top landings, lighting his way with a torch. He walked with a slow and measured tread which made the floorboards creak. At certain points he would stop to register his progress on a series of time-clocks. This made a loud click, and punctuated the sound of his steps. At five o'clock the housemaids started their day – cleaning, scrubbing, dusting and tidying; hurrying so as to become invisible before the first guests came down to breakfast. On the landings they moved with light nimble footsteps, like mice scuttling from one corner to another. At five-thirty in the summer, and a little later in the winter, the sounds came from the stables; the clanking of pails, water running into buckets, and the firm quick steps of Mr Brooks and the grooms. At six o'clock in the summer, and while it was still dark in the winter, the horses, wearing their blankets, moved off in pairs. The start of early morning exercise made a particular echo. At first it was the metallic sound of hooves on cobbled paving, echoed by the wings of the house: then the softer note as the hooves touched the gravel of the drive . . . At nine o'clock Lee went up to the first floor and performed his first ritual of the day. With a flourish he would pick up a large drumstick and, slowly at first, but working up to a fine crescendo of noise, he sounded the gong for dining room breakfast. The opening bars of this were like thunder rumbling in the distance, then the crash of the storm and, to give it a note of artistry, the sound would be made to roll and fade out slowly. Lee performed this function, as he did everything else, immaculately and with a sense of style. After this everyone, at least officially, was awake and the day started in earnest.'

The children's life was pre-ordained. In the holidays they were taken riding in the morning, and out in the tub-cart in the afternoon. They were given no option about the drives, although they often rebelled against their monotony. Later there was five o'clock nursery tea and afterwards the children were sent down to their parents and their guests. Nancy would then begin to play with them. Her play was inspired and there was something magical about her highly inventive imagination. Because of her 'roguish' sense of humour children found Nancy both compulsively funny and entertaining. She had no interest in the class of the child, its background or its demeanour. All Nancy was interested in was the adaptability and trusting acceptance of childhood. Boisterous games of charades and mimicry were still the order of the day, yet there were other times when she would take them into the boudoir, turn out the lights and tell them her 'nigger' stories. These paternalistic anecdotes of her Mirador childhood featured the 'Uncles' and 'Aunts' in their 'Rastus' image. Nancy did not mean to offend: she believed totally in the order of Mirador's benevolent tyranny. She acted out every part, making her black characters sound histrionic, childlike, yet imbued with a fundamental wisdom.

The Astor children soon became used to being surrounded by the famous and they were quick to remark on their personal habits and mannerisms. Michael Astor remembers: 'Mr Lloyd George was distinguished in our eyes for his exceptionally long hair. Lord Balfour was tall, kindly and detached, as a grown-up should be. J. L. Garvin had an engaging but odd way of speaking, and looked as if his eyes would pop out of his head. Lionel Curtis, with his shaggy grey head, looked to us like a man who probably knew everything there was to be known, but he gave himself away by his jokes which, we could have told him, were not faintly funny.'

Both Nancy and Waldorf believed strongly in the feudal system and, as there was no village at Cliveden, the club and recreation rooms, which during the First World War had been part of the Canadian War Hospital, became the centre of social life. The Three Feathers public house stood outside the gates of Cliveden – a continuous reminder to Nancy that prohibition was but a dream. Indeed the club house had a liquor licence and had its own bar, billiard room, kitchen, concert hall and stage.

Nancy's popularity in the House of Commons was currently not as high as it had been. Her moderate licensing bill was now law but she was still embarrassing the House with her continuous references to the joys of seeing real prohibition in force. Therefore this was not a good time for her to face a general election – but suddenly there was no choice. Bonar Law had become Prime Minister in 1922 but by May 1923 cancer of the throat was diagnosed and he resigned and was succeeded by Baldwin. Owing to division in the party a general election was held on 7 December 1923, barely a year after the previous election. This time there was no second Conservative candidate and Nancy battled against her old Labour rival, Captain Brennan. The contest between them was close and Nancy's majority was reduced to 2,676. The political situation was now confused with the Conservatives having 258 seats, Labour 191 and a revived Liberal party 159. This situation ensured that Baldwin or Ramsay MacDonald could become Prime Minister with Liberal support or Asquith could return to office with Conservative or Labour support. Asquith decided to give Liberal support to a Labour government, the Baldwin government resigned and Ramsay MacDonald headed the very first Labour government whilst Baldwin was re-elected Conservative opposition leader.

Nancy did not seem particularly dejected by this reversal and untactfully pointed out, in a letter to *The Times*, that the Conservative defeat was probably due to their indifference to social reform. She was also pleased that more women MPs had been elected. The already existing two Conservatives were joined by the Duchess of Atholl; Mrs Wintringham the sole Liberal woman MP was joined by Lady Tarrington and the Labour party welcomed their first three women MPs – Margaret Bondfield, Susan Lawrence and Dorothea Jewson. Another triumph involved Margaret Bondfield being appointed Parliamentary Secretary to the Ministry of Labour. This was the first appointment of a woman to a Ministerial post in Britain and

Nancy was generally delighted by the advancement of women in politics. As for going into opposition, Nancy regarded this as another challenge – and another fight.

Nancy Astor's political style at this time combined a bewildering mixture of jeering and exhortation, idealism and badinage. For instance, her speech supporting the Legitimacy Bill of 1924 contained an excellent aphorism: 'Laws cannot make people moral, yet the more moral the people the higher the laws.' Yet how typical it was of Nancy to let her feelings always run away with her when she was angry. When the Labour government spokesman announced that no help would come from the government on the Welsh Temperance Bill, Nancy shouted at him 'My own party may be reactionary, but at least they are honest.'

Nancy never entirely mastered the rules of parliamentary etiquette – and nor did she particularly care to. Gilbert Campion, a clerk in the House of Commons, worked closely with Nancy at that time and he remembers:

'In one branch of practice, the drafting of questions to Ministers, I happened to have my closest personal relations with Lady Astor in her early days. It is the duty of the junior Clerk at the Table to "vet" questions to Ministers given in by Members and try to apply the rules on behalf of the Speaker (who has better things to do). This is a somewhat delicate function (made more difficult in those days by having to be carried on at the Table of the House in whispers so as not to disturb Members speaking or listening) and it was under those conditions fruitful of misunderstandings. (It is now carried on outside the Chamber.) Lady Astor's questions were often, as might be expected, in the nature of propaganda – on behalf of temperance, etc. – which the rules particularly discouraged. These could however generally, with judicious trimmings, be squeezed through. But there was another type of question which was not so amenable. It would begin in some such way as this "Is it true that, as stated by the *Daily Blank*, the American Secretary for the Interior proposes . . . ." This type of question would give any experienced Member a shudder and it is, indeed, like walking over the grave of Erskine May, three at least of whose fundamental rules it contravened. On the reappearance of this type of question I would try to get it through, while making the question innocuous, if given a free hand. But innocuousness was seldom what Lady Astor wanted. A whispered wrangle would ensue. On one of these occasions when my senior colleague, Sir Horace Dawkins, had been drawn into my support, Lady Astor left the Table, registering frustration and rapping out not so very *sotto voce* "You two are the stickiest old men I ever came across." '

Nancy's parliamentary approach was still very unconventional as the following exchange shows. The dialogue occurred as a result of an altercation with a Labour MP, a Mr Hayday, who had the audacity to interrupt her in mid-flow to ask if there was a working mother on one of her committees.

NANCY :	I hate that assumption that a working mother is different from any other mother. A mother is the same in all walks of life.
HAYDAY :	In society gatherings puppy dogs take the place of children.
NANCY :	If I told all I know about the Hon. Member, I would give the House something to think of today. I would go into some of the company that the Hon. Member has kept that would not reflect credit on him nor on his party.
HAYDAY (rising) :	I really think this is going beyond the bounds.
SPEAKER :	I think so too, and the noble lady ought to withdraw.
NANCY :	He asked for it.
COMMANDER KENWORTHY :	The noble lady has made innuendoes against the Hon. Member. The House ought to have an explanation or else a withdrawal.
NANCY :	I am quite willing to withdraw. But the Hon. Member's reference to toy dogs was also insulting.
SPEAKER :	If the noble lady will accept my advice, often given to her, she will not entangle herself in such discussions. She should address me personally and avoid all this.
NANCY :	I quite agree (laughter). I wish I could accept

	your advice, but I do not suppose that any member speaks under more provocation than I do.
SPEAKER :	I cannot agree that the noble lady is not herself sometimes provocative.
NANCY :	I agree to that, too.

5 Tickling the House

Nancy's bright exterior still masked her sensitivity and she was very badly hurt by an episode that occurred over a picture Waldorf had commissioned. The picture was to be a gift to parliament and depicted the historic introduction of the first woman MP – Nancy Astor'. At first the Commissioner of Works indicated to Waldorf that the gift would be acceptable and Nancy sat for the painter, Charles Sims. In the summer of 1924 the picture was completed and Waldorf presented it to the House where it was hung on the wall by the main staircase that led to the Committee Room lobby. Trouble started almost at once.

The protestors declared that it was a dangerous precedent to have a picture in the House showing living members of parliament. In fact this was merely a cover-up for Nancy's enemies to have her picture removed. They clearly felt they could not allow the picture to remain. Nancy, in their view, was far too arrogant anyway and the portrait would merely condone this. Eventually, Waldorf unwillingly agreed that the picture would be withdrawn if the protests continued. Whilst an enquiry was held, a dust sheet was placed over the picture. Eventually some-

6   The Ghosts: 'But why?'

one childishly scribbled on the canvas and the painting was abruptly removed. There was no doubt that Nancy was deeply hurt, but she was determined not to show it. The picture was eventually hung in the Bedford College for Women in Regent's Park and it is now on permanent loan by the House of Commons to America. Later Nancy defensively told Maurice Collis: 'They missed the whole point. It was not a picture of Lady Astor; it was never intended to be a picture of Lady Astor. It is a picture of an historical event. The people who kicked up the row thought they were hitting at me. But what they were hitting at was an idea, the idea of women in parliament. But the idea is still in the House of Commons and they will never get it out.'

In Autumn 1924 Ramsay MacDonald, widening his efforts for European peace, began treaty negotiations with Russia. Unfortunately this move was to initiate yet another election for although the Bolshevist regime had been officially recognised, most Liberals were horrified by the revolution. They withdrew their support from the Labour government and Ramsay Mac-Donald was forced to go to the country.

Then, a happy intervention occurred for the Conservatives in the shape of a forgery – the Zinoviev letter which caused much disquiet and was taken very seriously. Zinoviev was president of the Communist International and in his so-called letter he appealed to all English Communists to influence the army to revolt. The country panicked and voters identified a horrified Labour party with the 'Bolshies' whilst the Conservatives walked into a comfortable victory. Nancy doubled her majority in her fourth election, and the majority in the House of Commons was as follows: Conservatives 414, Labour 150, Liberals 39.

Unfortunately the female membership of the House of Commons was diminished by the election. The three Conservative members were returned but the Liberal, Mrs Wintringham, was defeated as were all three Labour women members. One new Labour member, Ellen Wilkinson, was elected and quickly became known as Red Ellen. Similar in personality to Nancy Ellen was totally alien to Nancy's own political views. Ellen was very far left, had originally been a member of the Communist party and had, in 1921, been to Russia. Strangely, Nancy and Ellen became very close friends. Ellen suffered from manic-depression and no doubt saw in Nancy a strength that she lacked, whilst in Ellen, Nancy saw the vigour and courage that she always so much admired.

Meanwhile, A. G. Gardiner was writing about Nancy in the *Daily News*, as follows:

'It is not her opinions that make her so unprecedented a figure in the English public scene, but the gallop of the spirit with which she enters the lists, her terrific pugnacity and her gay indifference to the formal respectabilities of behaviour. "The House of Commons," said Bolingbroke, "loves the man who shows it sport." And wherever Lady Astor's "View halloo!" is heard, there is the assurance of sport. She is as ready to back Mr Baldwin or Mr MacDonald as she was to pull the coat-tails of Sir Frederick Banbury, and she has declared that she would go to Timbuctoo for the joy of fighting a brewer.'

Nancy's streak of cruelty, however, remained, particularly when she considered she had been thwarted. In 1925 she discovered a very old friend and admirer had arrived in the House as MP for Dartford. He was Angus McDonnell, now calling himself Colonel McDonnell after serving for a period with the Canadian Army. He gave his maiden speech on 2 April 1925 and although the speech was probably not particularly inspired, it was a sound one on a subject which McDonnell knew a great deal about – supply. Angus McDonnell seconded an amendment which claimed that current mass-unemployment could be relieved by emigration to the Colonies with the object of exploiting their largely uncultivated territories. Nancy, however, had never forgiven McDonnell for his temerity in marrying without her blessing. Naturally she overlooked the fact that he had worshipped her for years and that in his eyes she could do no wrong. His devotion to her had not changed when they met outside the Chamber. Instead of building McDonnell's confidence, Nancy made a remark that bitterly hurt McDonnell and finally destroyed his devotion. 'Angus,' she said with reference to his maiden speech, 'I'm sorry. You'll have to do better than that.'

This new parliament lasted rather longer than its predecessors and Nancy, enjoying a wave of popularity, worked hard. She introduced two private members' bills to do with social reform, but unfortunately neither passed its second reading. The first bill related to the control of prostitution and the second to raising the school leaving age. But Nancy was undaunted and she kept her reputation intact.

In 1926 further light was shed on Nancy's day-to-day political and social life with the publication of Will Thorne's autobiography. He wrote:

'One evening in the House of Commons Lady Astor asked me if I would like to dine with her to meet the Prince. I agreed on one condition, that I should be allowed to wear my everyday clothes. Her reply was that I could wear any clothes that I liked. I decided to go. When I reached the house in St James's Square several magnificent motor cars were lined up outside and crowds of people were waiting to see the guests arrive. Finally, I plucked up courage and pushed through the crowd, marched up to the door, conscious all the time that I was a little out of place. The door was opened by servants in gorgeous livery. They looked at me with amazement and I am sure they wondered who I was. My hat, stick and coat were taken and I was escorted to the grand staircase, at the top of which was Lady Astor, beautifully dressed and crowned with a glittering diamond tiara. She gave me a hearty welcome and introduced me to some of her friends. The silvery notes of an oriental gong summoned us to dinner. At the time I was speaking to Lady Astor's sister. I offered her my arm and escorted her to the table, where Lady Astor had seated me near the Prince of Wales. The general atmosphere of luxury gave me a rosy glow. I looked at the beautiful women around me and turning to Lady Astor's sister remarked that the beauty of it all reminded me of a song I had often heard in the East End. She was curious to know what it was and finally persuaded me to hum the song.'

But there were still strange conflicts and compromises in Nancy's nature which most people found very disturbing. For a prohibitionist, Nancy seemed both hypocritical and compromising over alcohol. Although it was true that she and Waldorf were totally abstemious, wine and brandy flowed for the guests. Edwin Lee told Maurice Collis that the Prince of Wales had been very wary of the Astor dinner parties, imagining that they would be dry. Lee recounted :

'I remember the first time the Prince of Wales came to dinner. That was before he knew the ways of the house. His equerry, Major "Fruity" Metcalfe, rang up first. He said to me: "His Royal Highness knows Lady Astor's principles. I am sending a bottle of his favourite brandy along with him. He hopes that you will be able to let him have a glass or so of it at the end of dinner." I replied "It is not necessary, sir, to go to such lengths. While it is true that her ladyship dislikes liquor and neither she nor his lordship takes any, their guests are always served with the best. I have been ordered to offer His Royal Highness some 1828 brandy." On learning of the famous brandy, Major Metcalf immediately withdrew his suggestion. I rather think the Prince was told what to expect, for after dinner when I asked in the usual way: "Will your Royal Highness have port, liqueurs or brandy?" he looked up at me with such an amusing face. "*Your* brandy," he said.'

Yet Nancy must have been conscious of her compromise because her old enemy, Sir Frederick Banbury, delighted in continually pointing out the dichotomy. James Stuart, a protégé of Nancy's, an ex-oil driller in America, and an ex-officer of the Royal Scots Greys, was the first to witness an attempted stand at Cliveden against alcohol being served. When a dinner party was given which included Stuart's former chief, the Duke of York and his wife (now the Queen Mother) Nancy decided to serve no alcohol whatsoever. Stuart, who was acting host in Waldorf's absence due to rheumatism, immediately protested and told Nancy: 'Well, if I'm to act as host, I only do so on condition that there's champagne for the Duchess – and me – at my end of the table, and I strongly advise you to have some at your end for the Duke. That is, if you ever want them to come here again. Have you ever thought of inviting the Prince of Wales? I wouldn't try giving him a pussyfoot dinner.' Nancy then decided against her non-alcoholic dinner for 'social reasons'.

But in other aspects of social reform, Nancy was progressive and incisive. This was particularly evident in her relationship with Labour party member Margaret McMillan. Nancy first met her in July 1926 and was initially sceptical. Margaret and Rachel McMillan had become members of the Independent Labour Party in 1893 and Margaret had campaigned, primarily in Bradford and later in London, to establish official health supervision in schools. Clinics were established with the help of the LCC just before the First World War; camp schools were begun and nursery schools were pioneered. Nancy's scepticism was short lived. Her doubts had been based on the fact that Margaret McMillan thought the only way she could pioneer her social causes was through Socialism. Nancy could not agree with that but she did agree with the educational work that Margaret McMillan was doing. Another factor that linked them strongly was that Margaret McMillan was also a deeply spiritual woman – although in a very different way from Nancy. Margaret's sister, Rachel, died in 1917 and for the rest of her life Margaret worshipped her sister, elevating her memory to such an extent that she believed Rachel was a mysterious and spiritual force still working with her – and contributing to her work. When Margaret became friendly with Nancy she assured her that Rachel had blessed the friendship with her approval.

Nancy backed Margaret McMillan with as much parliamentary muscle as she could gather. She brought to the attention of the House the importance of nursery schools and she also interested Waldorf in the McMillan campaign. She took him to one of the Margaret McMillan schools and training centres in Deptford and, as a result, Waldorf bought some land. Nancy fund-raised and the concept of the Rachel McMillan College was born. She also interested Queen Mary, arranged royal visits and eventually laid the foundation stone. Queen Mary opened the College in 1930; in the next year, 1931, Margaret McMillan died. As she died she left a message for her friend and patron, Nancy. 'Tell her,' she said, 'I have no fear. I am happy.'

With her employees, however, Nancy was often tyrannical and few of them had the courage to stand up to her. But there were exceptions – Rose Harrison who was shortly to join her as her personal maid and Miss Benningfield, her secretary and a fellow Christian Scientist. The following memo, written after Miss Benningfield had left Nancy's employ, is typical of her awareness of Nancy's personality and its problems. She was writing to Nancy after a worried visit from Nancy's current secretary who was also a Christian Scientist and who had previously worked for Philip Kerr.

'Well – Miss X has been here with me this evening & we've had a lot of talk. She's very depressed and discouraged, &, as ever in such cases, the most amazingly futile molehills seem to her like the whole of the Rocky Mountains. She feels that you have no confidence in her, & that until you can trust her a little more she won't be able to give her best or to please you in any way. From what I know of your beloved, bewildering & exasperating character, I think she is right! . . . I know that one question with you is now "Will she do for me" or "is she the kind of employee I want"? And to that question of course there are two sides. There is a good employer & one who is difficult to serve. Miss X is used to a very high standard where her employer is concerned. Mr Kerr must be a most considerate & just & thoughtful creature to work for . . . a very perfect gentle knight among employers. She's used to a certain amount of approval & satisfaction "for value received" & she's used to thinking of Mr Kerr and herself – voila tout. Now, suddenly, she's plunged into the whirlpool of St J Sq. where everything she does is in relation to what about a dozen other people are doing. She is faced with a mass of detail. She gets no sympathy, or encouragement, or patience, or consideration. Her chief faults are ignorance of your character and bewilderment. She's giving you her very best & is trying hard to learn your ways. *You'll have these difficulties with any secretary you take on . . .*'

In October 1926 another shattering blow was delivered to the Grenfell family when Ivo was killed in a car crash. This tragedy rocked Lady Desborough but it also brought her closer to Nancy. They exchanged correspondence and after Nancy visited Taplow Court, Lady Desborough wrote, 'We'll never refer to "byegones", but I suppose the world has never taken so much trouble in its life to make mischief between two people as between you and me! And I do want to tell you, dear Nancy, that I am so glad we have got it all right, directly we got to know each other. I shall always be fond of you now.'

But it was not the world that made 'trouble' between Lady Desborough and Nancy – it was Nancy's own insecurity and jealousy. Lady Desborough, however, was either in ignorance of this – or tactfully had decided to ignore the real reasons behind the problems of their relationship.

7

Friendships

Discussing Bernard Shaw, Nancy Astor said that his 'greatest gift had been in breaking down things.' Her relationship with G.B.S., as she always called him, was one of mutual respect and admiration. Nevertheless it was an extraordinary relationship because they had so little in common. She did not read his works, although Shaw read them to her and valued her opinion of them. For his part, Shaw had no use for her politics and he was totally absorbed in battling against institutions such as parliament and the universities which he considered useless and abhorrent. Nevertheless they were both highly extrovert and emotional personalities and it was these traits that bound them together.

Nancy and G.B.S. had known each other slightly for many years but it was not until 1927 that their friendship blossomed. The Shaws, Bernard and Charlotte, came to Cliveden for the Christmas weekend but stayed instead for three weeks. Charlotte's letter to Nancy of 28 January well expressed the Shaws' enthusiasm. G.B.S. added a postscript.

> 'Here we are, dear friend, safe & sound & we both agree that all that has occurred during the last 3 weeks is a wonderful & impossible dream, & that now we are awake again to the buffets and storms of life. But the lovely flower is alive & well to witness that we lie!
>
> 'My love to David.
>
> 'Ever C. F. Shaw.
>
> 'All the same, I don't believe it ever happened. I ask you, is it likely? G.B.S.'

The euphoria continued, despite the fact that Shaw poured considerable scorn on Christian Scientists and even went to the extent of writing in a letter to Nancy, 'My Charlotte, I regret to say, is in bed with a swamping headful of sin and error, known to the mob as a bad cold.' Amazingly Nancy did not take offence. Neither Nancy nor G.B.S. could entirely understand why their friendship was so strong and, referring to Charlotte in a letter to Nancy, Shaw wrote: 'She is very fond of you. So am I. I don't know why.'

Shaw began to regularly attend Nancy's social functions although both he and Charlotte seemed loath to join in the drama and music that Nancy so loved. Thomas Jones, then Deputy Secretary to the Cabinet, shared the Shaws' reluctance and wrote in his diary on 26 December 1927 an account of a typical Christmas with the Astors.

'Lunch at 1 o'clock with orders from Lady A. that no one was to use more than one plate for all courses so as to reduce work in the kitchen. We are nearer 30 than 20 at meals. About 3 o'clock after some gramophone with remarkable records (Temple boys, etc.) Astor and I and a Mr Judge from Plymouth went a two hour walk, despite some rain, through the grounds of "Dropmore" to Burnham Beeches and back, calling en route to see a Roman Camp. Tea at 5 and about the whole household, family, guests and domestics, filed into the library and Ruth Draper delighted us with: A German Lesson, the Scottish Immigrant on Ellis Island, the French Dressmaker, the Visit to an Art Gallery, and the Children's Party. Then Christmas Dinner, turkey and plum pudding, sweets and crackers and coffee. Then from 9.15 to 11.30 or so we had a characteristic Astorian evening of dance and song all jumbled up in a rollicking way. I should have said that practically all the guests, before dinner, had arrayed themselves in fancy dress, as well of course as the Astorians. Bernard Shaw and I were the only exceptions among the men and Mumsie and Mrs G.B.S. among the women. I wished I had brought the LL.D. gown with me. Tristan put on my new dressing gown, and Elphin had a mask of a benevolent "Punch" and a black robe, rather like a priest's or monk's – he looked the most kindly old gentleman, and was secretly very proud of himself, while T. was far less at ease. Lady Astor was an extraordinary figure – a racing tout in ill-fitting coat, vest, trousers (black and white check squares), face of a low-caste Jew, glasses slung along her side, small bowler hat. The carpet was rolled up in the Library, the records turned on, and she did all sorts of turns with uproarious results, talking the race course jargon all the time. There was lots of dancing and Elphin was made to whizz round more than once as her ladyship's partner – the Shaws and Joneses soberly looking on. About 10.30 I imagine dancing ceased and Mrs Paul Phipps (sister of Lady Astor) started negro folk songs and spirituals with banjo accompaniment and Ruth Draper and others joining in, song after song, until at 11.15, when R.D. got up to talk to her sister in New York, I got Billy to motor us home through a blinding snowstorm. And so to bed at midnight.'

Shaw accompanied Nancy to Margaret McMillan's nursery schools and he often came to Cliveden. There is a famous photograph of him there, standing on the terrace dressed in his usual uniform of Norfolk jacket, knickerbockers and cloth cap. He was now at the height of his fame and at the start of his friendship with Nancy he was writing *The Intelligent Woman's Guide to Socialism and Capitalism*.

During the winter of 1928–9 Shaw was writing *The Apple Cart* – much of which he wrote during various visits to Cliveden. Thanks to Nancy's policy of giving her guests freedom rather than schedules, Shaw knew he would enjoy peace and tranquillity as a background to his writing at Cliveden. After finishing a play, G.B.S. usually ran reading parties, and he refers to one of these in the letter he wrote to Nancy on 11 February 1929. Nancy was now fifty and still strikingly beautiful.

'Loveliest Nan. As to that list – what about Balfour? What about T.J. (an authority on Cabinet procedure who needs cheering up)? What about Elliot (for dinner and the last act; he heard the first)? What about Mosley and his Cynthia (to represent the Labour Party)? Griggs has suffered it all before: need we plague him again? Ward dear lad, is only one of many journalists; but why not Geoffrey Dawson: wouldn't you like to see him wriggling on my skewer?

'Are you on visiting terms with Ellen Wilkinson? Dare she

– if you asked her? I should rather like to know how my lampoon would strike her – whether she would detect portraits which don't exist. However, unless she would amuse *you*, disregard this suggestion, as I can easily get at her when I read for the Webbs and the Fabian lot.

'I shall have read the play professionally and privately to Sir Barry Jackson and the producer this week (it has come back from the printer); so there is no *need* to have him, though he might like to come and look at you under cover of the play.

'I can't think of anyone else for the moment; but I presume you don't want a mob.

'I hope you have not been devoured by wolves, though you would be if I were a wolf. Here it is blastingly, blightingly, blitheringly cold : 8 degrees of frost in the sun out of the wind at midday, and 1,000° below zero *in* the wind.

'Probably Charlotte, who is up and about the house, is writing.

'In haste : the post goes at 4.30 in this village.'

Yours G.B.S.

'PS. Waldorf is bringing in a bill to get Lady Rhondda into the House of Lords to cheer him in your absence. What about her?'

Meanwhile, Baldwin's large majority government was becoming weary and complacent. So was Baldwin himself and he seemed unaware of the restlessness of the country. Nancy had strongly supported the 1928 Franchise Act which gave votes to women at 21 and everyone expected that those votes would be Conservative. In April 1929 parliament was dissolved and on 30 May polling took place. Nancy's opponents were William Westwood representing Labour, and T. H. Aggett, for the Liberals. The miners' strike was still casting a shadow over the country and suddenly the Tories woke up to the fact that they had a fight on their hands.

G.B.S. wrote this letter to Nancy from Dubrovnik on 18 May 1929 :

'You are in a difficult position : a violently Radical Conservative, a recklessly unladylike Lady, a Prohibitionist member of

146

a Trade Party, and all sorts of contradictory things, including (on the authority of the late Speaker) the most turbulent member of the Party of Order. The only tune to which you can win in a seafaring constituency is Jack's Delight is His Lovely Nan. In that sign you will probably conquer in spite of all the sober and virtuous publicans and brothel keepers who minister to the paid off mariners of our historic port. Knowing that you are on the side of the angels, they will give you a vote to set against their profits in the books of the recording angel, believing that you are too jonnick [sic] to cut any ice in parliament on your own account. Therefore be extreme on the Drink question for if you compromise they will be afraid you might really hurt them whereas if you go all out for a Dry England they will laugh at pretty Nancy's way and feel sure that you might as well try to dry England with blotting paper as with Prohibition. On the social question, just read chapters of my book [*The Intelligent Woman's Guide to Socialism*] at random and give them chunks of it : they will neither know nor care whether it is Socialism or Conservatism if you don't tell them. Give them what you like, and they'll probably like it too; and leave it to the others to "give em much" (Peche Melba). Tell them you are making enemies all the time because you can't suffer fools gladly and are up against 600 of them every working night of your life, and that under God your refuge is Plymouth, and if Plymouth turns you down it will shut the gate of mercy on mankind. In short, dear Nancy, let yourself rip and were all your pearls : prudence is not your game; and if you ride hard enough for a fall you won't get it.'

This was one of the soundest pieces of advice Nancy had ever received. Charisma was the only quality on which she could possibly win this election and she was now determined to apply as much of it as she could – as quickly as she could. Three days before the election Nancy decided to electioneer in a red stronghold. The *Daily Express* described the ensuing scene :

' "So you are a pack of Bolshies, eh ?"

'Lady Astor stood with her feet squarely planted, a large umbrella clasped by the ferrule in her right hand, like a club, and her smart cloche hat at a rakish tilt.

'She stood completely alone in the courtyard of the worst tenement of the worst street in Plymouth, a Communist stronghold, and glowered at balcony on balcony above her packed with more than a hundred shouting, shrieking, hostile women. "So you are a pack of Bolshies, eh?" she challenged, waving the umbrella threateningly.

' "Better get away, Lady Astor," I warned, for a hefty woman with sacking over her head was reaching for a cabbage.

'She spun round fiercely. "Leave this to me." A man caught her roughly by the shoulder, and she raised the umbrella. He ran like a hare, and then she faced the crowd.

' "Too proud for the working woman, am I?" She laughed merrily, and struck an attitude, nose perked comically, and danced affectedly up and down outside the tenement.

' "They say I drink gin-and-bitters," she cried. "Hoy, you up there – " she pointed to a woman who had been shouting herself hoarse. "How many gin-and-bitters have I had with you, Pleasant?"

'A little dog flew snarling at the crowd. Somebody threw a brick at him. Like an avenging angel with her umbrella, Lady Astor dashed up, saved the little dog, and then, with arms akimbo, harangued the crowd. Her words burned like acid. With their own words and phrases she flayed and slashed at them.

' "Twenty years you have known me," she said. "Twenty years; and this Westwood man is brought against me. Who and what is he? He has only just come, and we do not even know what he looks like. I tell you, Cook says this is the beginning of the revolution. They are out to smash the British Government. Believe me, don't believe darned idiots who come round touting fake promises."

'There was a moment's silence, and then they cheered her – cheered her like mad, and as her car left the place, roared and roared again : "Good old Nancy!" '

Shaw had been totally correct when he advised Nancy 'If you ride hard enough for a fall you won't get it.' Nevertheless, Nancy only just retained her seat and polled 16,625 votes against Westwood's 16,414. The Liberal candidate received

5,430 and very probably saved Nancy's seat. The situation in the House of Commons was now Labour 287, Conservative 260 and Liberal 59. Labour was returned with Ramsay MacDonald as Prime Minister, backed by the Liberals with Lloyd George as leader. There were now fourteen women members in the House of Commons, made up as follows: three Conservative, nine Labour, one Liberal and one Independent.

Nancy invited all these women MPs to a rather extraordinary lunch, shortly after their swearing in at St Stephen's. With sudden ardour, Nancy fully adopted the feminist cause for the first time – but she adopted it with familiar and characteristic exaggeration. Having told them that she understood how irritating it was to have an American pioneer as first woman MP in the House of Commons, Nancy then went on to launch a long diatribe on forming a women's party. The nine Labour women MPs were then calmly told by Nancy to drop their political allegiances completely and form the backbone of her proposed Women's Party. One of these Labour women MPs, Mary Agnes Hamilton, remembered that:

'This notion did not appeal to us. It would not, at any time, have appealed. Least of all did it appeal in 1929. We were "true believers". Sex equality, while an important item for long in the programme of our Party, was only one element in our creed. The timing of the proposal, further, seemed incredibly naive. In the new Government, Margaret Bondfield was a member of the Cabinet, and Susan Lawrence a junior minister. The Government had a tremendous task, in the social, the economic, and the international field; we were here to help in that task. Why, at this juncture, should we hive off and form a specifically female organisation?'

The ensuing row was lively but not malicious and this was thanks to Nancy's good humour. Even she must have realised that she was shooting a very eccentric line. So ended Nancy's first and last attempt to found a unified feminist political movement.

Bernard Shaw was now a staunch friend of the Astors. He admired Nancy's vivacity but most of all he admired her audacity. Shaw loved people who were unique and who did not kowtow to any established way of thinking. This was the main reason why he became so attached to Nancy, and why their friendship persisted for so many years. He would sometimes support Nancy and Waldorf on public occasions, although his speeches were often as eccentric as Nancy's. Typical of his manner was the opening of Astor Hall, a residential hostel for students of Exeter's University College:

'The extraordinary devotion of my friends Lord and Lady Astor to the City of Plymouth has always been a source of astonishment to me because I have never been able to understand in what way the citizens have deserved it. I have a strong impression that a large number of them resent it extremely. Lord Astor is evidently carrying on a struggle against the inevitable consequence of his own public spirit. After a few more years I believe he will be the most unpopular man in south-west England. Possibly, however, those who come after him, his sons, for instance, if they abstain from doing anything for the people of Plymouth, and make as much money as they possibly can, may restore the popularity of the Astor family ... Many of you think I am an enthusiastic advocate of University education, whereas I am fully convinced that English University education is destroying civilisation and has for some centuries been making decent government and decent life for the people impossible. The thing to do with these venerable institutions, particularly Oxford and Cambridge, in spite of the beauty of many of their buildings, is to raze them to the ground and sow the foundations with salt. If it is too much trouble to knock them down, use them as asylums for lunatics ...'

Nancy responded to Shaw's speech. She pointed out that there were few people who could speak as G.B.S. did – and she added that perhaps it was as well for the world that there were.

Shaw introduced Nancy to T. E. Lawrence, who, at forty, was masquerading as Aircraftman Shaw in a camp near Plymouth. Lawrence was attracted to the famous and, besides Shaw, he knew Lionel Curtis and Philip Kerr. Nancy first met Lawrence in 1924 but their friendship became closer when Lawrence moved to Plymouth. Shaw obviously thought highly of him and invited Lawrence to a reading of *The Apple Cart*. Lawrence wrote to Nancy on 12 March 1929: 'Dear Lady Astor, I'd immensely appreciate hearing that G.B.S. reading, and if I can possibly wangle leave for Saturday and Sunday I will attend (probably in uniform, but I shan't mind your being differently dressed) on the 23rd. If I do not turn up, then please blame the RAF rather than my expectant self. Yours sincerely, T. E. Shaw.'

Lawrence did not normally like the company of women, but in Nancy he found a great friend. He had now recovered from the nervous breakdown he had suffered after the Arab campaign and was no longer contemplating suicide. In his role as Aircraftman Shaw, Lawrence believed that a life of spartan, dull routine would keep him sane and away from the yawning precipice of black despair that was always awaiting him in his idle moments.

Like Shaw, Lawrence felt completely at ease with Nancy and was able to relax in her house, and read without interruption. Bill Astor told Maurice Collis: 'In their house Lawrence was relaxed and easy, fond of children, patient with young people, sometimes very witty, sometimes playing practical jokes, a different man altogether from the shrinking and uncouth eccentric he appeared to many people.' Once again, as in Nancy's friendship with Shaw, the relationship was unlikely. However, one clue to the enigma was the fact that Nancy regarded Lawrence as a hero – a psychologically wounded hero – and an intellectual for whom she had enormous respect. From Lawrence's point of view he was attracted to Nancy because of her great appetite for life and because of her strength. Nancy told Collis: 'When Lawrence was stationed near Plymouth he used to come in often and see us after dinner. If interested, his conversation was brilliant, but he was often silent. I used to ride pillion on his motorcycle and go long distances very fast. He liked it because I could balance without touching him. My last ride with him was only a fortnight before his fatal accident.' Nancy's maid, Rose Harrison, described one such episode as follows:

'Suddenly both of them got up, rushed outside, jumped on his bike, her riding on the pillion, and drove off at top speed in a cloud of dust down the drive. They were away only for a few minutes, but it seemed an eternity, and his lordship was beside himself with worry and embarrassment. They came back, if anything faster than when they'd gone away, and stopped in a skid on the drive. "We did a hundred miles an hour," she screamed, but she didn't get the enthusiasm back that she expected. I know I was thanking God for having answered my prayers. His lordship just stalked away furious. Unfortunately that kind of reception didn't stop her. There was always a next time and we knew there would be.'

Waldorf's reaction to Nancy's friendships has always been obscure. He partly indulged her, understanding that she needed the stimulation that he could not give her, but at the same time Waldorf resented her friends because of their influence on her. He may have also realised that part of Nancy's nature was flirtatious, despite her extreme fastidiousness over sex and her constant withdrawal from sexual confrontation. Probably Lawrence also saw Nancy as a mother figure – but as a dynamic and non-repressive mother. Nancy also found Lawrence attractive because she knew she was safe. As a homosexual he would make no demands on her and she could flirt with him without committing herself to anything. Years later Nancy told her niece, Nancy Lancaster, that Lawrence 'was a beau, and I've always liked beaux.' Providing, of course, they kept their distance.

Lawrence's letters to Nancy were depressive, and he played 'hard to get'. When she was elected in 1929, Nancy asked Lawrence to Cliveden and to Elliot Terrace in Plymouth. Lawrence replied 'Alas! I can't come to Cliveden. Nor will I see Elliot Terrace. Thank you all the same. The best way to be content in the service is to stick to it, taking only such reliefs as one's own pocket affords. The helplessness of money: that's a very often forgotten point.'

Lawrence found Nancy a distracting alleviation to his own self-imposed misery. His frame of mind is best summarised in this letter to Lionel Curtis, written some years earlier, on 14 May 1923:

'I should have written before, but a split thumb, and a sudden discovery of the authorities that I belonged to a criminal class, have put me out of the mood for subjective writing – and since politics passed out of me the only theme between us is myself.

'There was one injustice in your letter. My crying-out here was not at the fowl [sic] talk. To me it's meaningless, unobjectionable, on a par with heedless fair-talk. The RAF was fowl mouthed and the cleanest little mob of fellows. These are fowl mouthed, and behind their mouths is a pervading animality of spirit, whose unmixed bestiality frightens and hurts me. There is no criticism, it's taken for granted as natural, that you should job a woman's body, or hire out yourself, or abuse yourself in any way. I cried out against it, partly in self-pity because I've condemned myself to grow like them, and partly in premonition of failure, for my masochism remains and will remain, only moral. Physically I can't do it : indeed I get in denial the gratification they get in indulgence. I react against their example into an abstention even more rigorous than of old. Everything bodily is now hateful to me (and in my case hateful is the same as impossible). In the sports lately (they vex us with set exercises) I was put down to jump, and refused because it was an activity of the flesh. Afterwards to myself I wondered if that was the reason, or was I afraid of falling ridiculously : so I went down alone and privily cleared over twenty feet, and was sick of mind at having tried because I was glad to find I could still jump. It's on a par with the music for which I'm hungry. Henry Lamb is in Poole, and will play wonderfully to me if I go over : and I won't go, though I'm so starved for rhythm that even a soldier's stumbling through a song on the piano makes my blood run smooth. (I refuse to hear it with my head.)

'This sort of thing must be madness, and sometimes I wonder how far mad I am, and if a mad-house would not be my next (and merciful) stage. Merciful compared with this place which hurts me, body and soul. It's terrible to hold myself voluntarily here : till the burnt child no longer feels the fire. Do you think there have been many lay-monks of my persuasion? One used to think that such frames of mind would have perished with the age of religion : and yet here they rise up purely secular. It's a lurid flash into the Nitrian desert : seems almost to strip the sainthood from Anthony. How about Teresa? I consume the day (and myself) brooding, and making phrases and reading and thinking again, galloping mentally down twenty divergent moods at once, as apart and alone as in Barton Street in my attic. I sleep less than ever for the quietness of night imposes thinking on me : I eat breakfast only, and refuse every possible distraction and employment and exercise. When my mood gets too hot and I find myself wandering beyond control I pull out my motorbike and hurl it at top-speed through these unfit roads for hour after hour. My nerves are jaded and going near dead so that nothing else than hours of voluntary danger will prick them into life: and the "life" they reach then is a melancholy joy at risking something worth exactly 2/9 a day.

'It's odd again that craving for real risk; because in the gymnasium I funk jumping the horse, more than poison. That is physical, which is why it is: I'm ashamed of doing it and of not doing it, unwilling to do it: and most of all ashamed (afraid) of doing it well.

'A nice, neurotic letter. What you've done to deserve its receipt God knows ... perhaps you have listened to me friendly-like at earlier times. Sorry and all that.

'You are a kind of safety valve perhaps. I wish you were an alienist, and could tell me where or how this ferment will end. It makes me miserable on top of all the curiosity and determination: and sets me so much aside that I hardly blame the powers for jumping on me with their dull punishments.'

The distinguished and celebrated people who gathered around the Astors clearly attracted the aspect of Lawrence's personality that craved for fame and for the continuance of the 'Lawrence of Arabia' legend. Admittedly, Lawrence's other self continually chastised this publicity seeking and had created the abrasive Aircraftman Shaw role. Nevertheless, his ego often broke through his exile from glamour, and his most controversial biographer, Richard Aldington (whose book Nancy was later to fight to suppress) wrote: 'Lawrence was always most careful to foster the illusion that he was frantically avoiding publicity, which naturally created the suspicion that he had something of great public interest to conceal.' Even Lawrence's great friend, George Bernard Shaw, wrote: 'When he was in the middle of the stage, with ten limelights blazing on him, everybody pointed to him and said: "See! He is hiding. He hates publicity." '

But Lawrence had far more grim objectivity over his double standards and secret needs than Nancy. Lawrence was a masochist and probably enjoyed punishing himself, yet he instinctively realised his frailties. Nancy buried the fears of her own self-knowledge under a welter of activity and manipulation of her own brand of Christian Science. Perhaps Lawrence was aware of this frantic self-deception and drew closer to her because of it. They were both people of sensation, hell-bent on a spiritual path of their own construction.

Lawrence often declared that he was incapable of falling in love but this fact did not seem to prevent people falling in love with him, or so he claimed, and in 1933 he told Nancy in a letter that he had received over the Christmas season declarations of love from four women and two men. But Nancy declared no direct love for him although there was something of her previous relationship with the Grenfells in their correspondence. Lawrence's literary tastes were also shared by Nancy and much of their correspondence is devoted to their common interest in books. Lawrence's literary style is very commanding and in his dedication to S.A. in *Revolt in the Desert* (omitted from popular editions) Lawrence movingly writes:

> 'I loved you, so I drew these tides of men into my hands and wrote my will across the sky in stars to earn you Freedom; the seven pillared worthy house, that your eyes might be shining for me when we came ... Love, the way-weary, groped to your body, our brief wage, ours for the moment before earth's soft hand explored your shape.'

This erotic description was not inspired by a woman and, with the exception of Nancy and Charlotte Shaw, Lawrence was a determined woman-hater. 'Women,' Lawrence wrote, 'I like some women. I dont like their sex. It's as obvious as red hair: and as little fundamental, I fancy.' Later he added: 'Surely the sex business isn't worth all this damned fuss? I've met only a handful of people who really cared a biscuit for it.'

Lawrence's correspondence with Lionel Curtis continued, sometimes going to such heights as this outburst '... surely the world would be more clean if we were dead or mindless? We are all guilty alike, you know. You wouldn't exist. I wouldn't exist without this carnality. Everything with flesh in its mixture is the achievement of a moment when the lusty thought of Hut 12 has passed to action and conceived: and isn't it true that the fault of birth rests somewhat on the child? I believe it's we who led our parents on to bear us, and it's our unborn child who makes our flesh itch. A filthy business all of it, and yet Hut 12 shows me the truth behind Freud.'

But much of Lawrence's correspondence with Nancy was sympathetic, companionable yet cynical, as is demonstrated in this letter.

30/5/29

RAF Cattewater,
Plymouth.

'Dear Lady Astor,

I have heard of your worries lately, [a reference to Nancy's election problems] and how the sons of Belial have been making loud noises. I am very sorry: though I hope that you are worldly enough not to wish for gratitude or even fair play from mankind (in which womankind is included). Still, I suppose it hurts, when you have done your best for a place and meet only misrepresentation. Once MPS were supposed to do their best; now they are only supposed to do what their constituents wish, or their leaders order. Do, please, read the education of Henry Adams, as an antidote to success or failure. I hope it will be successful, all the same. I dislike die-hards, & drink-hards, and would like you to get it.

'Sandwich and Cliveden are both beyond reach. So is Philip Kerr, who lives mostly in heaven, I think. Alas: selfish of him. He should join the RAF.

Yours, T. E. Shaw.'

A month later Lawrence wrote:

30/6/29

'Dear Lady Astor,

I will do my best to come on Wednesday at 8.30 – do my best, because probably I will have to fly to Portsmouth on Wednesday. We should be back in time for me to change & come over. I shall be stone deaf, dizzy, sick and stupid. You, alas, will say that you notice no difference ... Mrs Shaw sees only my virtues. I think she is a very understanding soul. She and G.B.S. mix like bacon and eggs into a quintessential dream. I would rather visit them than read any book or hear any music on earth.

Yours sincerely, T. E. Shaw.'

Lawrence's critic, Richard Aldington, wrote: 'There is one achievement which nobody can deny Lawrence, and that was his capacity to convince others that he was a remarkable man.' But Aldington is too harsh. Lawrence *was* a remarkable man, both as a soldier and a man of letters. Certainly some parts of his legend were fabricated, as was his claim that he had been offered the position of High Commissioner of India. Bernard Shaw also admits that Lawrence was 'a born actor and up to all sorts of tricks.' But Lawrence's main problem was that he did not know where his fabrication ended and the truth began. Despite this he was a very courageous man torn apart by inner conflict and guilt. He chastised himself (and had others do it) partly because he was a masochist, partly because of an awareness of his faults and partly because he was still bearing the secret of his own illegitimacy.

Nancy, successful, fashionable and rich was the ideal woman friend because she accepted him, admired him and never disbelieved in the legend for one moment. He also shared Nancy's love of excitement and on 31 December 1930 part of one of his letters to Nancy read, '. . . I feel inclined to send a postcard to Sandwich, explaining how much I enjoyed that night at Cliveden, and what an excellent ride back I had (including a race across the Plain with a sports Bentley: Well, not so much a race as a procession for the Bentley which did only 88. I wished I had had a peeress or two on my flapper bracket.)'

Lawrence always struggled against exhibitionism and because of the Astors' fame this was a hard struggle. He was also paranoid and quite capable of inventing fantasies. Therefore the following account of how Lawrence was barred from mingling with the famous must be questioned as to its accuracy. In September 1929 the air-race for the Schneider Trophy was held and Lawrence claims to have been criticised by Lord Thompson, Minister of Air, for hob-nobbing with the famous. He asserted that he was an old friend of the Italian air ace Ihalo Balbo, which seems very unlikely. Lawrence also stated that Lord Thompson was infuriated by seeing Aircraftman Shaw talking to such prominent figures as Austen Chamberlain, Nancy Astor, Winston Churchill, Lord Birkenhead and Sir Philip Sassoon. Lawrence further claimed that this resulted in his official dismissal from the RAF although this was rescinded by 'influential' intervention. He then stated that he was only allowed to remain in the RAF providing he did not see or communicate with his famous 'friends'.

In reply to an invitation to Plymouth by Nancy, Lawrence wrote 'Dear Lady Astor, What an undisciplined person you are! I was given positive orders to cease from meeting you, so far as that lay in my power: so I can't come and see you.' Lawrence added that the authorities agreed that he should go on seeing Shaw, and that Shaw was furious at this because he was not on the influential list. However, this seems to be the most unlikely part of a quite extraordinary story.

Rose Harrison had now become Nancy's maid after spending some years working for her daughter, Wissie. Rose became increasingly indispensable to Nancy over the years. She was one of the few Astor servants who really stood up for themselves and there was no doubt that she quickly won Nancy's respect. Despite this Nancy behaved extremely self-indulgently with Rose, sometimes displaying a child-like dependency on her. Temper tantrums and small, selfish acts were the main problems that Rose had to face as Nancy relaxed from her public engagements and political tension. Rose Harrison writes:

'Black or white, that was Lady Astor. That there was so much white was the wonder. She was spoilt from birth, for despite what her mother is supposed to have said, "I've had eleven children, all unwanted," the Langhornes were made to feel very much wanted, with everything that money could buy and the other things that money couldn't, like love and happiness. She enjoyed the outdoor life and the débutante scene in New York. All right, her first marriage was not a success, but to what extent did she try and make it one? She ran back home a number of times, beginning with the second night of their honeymoon. She blamed the drink, but a lot of men drink, particularly if their wives are a bit unstable.'

Rose Harrison was one of the most perceptive commentators on Nancy's personality. She was heavily critical of her, but so was Nancy of Rose. They had traumatic rows, encounters that often ended on the borders of physical violence. Yet Nancy realised that Rose completely understood and would remain with her against all odds. Rose continues:

After she was separated, and later divorced, from Mr Shaw, she toured round Europe so she could forget the unpleasantness. Then she had the wonderful good fortune to meet and marry his lordship, a great gentleman, a kind husband, and one of the wealthiest men in the world. From what I've heard of their early years together he lavished everything upon her, love as well as his worldly goods. She was pampered in every way. I reckon that treatment would have destroyed most women, but that her ladyship survived it and became the great person that she did shows a phenomenal strength of character that her worst enemy couldn't help but admire. From what I knew it was her love and feeling for others that saved her from becoming a spoilt darling. Cleverer people than I have talked about her as a supporter of causes. I believe that behind every cause was a person, someone she could identify herself with. She never talked politics to me, she only talked people, and I would later see the plight of these people turned into causes. She is famous for those she entertained. There's no doubt she enjoyed meeting them. Entertaining with her was like an industry. Many people are said to have used her for their own ends, but she used many of them to make the lot of the poorer and more insignificant easier.'

Nancy's fastidious attitude to sex was also understood by the faithful Rose although she over-simplified the tremendous inhibitions her mistress felt.

'She was hot-blooded by nature. She had five children. Yet she was fastidious and so was her husband. They disliked even the most witty or sophisticated reference to anything of a sexual nature and coarseness was not tolerated. Any guest who wandered over the border of what they considered acceptable would never be asked to come again. This was common knowledge among their class and few ever were indiscreet. In a way I suppose her ladyship was like Queen Victoria in her attitude to sex. To them both it was an intensely personal thing. A remark of Lady Astor's that was often quoted was, "I can't even tolerate seeing two birds mating without wanting to separate them," and this was often used to try and show that she was frigid. I don't see it that way. She was an inveterate match-maker, not with her own children, but with other people's. She liked good-looking, virile young men, but the parading of sex embarrassed her, so did vulgarity.'

Rose is also revealing about Nancy's calm acceptance of the blanket of love and security thrown around her by Waldorf. There is no doubt that Nancy took Waldorf very much for granted.

'Her ladyship's attitude towards Lord Astor was one of easy acceptance; she took without question or appreciation all that he gave her. Of course, she loved him, if ever she'd thought about it, but she didn't give herself time. She mimicked him as she did all of us, sometimes cruelly. She was impatient if ever he was ill. She would blame it on to his lack of faith. If she'd given to him a tenth of the time she gave to her religion, Christian Science, he would have been a much happier man.

'Once again it seems I'm criticizing her ladyship. I'm not, for while to some extent it was in her nature, there were also circumstances which kept her away from him. She had a busy political life which he could only share in the shadows. She had this passion for entertaining people which early in his own political life he must have encouraged, so when it became a near-fetish, it was to some extent his fault. He could also have tempered it, but it seemed that everything that gave her ladyship enjoyment gave him happiness. Perhaps after the war, when her ladyship gave up her seat in parliament, he hoped that they would settle more together, but it was too late. He by then was a sick man; sickness was something that Christian Scientists have to ignore and my lady was impatient with her new life. "What shall we do with her, Rose?" his lordship would say to me, and we'd set forth on a succession of travels to try to soothe her itching spirit. In a way, my lady was like a man who has devoted his whole life to his work, has found no time to interest himself in anything outside, so when he retires he finds he is lost. When she left parliament she found herself in a similar predicament. She still had people and friends to interest her, but it was a long time before she was able to come to terms with herself.'

In 1929 there came the greatest test of Nancy's faith. Wissie fell from her horse while hunting and at first the doctors thought that she only had a minor injury. However, a later diagnosis indicated that she had a serious spinal injury and an orthopaedic surgeon was recommended before further damage was done. This recommendation faced Nancy and Waldorf with a grim decision. What was it to be? Christian Science or conventional medicine? Finally Nancy decided that the only acceptable doctor would be Sir Crisp English who had operated on her and Philip Kerr – and set them on their spiritual paths.

When English arrived he was furious, pointing out that he was an abdominal surgeon and not capable of dealing with a spinal injury. He added that the delay caused by his involvement – twelve hours – was inexcusable in the light of Wissie's suffering. Immediately the Christian Science resolution of Nancy and Waldorf failed – and the leading London orthopaedic surgeon, Thomas Fairbank, was called in. He immediately placed Wissie in plaster of paris, and she made a perfect recovery.

Nancy decided to blind herself to the presence of the doctors – and later she denied their presence altogether. In 1944, for instance, she told Henry Tiarks that doctors were unnecessary and a hindrance to the truth. He reminded Nancy about Wissie's accident and how much help Wissie had received from medical science. But Nancy completely denied that any doctors had been present and when he mentioned the names of Crisp English and Fairbank she refused to admit that they had been there. Philip Kerr condoned her action when he wrote on 24 December 1929: 'Just a line to thank you again for what you did about Wissie. It was, I think, a real step in advance; the right answer to the Fisher book & the new attacks on C.S. [H. A. Fisher's book had recently appeared attacking Christian Science.] I welcome these, they are the tests and proofs of all true religion, & C.S. will be all the stronger if it is able to sustain them humbly and without fanaticism but with demonstration of power.' Naturally, there was no mention in Philip Kerr's letter of any doctors. Charlotte Shaw also wrote to Nancy, keeping the fantasy going. She linked Wissie's recovery to faith healing and on 12 January 1930 she wrote: 'Splendid news that Wissie is back at Cliveden. It seems extraordinarily different thinking of her there. The thoughts seem to go to her so much more willingly – to her own home – where I can picture her. I do long to have a talk straight – not letters – with you about her. It seems long to wait until the 31st, but I suppose it has to be. It is something I could say which *might possibly* help. But of course I know you are up to every possible thing that can be done, far more than I can be.' Charlotte Shaw had been to Christian Science meetings with Nancy and so it is possible that she had been influenced although there is no record that she was a convert.

In 1928 Asquith died and in 1930 Lord Revelstoke also suc-cumbed. He had never married and had continued to love Nancy. There was change in the air and Nancy felt uneasy. Philip Kerr became the 11th Marquess of Lothian and changed his name to Philip Lothian, whilst Horatio Bottomley emerged from prison and started a new magazine called *John Blunt* in which he recommenced his attacks on Nancy. His leading article in the first issue was 'I HAVE PAID BUT . . .' He was no longer taken seriously, however, and the magazine soon folded.

Nancy was once again threatened with far more serious and damaging criticisms than Bottomley could ever provide. On 19 April 1930, the Socialist intellectual, Harold Laski, published a severe attack on Nancy in the *Daily Herald*. Entitled – 'Lady Astor: The Pollyanna of Politics', the article was the worst attack Nancy had undergone. Laski made a number of points. Of her first election in 1919 he said:

'Why she was elected it is difficult to say. She had done nothing for women's emancipation. She had no special know-ledge of any social or political problems. But she was rich and entertained lavishly and was just the person required for a Tory member . . . It would be difficult to argue that Lady Astor has made any mark on the House. Her attitude is of the type that in New York makes a millionaire's wife notable for smartness in repartee. Her speeches are generally amiable, but do not display any direct familiarity with the things of which she speaks . . . I suppose that no new lion has ever come to London without being at her house. In one corner you can see Mr Guedalla polishing his latest epigram; in another the Sitwell family is trying to be mistaken for the Lake poets; in another still is Lord Cecil looking like a Laudian archbishop.

It is endlessly good fun. It gives the socialist attendants a consciousness of recognition, while the aristocracy is able to feel the full limit of its generous condescension.'

But Laski saved his real attack for the end of his article. 'She really thinks that the Tory party means to unite the classes in a great national fellowship of mutual benefit. For her a declaration of goodwill is equivalent to the realisation of justice.'

Considerably wounded by this criticism, Nancy immersed herself in her anti-drink campaign. In May 1930, when beer and excise duties were being discussed, she criticised the Chancellor of the Exchequer for being too weak. She considered the higher the duty, the greater the propaganda for temperance. Her old enemy, Winston Churchill, pointed out sharply that it was 'nothing less than brazen', in the face of the prohibition mess in America, to continue the campaign against drink.

Nancy then made a silly mistake. She blandly stated that the reason England had lost the Ashes was because their cricket team drank and the Australian team did not. The comment raised considerable controversy and she was heavily criticised by both teams as well as the general public. Teetotallers wrote to Nancy in droves for advice and the *Yorkshire Telegraph* published the following open letter from one such person in November 1930. It read: 'Dear Madam, picking up a magazine six or seven years old, I came across an article written by you entitled "England and the Dragon", in which you condemned the sale of alcohol. You, madam, with a great income and an assured position in life, can well afford to denounce the drink trade. But I, a lifelong teetotaller, am compelled by lack of income and indifferent circumstances to earn my living in a pub.'

Nancy's popularity and standing in the House of Commons were now on the wane. The twenties had been her heyday but the thirties looked bleak. It was as if she was burnt out – as if this perpetual dynamo of a woman was now becoming synthetic and mechanical. Worse, however, was to come, when Bobbie, Nancy's much loved eldest son, found himself in serious trouble. Rose Harrison knew Bobbie well and her assessment of his personality sounds depressingly accurate:

'To me one of the greatest and most lovable qualities of my

lady was her ability to forgive people who had, in her eyes, done wrong. Drink and sensuality were the two big ones in her sin book yet in London and Plymouth she's brought back drunken servicemen rather than let them get caught by the military police, and the compassion that she showed to Mr Bobbie was by any mother's standards remarkable. If only she could have left it at that it would have been better for him. Unfortunately she couldn't leave religion alone and exhorted him too much in that way. It took the gilt off the gingerbread. The children too were wonderful to him then, and for the rest of his life. To hear them speak of him today is to listen to nothing but praise for his charm, wit and courage. There's no question but that he was devoted to his mother, though they were constantly at cross purposes and many's the tear I've helped mop up after he'd been with her. In her later years, he was particularly attentive and seldom a day passed when he didn't telephone or visit her.

'Yet somehow I couldn't like him in the same way that I did the other children. He was too changeable for me. He'd come into his mother's room, sometimes he'd be pleasant and delightful and others he'd try and corner me in conversation and make me say something indiscreet about my lady or the other servants. I always felt on my guard when I was with him. It may have been something to do with a happening very soon after I joined her ladyship. I was waiting outside her room on the landing near a bathroom at Sandwich while she was dressing, and he came along and started talking to me. Suddenly from out of the blue he said, "I bet you were glad to leave Lady Cranborne, weren't you, Rose?"

' "No, Mr Bobbie, I wasn't," I said, after a moment's bewilderment. "While I was with her I was very happy and she was always kind to me."

'He smirked at that and went away. A few seconds later the bathroom door opened and out walked Lady Cranborne. He'd known she was in there and had tried to make me say something that would have caused her a hurt. I took the incident as a signpost of the direction his mind worked in and was ready for the other occasions as they happened.'

Rose eventually grew to understand and even admire Bobbie's

sad and self-destructive personality. For Nancy there was no question of any lack of devotion to him. She loved him very deeply and Bobbie was the only member of the family who was capable of really hurting her. Bobbie reciprocated his mother's love and was very dependent on her. He had a similar personality to his mother although his humour was much more cruel. But Bobbie drank heavily and had done so from an early age. After leaving school he had joined the army and had eventually become a senior subaltern in the Royal Horse Guards. But now he had been found drunk on duty and was being forced to resign his commission to avoid a court martial. There were no recriminations, and after Bobbie's resignation he was immediately invited to Cliveden and there both Nancy and Waldorf provided loving security for him. The bombshell had not yet arrived.

8

⁂

Nancy in Stalin's Russia

In March 1931 Nancy and Waldorf celebrated their silver wedding at Cliveden and were presented with a silver model of Drake's ship *The Golden Hind* by the City of Plymouth. Then, later that spring, Shaw received an invitation to visit Russia. As he openly described himself as a Communist, it was not surprising that Russia regarded this important writer as an ally. *The Apple Cart* had impressed the Soviet authorities and in Russia, Shaw had quickly risen to the status of a popular hero. Shaw knew that Charlotte's health was not up to the journey or the midsummer heat and so he asked the Russian Ambassador if he could take some friends to accompany him on the trip. The Ambassador agreed and Shaw invited Nancy and Waldorf as well as David Astor, Philip Lothian, Charles Tennant (a Christian Scientist) and an old friend of Nancy's, Gertrude Ely.

Ten days before the retinue was due to depart, Bobbie was apprehended for a homosexual offence. The Astors were told by the police that a warrant for their son's arrest would be issued in a few days – thus allowing the son of such famous parents to leave the country. Perversely but courageously Bobbie refused to do this and the warrant was issued. Philip Lothian wrote to Nancy saying: 'I've no doubt that the right thing is for Bobbie to face the music – which I think means a period of gaol. It is really exactly what we have all known he needs – a period where he will have to work and be kept from idleness and false pleasures. It's just the charm of sensuality destroying itself. From the Science point of view it is a blessing for him & but preparation for healing. Scientifically you can rejoice in it.'

Having imparted this piece of ludicrous and damaging advice, Lothian went on to say,

'From your point of view & Waldorf's we are all clear that there is no reason why what mortal mind will claim to be grief, shame, outraged pride, the sympathy or censure of your friends or enemies, should touch you or Waldorf at all. The tempest may roar but Jesus saw that there was really calm & I can see & prove this also. You can go through this wondering how it can touch you both so little and how the whole experience is going to bless Bobbie & yourself & Bill, Wiss, David & all.

'I don't see how you & Waldorf can go to Russia on Saturday whatever happens. So far as I am concerned I should like to be about in so far as I can be any use to you or W. But Mind will adjust the situation about G.B.S., Tennant, Gertrude Ely, David & myself. If you have any news, tell W to telephone & I will see G.B.S.

'Gosh, mortal mind has planned a good one this time – But it can only work out for the greater good of everybody, Bobbie, yourself, W & the family & Science itself. Best love from Philip.'

Waldorf used all the influence he had to keep Bobbie's arrest out of the press. He enlisted the support of Garvin, who was friendly with Beaverbrook, and the whole business was effectively hushed up. But the price of editorial silence was that the trip to Russia must go ahead. Fleet Street was very unwilling to forsake all the excellent copy that could be extracted from Nancy's antics in that most emotive country. Miserably, and knowing that she was being manipulated, Nancy went ahead with her plans whilst her beloved son was sentenced to four months in prison.

In Warsaw, Gertrude Ely had to turn back as her passport had not been visa'd for Poland. Two new members of the entourage were then included – Maurice Hindus, an American author of Russian origin, and Maxim Litvinoff who was going to Moscow for a holiday after a League of Nations meeting in Geneva. By 20 July 1931, the party had reached the Polish-Russian frontier and Waldorf recorded in his diary:

'The situation at the frontier is ridiculous and theatrical. There are two frontiers: a Polish and a Russian one with No Man's Land in between. Each frontier is guarded by armed sentries. There is heavy barbed wire to prevent anyone crossing. As one reaches the frontier (going either way) an armed guard mounts the train. At the USSR frontier is an erection with mottoes under which the train passes. I believe it is to the effect that Communism abolishes all frontiers, which seems cynical as almost immediately after crossing the frontier a Communist demands passports etc. and shows a very rigid frontier. The Custom house is full of posters and cartoons directed against capitalist countries. Whilst waiting at the customs we went and spoke to half a dozen girls, great strapping wenches, bare legs, each with a shovel. They were there because of technological unemployment – the introduction of machinery into their village. Nancy got an interpreter and began talking to them and soon hit on common (feminist) ground. A crowd of them gathered. Litvinoff joined in. To his amusement they asked him if he were also English. Stalin was the only leader whose name they knew.'

Temporarily Nancy was back in her element – but only superficially. Throughout the busy and arduous tour, her thoughts were with Bobbie and how he was faring in prison. But she thanked God for their frenetic journeying, for at least it burnt up her energy, leaving her exhausted and free from too much morbid introspection.

On Tuesday, 21 July, Waldorf confided to his diary:

'Breakfast on the train. The USSR certainly have made everything most comfortable.

'The arrival at the [Moscow] station was unique.

'If one had told the late George Edwardes or the present Cochran to stage G.B.S.'s arrival in "Red" Moscow and his reception by the Proletariat they would have staged exactly what happened.'

The Daily Herald also recorded the occasion:

'A brass band and a guard of honour of Soviet soldiers supplemented a crowd of several thousands of people who greeted Mr Bernard Shaw when he arrived at the Alexandrovsky station, Moscow, today.

'Among the people on the platform were M. Lunacharsky, former Commissar for Education, M. Khalatov, head of the State Publishing Trust, and M. Karl Radek, a leading journalist.

'When Mr Shaw appeared in the doorway of the special car in which he had travelled, the crowd broke into wild applause. Mr Shaw smiled and waved his hat.

'Then two lines of soldiers were formed to enable him to pass through the crowds.

'Lady Astor, who had travelled by the same train, received less attention. She patted a Russian baby on the head while Mr Shaw acknowledged cheer after cheer.

'Outside the station the streets were packed with thousands of people, above whom dozens of Red banners waved.

' "Hail, Shaw!" roared the crowd.'

The group stayed in the Metropole Hotel and their first expedition was to Lenin's tomb, to see his mummified corpse lying as if asleep with his hands exposed and his head resting on a red pillow. A dramatic and rather theatrical reddish glow came from above the coffin. They also saw the Garden of Culture and Rest and the other well known sights of Moscow. Waldorf wrote: 'G.B.S. is presented to the Proletariat at the theatre, in the park, etc. I hear that the only two other people who had anything like a similar reception were Gorky and Fairbanks (with Mary Pickford).'

The visit was to last nine days and the itinerary was very crowded. The Shaw entourage were taken to the Kremlin, to the theatre and to the Museum of the Revolution. Shaw, determined to cut a dash, told reporters 'I would like to stay nine years, but we are busy people and I can only spare nine days.' As he came out of the Museum he told reporters 'I think your government are mad to have a Museum of Revolution. It is most dangerous from their point of view. All governments hate revolutions and will do everything they can to prevent them or crush them. The courage of the Russian Government seems to me foolhardy.' Shaw was trying to be ponderously humorous but his comment was immediately censored and went unrecorded in the Russian press.

On Wednesday 22 July the garrulous English visitors were

taken to a prison. Waldorf wrote that they were then taken on to 'a settlement for criminals, 18 to 26 years of age. It's for *real* criminals, not first offenders. They live without restraint in a colony and are taught trades and paid regular wages.' They watched the prisoners making skis, skates, racquets and textiles amongst other items, and they were told that about twelve per cent of the inmates escaped. The propaganda continued with the group being told that when there were vacancies in the settlement the Committee of the Community chose the worst prisoners to fill them. Liberty, work and autonomy were the key words behind the programme, and Waldorf commented, 'Like so many strange things in this strange country it seems to be working.'

After dinner a book was passed to G.B.S. for his signed comments but he sidestepped detail by merely observing: 'For what I have received may the Lord be thankful.'

Then Nancy was handed a telegram. It had been sent to her by a Russian professor named Krynin who was currently based at Yale. He wanted Nancy to use her influence in getting his wife out of Russia to join him in America. Nancy at once showed the cable to Litvinoff who firmly stated that she must take it to the GPU. Nancy was now thoroughly involved and determined to confront the authorities. But once again Waldorf stepped in, pointing out that the GPU would naturally have already seen the content of the cable which had not been complimentary to the Soviet Union. Waldorf pointed out to Nancy that the woman's fate could not be changed by their intervention. Reluctantly, Nancy accepted Waldorf's judgement. Waldorf adds in his diary that the appeal 'was also addressed to Shaw who ignored it.' Waldorf was not a jealous man but there does seem a note of sardonic satisfaction in his reference to Shaw's apparent failure to be humane.

Years later Nancy told Maurice Collis:

'Molotov met us at the station. Shaw was received like a film star; the Russians, regarding him as the great writer of the age, had been most delighted at the warm way he had written about Lenin. But he understood about as much about politics as I do about the writing of plays. At the hotel G.B.S. had the best room; I was somewhere in the attic. The reception delighted him; he was very vain. One of the things he wanted to do was to call on Lenin's widow. For some reason the Russians kept putting this off. Eventually we were taken to a cottage outside Moscow. Here Lenin's widow and her sisters showed great joy in welcoming G.B.S.'

The group then travelled to Leningrad where they saw the Winter Palace and the Hermitage and on 24 July Waldorf recorded in his diary:

'Propaganda – propaganda – nothing but propaganda. Jolly well done. When I saw the workers shot down by the troops, trampled on by Cossacks in the film, I felt like waving the red flag. When I saw the ideals of the industrial development of Russia dramatically pictured, when I saw the factory government in the hands of myself (a worker) instead of a tyrannical boss, when I saw the horrors of war, of young Russians and young Germans each intoxicated with ideas of patriotism disembowelling each other – then I too felt like becoming a Red Pacifist.'

The tour continued with Waldorf exuding disapproval of a speech made by Shaw, during which he praised the Russian Five Year Plan and pointed out that England should be ashamed not to have thought of this policy and initiated it herself. Shaw then generously turned to the Astors and Philip Lothian, pointing out that it was not their fault that they were capitalists, landowners and exploiters. They were victims of the British system. But soon, he added encouragingly, the British proletariat would change the situation. Quite what would happen to the Astors and the Lothians after the revolution was not clear but no doubt they would be protected by G.B.S.

Waldorf's diary entry read: 'Late for dinner. Then to an official function to G.B.S. a huge ball. 2,000. Lots of speeches. G.B.S. replied. A bad effort.' Later he writes: 'So strict is the censorship and propaganda that even G.B.S.'s speech, which we all thought too unqualified and unguarded, was doctored.'

On 29 July they returned to Moscow where Stalin had asked to see Shaw. Nancy, Waldorf and Philip Lothian accompanied Shaw to the interview which was to last two hours, twenty-five minutes. It took place in Stalin's study. Years later, Nancy remembered, when talking to Maurice Collis:

'Going to visit Stalin in the Kremlin was like going into Sing Sing. The place was more like a prison than a palace. Stalin never received visitors from abroad normally. One of the questions he asked G.B.S. was: "How do you account for England getting possession of so much of the earth?" To which G.B.S. replied "I'm an Irishman and know nothing about England." When G.B.S. did not want to answer a question he always said he was an Irishman. I answered for him. "I believe the translations of the Bible we distributed did it. That along with the justice and mercy we brought." Stalin replied: "If we don't do that we fail?" '

Waldorf noted in his diary: 'He has a clear rather kindly eye, is a man of very few words, is supposed to owe his position to an iron will and to a close association with Lenin. He seemed shrewd rather than big mentally. He had quite a sense of humour and knew how to parry questions he did not wish to deal with. G.B.S. began the interview by explaining why he had brought us to it, and nice things about Nancy, Philip and myself.'

During the course of the interview, Nancy shocked everybody by asking Stalin why he had slaughtered so many of his people. At first the interpreters were anxious not to translate the question but eventually Stalin, curious at the alarm and confusion, demanded to know what question Nancy had asked. When told, he replied quietly that some slaughter was inevitable when the constitution of a country was fundamentally disrupted and that the violent death of a large number of people was necessary before the Communist State could be firmly established.

This version of the encounter was the one remembered by Shaw and related to his biographer, Sir John Ervine. Waldorf, however, remembered the incident rather differently in his diary: 'Stalin evaded by quoting a case when some engineers had been convicted of intercourse with some foreign country with a view to sabotage, and assured her that he hoped the need for dealing with political prisoners drastically would soon cease.'

The remainder of the interview involved a number of questions from Stalin about Churchill and his hostility to Russia. The assembled company assured him that Churchill did not represent the Conservative Party's views on Russia, and that he would not be given office in any future Conservative government. Nancy discussed child-care and welfare and claimed that Russian children were far too clean and well-drilled as opposed to her own childhood days in Virginia when she had 'run wild'. Stalin sanctimoniously replied that in England children were whipped whilst in the Soviet Union a parent would be sued in the courts on behalf of the child if struck.

Finally the discussion centred on why Lenin's proposals for a peaceful settlement between the Allies and Russia had not received a fair hearing.

On the group's return to their hotel they found the press waiting, who were in ignorance that they had all been given strict instructions not to speak to them by the Russian authorities. Shaw, always the showman, brushed the reporters aside and slowly mounted a huge flight of marble steps. They followed pleading with Shaw to give them at least a hint about what had transpired in the Kremlin. He ignored them until he had ponderously reached the top of the staircase. Shaw then turned, folded his arms and with heavy humour solemnly said: 'You want to know what happened? Well, I'll tell you. We discovered that Stalin has big black moustaches.'

Before the farewell speeches, Waldorf went to visit Madame Krynin, on whose behalf he was still quietly campaigning. She was in a desperate state, terrified that somehow her husband or son (or both) might be induced to return to Russia and that they would be severely punished on arrival. It occurred to Waldorf that Krynin must have gone to America on a limited work permit and simply had not returned in the time required. However, Waldorf decided it would be too dangerous to pursue enquiries in this sensitive area. Instead, he wrote to Khalatov saying that the lady had no complaint to make against the authorities about her treatment but was simply very anxious to join her husband in America.

On 3 August 1931 the group returned to England. En route Shaw made a statement in Warsaw to a reporter on the *Chicago Tribune*. He said, 'I am a confirmed Communist. I was one before Lenin and am now even more so after seeing Russia. Dictator Stalin is an honest and able man. There is no starvation in Russia. Workmen there are happier than in other countries.' This classic statement was followed by others, such as this to the American and English press: 'Russia has put her house in order, and we western capitalist nations have got to look out because we are not doing so. It is a very serious thing. It is all silly nonsense about Russia being a failure . . . I very much like black bread and cabbage soup. They agree with me and I had plenty of both.'

A storm of criticism instantly arose in England and G. K. Chesterton wrote: 'Shaw would long ago have become a grand old man but for his desperate attempts to remain an *enfant terrible* . . . Nevertheless, there is something impressive and touching about the entry of the veteran socialist into the first real socialist civilisation.'

Nancy also came in for criticism and a London evening paper reported: 'Lady Astor is having a hard time just now with the force of criticism directed against her for going to Russia. She has declined to express her views on the Soviet. The only reference to her which Lord Astor has permitted himself is that she never during her visit expressed herself as other than against the principles of Communism.'

The controversy heightened and Waldorf warned Nancy not to give any press interviews at all. Churchill dramatically denounced the Russian trip in the *Sunday Pictorial*. He held both Nancy and Shaw up to public ridicule, using irony as his main weapon.

'They like to have everything both ways. Thus Mr Bernard Shaw is at once a wealthy and acquisitive capitalist, and a sincere Communist. His spiritual home is in Russia but he lives comfortably in England. He couples the possession of a mild, amiable and humane disposition with the advocacy and even glorification of the vilest political crimes and cruelties. He indulges all the liberties of an irresponsible chatterbox babbling from dawn to dusk . . . He has laughed his sparkling way through life, exploding by his own acts or words every argument he has ever used on either side in any question, teasing and bewildering every public he has addressed, and involving in mockery and discredit every cause he has championed . . . Similar, though different, contradictions are to be observed in Lady Astor. She reigns in the old world and the new, at once a leader of smart society and of advanced feminist democracy. She combines a kindly heart with a sharp and wagging tongue. She embodies the historical portent of the first woman member of the House of Commons. She applauds the policies of the Government from the benches of the Opposition. She denounces the vice of gambling and keeps an almost unrivalled racing stable. She accepts Communist hospitality and flattery, and remains the Conservative member for Plymouth. She does all these opposite things so well and so naturally that the public, tired of criticising, can only gape. The Russians have always been fond of travelling-shows and circuses, and here was the world's most famous clown and pantaloon in one, and the charming Columbine of the capitalist pantomime. So the crowds were marshalled, thousands were served out with their red scarves and flags. Commissar Litvinoff, unmindful of the food queues in the back streets, prepared a sumptuous banquet, and the Arch-Commissar, Stalin, the man of steel, throwing open the closely guarded sanctuary of the Kremlin, and pushing aside his morning budget of death warrants and *lettres de cachet*, received his guests with smiles of unaffected comradeship . . . Here we have a power actively and ceaselessly engaged in trying to destroy civilisation by stealth and propaganda and, when they dare, by bloody force. Here we have a state, three million of whose inhabitants are languishing in exile, whose intelligentsia have been methodically destroyed, a state nearly a million of whose inhabitants have been reduced to servitude for their political opinions, and who are rotting and freezing through the Arctic night; toil to death in forests, mines and quarries for indulging in that freedom of thought which has gradually raised man from the beast.'

But Nancy did not reply to any of this criticism and the public found her silence bewildering. Then an enormous economic crisis overtook the country and the controversial Russian trip was swept out of the headlines. By the end of July 1931 a government economic committee reported that the Budget deficit, by 1932, would reach £120,000,000. Economies were introduced, including a £22,000,000 cut on unemployment allowances. The Trades Union Congress and the Cabinet fought this cut and Ramsay MacDonald resigned. A coalition government, headed by MacDonald, was formed on 25 August and a General Election seemed to be imminent providing the Liberals agreed to an early October date.

Nancy was very concerned. Her Russian visit had clearly made her unpopular and realising that she stood little chance at the hustings, Nancy suggested that Bill, her son, should stand instead. But Waldorf thought Nancy had left it too late to stand down now. Dr Thomas Jones, an old friend of the Astors and a Deputy Secretary to the Cabinet, was called in to advise on the situation. He confided to his diary:

'11.15 am. To 4 St James's Square. Shown upstairs. Lady A propped up with pillows, issuing instructions to a private secretary at lightning speed. The p.s. withdrew. Bed sprinkled with Bibles, large and small; daily papers on a side table; letters all over the place. My business was to try and persuade her to let Bill fight Plymouth in her place. She began at once on a high religious note – what did the Lord want her to do? She had for days been trying to discover this. Nothing else mattered. Waldorf had phoned from Plymouth to say it was not too late to propose Bill. I knew it was useless to tell her that the fight would be a hellish one for her – I did say so, with the expected result. Did I think that she could be killed or broken by anything outside her? It was the duty of all to help the country, to fight class consciousness and bitterness. The new House might need her for though she could not make speeches she would weaken the forces of hate. Only Waldorf on the spot could judge. I argued for half an hour, secretly admiring her more and more as she swept aside my appeals to prudence, health, the work needing to be done outside the House. I felt humble and ashamed in her presence. Flippancy was far away from her speech this morning. I sat at the foot of the bed looking straight into the eyes of the most remarkable woman it has been my fortune to know intimately. I kept thinking of Joan of Arc, precisely as when I saw Sybil

Thorndike play the heroine in Shaw's play. I could not get Nancy Astor out of my mind.'

This 'conversion' to Nancy's personality is an important record because it demonstrates the enormous amount of personal magnetism she had. When the going was rough Nancy fell back on her religion as a prop and, illogical as she was, found strength. Nancy may well have bent the tenets of Christian Science all over the place to suit her problems, but there is no doubt that her basic spiritual belief – her need to believe – was fundamental to her personality.

Nancy decided to stand and, re-charged, she found herself surprisingly successful. The poll on 27 October resulted in Nancy polling 24,277 votes and her Labour opponent, G. Ward, 14,073 votes. Indeed, overall, a great Conservative landslide victory occurred, one side-effect of which was Philip Lothian being offered the Under-Secretaryship of State for India, which he accepted with alacrity. Also there were now fifteen women members in the House of Commons and suddenly Nancy found herself with new confidence, new energy and, importantly, new popularity.

Bobbie came out of prison in November and went to Rest Harrow, their country house at Sandwich, with his mother. Philip Lothian wrote to him saying:

'Delighted to get your letter. Yes! A rest won't do your "mommer" any harm. She's had a lot of strain lately, though, as usual, she comes up smiling. Why our mothers are so fond of their children, I do not know. And the worse we treat them the more they love us. True mother love is the best revelation to man of what the Love of God is, & all the experts on religion say that even the purest mother love is only 30 cents on that! So go on giving her a helping hand. She needs it & nothing will make more difference to her life than to realise you have found a way of life which will bring happiness to both others & to yourself. Everybody is going to leave you alone together for a bit longer. But after that I shall come down & beat you at golf!'

At Rest Harrow, mother and son licked their wounds. For Nancy life had a feeling of renewal with much to offer, but for

Bobbie there was no renewal – only a bleak social wall around him. Cynically, he knew that, apart from his immediate family circle, he would be ostracised by the rest of society. Alcoholism was common enough but this in conjunction with promiscuous homosexuality was definitely 'not on'. To Nancy's dismay Bobbie continued to drink and his personality disintegrated.

Nancy's energies redoubled as her political life enjoyed its recharge and, typically, she was able to blind herself to Bobbie's deterioration by plunging herself into politics and their attendant social life. She held extreme anti-Nazi views at this time, views that were stimulated by the appointment, in 1933, of Adolf Hitler as Chancellor of the Reich. She became friendly with the Communist Irish playwright Sean O'Casey, a relationship that fell into the same category as her friendships with Shaw and Lawrence. In 1933 Shaw convinced Nancy that she should sit for the Hungarian sculptor Kisfalud de Strobl. But Strobl found Nancy too restless a subject and Shaw had to remonstrate with her on 12 May 1933. Part of his letter read:

'You must go to de Strobl's studio and give him one real sitting: that is, you must behave exactly like a professional model with her livelihood (half a crown an hour) at stake. The bust is a beautiful work: you will never get anything like it brought into existence again in point of beauty and refinement: but it lacks the final touch which will completely identify it with you ... He says the conditions under which he has worked have been frightfully distracting, difficult and distressing, as you are incapable of stillness and silence. I suggested chloroform, but I now appeal to one of your several better selves. He is a very fine workman and should be treated with genuine respect.'

Nancy returned dutifully to the treadmill and Shaw eventually bought the bust. The original idea had been for Waldorf and Shaw to present the bust to the Palace of Westminster but after the disaster of the portrait and its withdrawal, the plan was dropped.

Another interesting portrait of Nancy at this period came from the pen of the playwright William Douglas Home. He was one of a party of Eton schoolboys who had come on a nature ramble to the sweeping grounds of Cliveden. Nancy came out to meet them and she began to talk with one of their school-masters. Douglas Home writes:

'He, like most schoolmasters, when confronted by a woman, and, like all schoolmasters, and indeed most men, when confronted by Lady Astor, was giving a fairly creditable imitation of a rabbit waiting at some woodland cross-rides for a passing stoat.

'As I looked up from the clatter of the tea which was laid out on a long trestle-table on the terrace, Lady Astor, having abandoned her strictures on schoolmasters in general and on that one in particular, and having reloaded her verbal guns with lighter shot, then turned her broadside on the crowd of chattering small boys and raked the tea-table from end to end. She told us collectively first and then individually later, that we were the stupidest, ugliest, dirtiest boys she had ever seen. As most of us were of the opinion that we were some of the cleverest, prettiest, and best-groomed adolescents in our age-group, this initial broadside had nothing but a salutary effect. To those of us whose parents she knew she vouchsafed the information that she had warned them against having children which were bound to be morons and now she saw how right she had been. On the whole, as she worked her way down the table, she shot well. Only occasionally did a missile which had been launched from the mother ship as a laughing gas shell, burst on impact with all the destructive force of a high explosive, leaving the unhappy target purple in the face and fighting back an angry and embarrassed tear.'

Here was Nancy at her worst. Patronising, with a cruel, impish sense of humour that only the very strong or the very insensitive could stomach. And yet Douglas Home sees through this abrasive veneer when he continues:

'While she was thus engaged, I looked shyly up into a pair of kindly sapphire-blue, compelling eyes, which sometimes danced and sometimes filled with tears, as though in her dynamic little person, comedy and tragedy walked step by step and hand in hand. And suddenly, I was not shy at all.

'When we returned to Eton that evening in the bus, we most definitely knew that something had hit us – something that was beneficial to the health, provided one could swallow the initial dose. Some could and others couldn't. I discovered, when I met her again, ten years later, at the age of twenty-five, that I was one of those who could.

'To her dynamic personality, all humbug was a wicked waste of time. Invariably she put her own cards on the table in order to facilitate and hurry up the game. She expected other people to do likewise. If they didn't, she devised a simple remedy. She merely looked over their shoulders and then broadcast to the world what cards they held.

'She wanted no misunderstandings, no secrets. She preferred open covenants, openly arrived at.

'For the truth is that Lady Astor could not help speaking the truth. Of course, she had no tact, but very honest people seldom have. They look on tact, with some justification, as a form of intellectual dishonesty, a smothering of fact, a clipping of the buds of spontaneity, a compromise with fraud. She would have none of it. She was a seeker after truth, a debunker of hypocrisy, a scourge of sinners, so long as they exposed their sin as readily as she exposed her own.

'If she had a fault it was that since she applied this treatment indiscriminately she sometimes failed to bomb only military targets.'

There had been many tragedies in Nancy Astor's life. One of the worst, a tragedy comparable to the deaths of the Grenfell boys, was T. E. Lawrence's fatal motor-bike accident. His death, however, was predictable and although not proven to be suicide, was virtually just that. Since leaving the RAF in March 1935 he had become more and more withdrawn, trapped by the rigours of his own personality at Cloud Hill. As can be seen in previous correspondence, Lawrence had sublimated himself within the coarser structure of the RAF. He hated it – yet needed to belong. Now, without it, he was more helpless than ever.

Even whilst still serving, Lawrence was breaking up, becoming more and more of an isolationist. Nancy had worked hard to tempt him to Cliveden. She knew she could offer him two alternatives that, in previous years, had appealed to him. Either he could come to Cliveden and be absolutely private – or he could join in the social round, playing the role of the literary butterfly and witty conversationalist that had satisfied the Lawrence ego in the past. The previous Christmas, Nancy had cabled Lawrence pleading: 'IT WOULD BE A HAPPIER CHRISTMAS IF YOU COME HERE AND A WARMER ONE FOR YOU TO TRY IT.' But Lawrence remained at Cloud Hill, immune to any of the Cliveden temptations.

In sombre mood Lawrence had printed a number of cards bearing the legend 'TO TELL YOU THAT IN FUTURE I SHALL WRITE VERY FEW LETTERS.' Nevertheless he continued to write to Nancy, sometimes writing on the back of one of his cards.

On 2 March 1935 Lawrence wrote to Nancy saying: 'The RAF takes away from me the right to serve it longer, and I relapse into self-supporting life. My cottage 35/- a week, 24 hours a day. I am so tired that it feels like heaven drawing me; only there are people who whisper that heaven will bore me. When they told me that I almost wish I were dead for I have done everything in life except rest, and if rest is to prove no refuge, then what is left?'

On 5 May Lawrence's mood darkened still further and he wrote to Nancy: 'It is quiet here now, and I feel as though I were fixed in my cottage for good. It is as I thought . . . something is finished with my leaving the RAF. It gets worse instead of healing over.'

His only release was the one which Nancy had shared with him – to roar his motor-bike at top speed over country lanes which were quite inadequate. As Lawrence had written earlier, the feeling of self-imposed danger made a little adrenalin begin to race in his body again. It was not enough. Just over a week later Lawrence took his motor-bike over the sweet scented lanes of early spring. In his recklessness, he had not considered others. He braked hard to avoid a child – and crashed.

For six days he lay in hospital with such severe brain injuries that, had he survived, he would have lived as a speechless cabbage. No one saw fit to advise Nancy of the accident and the press only reacted to the disaster when, on the sixth day after the crash, Lawrence of Arabia died. Nancy was eventually told of his death on 19 May during a lunch party at Cliveden. She was overcome with grief: one of the most precious and exciting relationships of her life had abruptly been taken from her. The funeral was held on 21 May at Moreton in Dorset and Lawrence had left instructions in his will that there should be no wreaths. Nevertheless the men wore black ties and the women dark clothes; a child threw a bunch of flowers on the coffin at the very last moment and those old enemies Winston Churchill and Nancy Astor held hands and cried.

As Nancy spent her emotion she must have been remembering their shared excitement as she and Lawrence sped up the dusty lanes of Buckinghamshire, the roads a blur, the air tinged with oil and the scent of the hedgerows, and their ears filled with the lusty, danger-spiced roar of the bike's engine.

In June 1935 Baldwin became Prime Minister again and called a General Election. The main issue was rearmament, to counteract the mounting support for pacifism as expounded by such figures as Bertrand Russell and Aldous Huxley. The poll was fixed for 14 November and Nancy was once again opposed by George Ward. She was successful, winning 21,491 votes to Ward's 15,394. Bill Astor ran for East Fulham and succeeded in winning the seat for the Conservatives with a majority of 1,054. But the feminist cause suffered a considerable set-back with only nine women members being returned. Nancy was considerably depressed, not only by Lawrence's death, Bobbie's continued deterioration and the dearth of women MPs in the House, but by a feeling of unease – of being past her best.

9

❧❦❧

The Cliveden Set: A Myth
or a Reality?

The term 'Cliveden Set' was created by Claud Cockburn. Journalist, humanist and politician, Cockburn worked for *The Times* and later the *Daily Worker*. He founded and edited *The Week* which for a period was very widely read. *The Week* first appeared in 1933 just as Hitler was becoming an important and threatening figure. In 1936 Hitler marched a token force of troops into the demilitarised zone of the Rhineland in direct violation of the Treaty of Versailles. Churchill campaigned for a policy of rebuffing Hitler, but Baldwin was Prime Minister and the policy was appeasement. *The Times*, now owned by Waldorf's brother John, and edited by Geoffrey Dawson, wholly endorsed the policies of Baldwin and Neville Chamberlain. Because of this Cockburn waged a campaign against *The Times* and its proprietor, as well as Lord Halifax, Neville Chamberlain, Philip Lothian, Waldorf and Nancy.

Halifax was Cockburn's first target. Cockburn claimed that under cover of going to join Hermann Goering's hunting party in Germany, Halifax's real motive was to propose to Hitler that, in return for an Anglo-German truce, Great Britain would guarantee not to interfere with Germany's eastward expansion. Cockburn went on to allege that this scheme was the brainchild of a secret group which was subversively able to influence the policy of the British government. Cockburn then mentioned, for the first time, the name 'Cliveden'. This was the beginning of the end for Nancy. She would never stand for election again – nor would she ever regain the popularity which had only recently been restored to her. The article stated that 'Subscribers to *The Week* are familiar with pro-Nazi intrigues centring on

Cliveden and Printing House Square on the eve of the outbreak of the Spanish War. The expulsion of *The Times*' correspondent from Berlin put a spoke . . . in the wheel of certain Germanophile plans. The intrigue however continues with Lord Lothian, the Astors, Mr Barrington Ward of *The Times* and its editor Mr Geoffrey Dawson (né Robinson) at the heart of it.'

Cockburn continued by claiming that Lord Halifax was a guest at Cliveden just before he joined Goering. In fact he was not. The guests were Anthony and Beatrice Eden. Cockburn, however, turned his mistake to his advantage and reported that 'Among those present at the fateful meeting at Cliveden, where the plans were laid, was Mr Eden himself. He was asked there for a purpose which, it seems, he himself did not understand. He was asked in order to "associate" him with the intrigue. He expressed his immediate and profound opposition to the whole perilous business.'

Michael Astor denies that there was any such clandestine operation, and writes, in *Tribal Feeling*:

> 'The effect of the "revelations" by *The Week* had a chain reaction in the rest of the press. The validity of the charges raised against the Astor family were argued and questioned in London, Washington and New York. Although the charges made by *The Week* were withdrawn, as Cockburn himself later admitted, it is nevertheless true that there was a consortium of people, engaged in public life, which normally met at Cliveden or at 4 St James's Square, whose members shared a common view about the best methods of keeping the peace in Europe. Their views hinged on faith in the belief that Hitler treasured in his mind certain "reasonable demands" for the restoration of Germany as a state on an equal footing with the other great states, and when these "reasonable" demands were met a final and peaceful settlement could be reached without resorting to force.'

Michael Astor goes on to say that this view evolved into the policy of appeasement – a policy which could only have been disastrous to the Cliveden group in hindsight, for it meant one concession after another was made to Hitler, each time assuming that his latest demand was his final demand. Appeasement was not confined to the Cliveden group, for it had the support of most politicians (with the notable exception of Churchill) and the majority of the press. Michael Astor tries to define the so-called 'Set' by saying that it consisted of Neville Chamberlain, Geoffrey Dawson and his assistant editor Robert Barrington Ward, J. L. Garvin of the *Observer*, Philip Lothian and Waldorf and Nancy. With some reason the group felt they represented the views of the country. They had absolutely no conception of Hitler's real power and there is no doubt that they set up a highly influential politico-press pressure group.

But once *The Week* had turned this naively powerful lobby into a pro-Nazi set, the news spread fast. Claud Cockburn told Christopher Sykes:

'I think it was *Reynolds News*, three days later, which first picked up the phrase from *The Week*, but within a couple of weeks it had been printed in dozens of newspapers, and within six had been used in almost every leading newspaper of the Western world. Up and down the British Isles, across and across the United States, anti-Nazi orators shouted it from hundreds of platforms. No anti-Fascist rally in Madison Square Garden or Trafalgar Square was complete without a denunciation of the Cliveden Set.

'In those days, if you saw cameramen patrolling St James's Square at lunchtime or dusk, you could be nearly sure they were there to get a picture of the Cliveden Set going in or out of the Astors' London house. Geoffrey Dawson, then editor of *The Times*, and a prominent member of the "Set", comments petulantly on this nuisance in his diary. If you talked to American special correspondents, what they wanted to know all about was the Cliveden Set. Senators made speeches about it, and in those London cabarets where libel didn't matter, songsters made songs about it. People who wanted to explain everything by something, and were ashamed to say "sunspots", said "Cliveden Set".'

David Low further damned Nancy by drawing some famous cartoons of the so-called Cliveden Set. He called the Set 'The Shiver Sisters' whose motto was 'Any sort of Peace at any sort of Price.'

The gossip about the pro-Nazi Cliveden Set might just have faded away had Ribbentrop not suddenly appeared at St James's

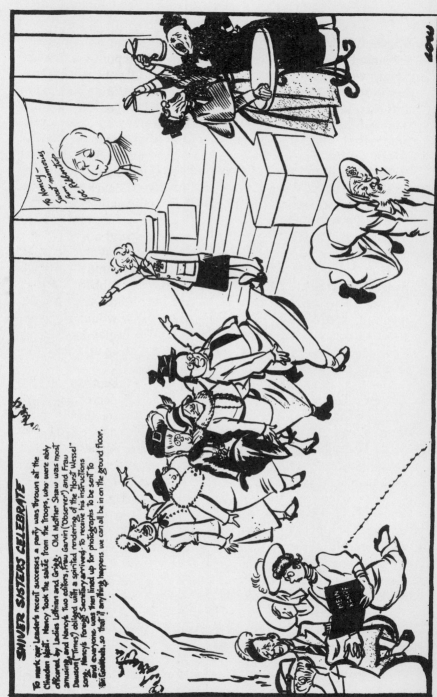

7 Where Our Foreign Policy Comes From

Square. The year was 1936 – and Ribbentrop had not yet been appointed German Ambassador. To be fair, as a political hostess Nancy would automatically have invited Ribbentrop to lunch and certainly Nancy could not have been anything less than anti-Nazi if her behaviour at lunch is to be judged. She was in one of her brash, tactless moods and behaved to Ribbentrop much as she had in William Douglas Home's account of her attack on the Etonian boys. She calmly told Ribbentrop that Hitler made himself look absurd in public and no one could take him seriously if he persisted in wearing a Charlie Chaplin moustache. Ribbentrop remained icily enigmatic about his Führer's outward appearance.

Some months later Dr Jones was asked to spend a long weekend with Ribbentrop in Germany. He had been invited because he was the Prime Minister's confidant and it became clear that Ribbentrop wanted him to act as a go-between. Ribbentrop told Dr Jones that he wanted Baldwin and the Führer to meet – a meeting at which the key to European peace would be held. Jones agreed, saw the Führer, and returned to England where he told the Astors that he wanted their help in setting up a meeting between Hitler and Baldwin.

On 2 June, Jones lunched alone with Ribbentrop at the Carlton. There, they discussed the proposed secret meeting between Hitler and Baldwin in relation to where they should meet. Baldwin could not publicly fly to Germany – and nor could Hitler publicly fly to England. However Ribbentrop told Jones that he could arrange for Hitler to come near our coast – perhaps two or three miles out from Dover or Folkestone.

Jones agreed to this off-shore meeting, adding that Baldwin would want Eden with him, and that the meeting should be arranged as quickly as possible. Also, if Baldwin would not agree to the meeting, then Lord Halifax should go in his place. Jones then proposed to Ribbentrop that they should journey down to Rest Harrow so that they could meet Inskip, who was staying with the Astors and who now held the post of Minister for the Co-ordination of Defence. Philip Lothian would also be there.

Jones confides to his diary some of the details of the journey and the ensuing dinner party:

'At 5.10 pm von R. picked me up at Tufton Court. He had

with him von Wussow and a valet. At 7.30 we were at Rest Harrow and dressed for dinner at once. Waldorf had gone to Geneva to preside over his Nutrition Committee. On the way down I had warned von R. that Inskip was an evangelical churchman. The dinner had not been going many minutes before he brought up the Nazi persecution of the Church in Germany. Von R. tactfully prefaced his defence by saying he knew the Archbishop of Canterbury and George Bell [Bishop] of Chichester, and went on to explain that a new Reformation was proceeding in Germany in the interests of religion. The orthodox Lutheran Church was petrified and had no message. Out of the present confusion a new and better Christian Church would emerge. It was absurd to imagine that there was not enough vitality in Christianity to surmount the present troubles. Which of its many heterodox variants now clashing with one another would triumph no one could prophesy. Nancy broke in with "The Roman Catholics made God material and the Communists make man material." '

After dinner an intense discussion took place with Inskip questioning Ribbentrop and finally professing himself impressed. Ribbentrop then went on to stress how important it was for Germany and England to collaborate and create a 'new centre of crystallization' for the smaller European powers. He hinted that some of these had already approached Germany secretly.

Ribbentrop went on to point out that a party of English Trade Unionists were currently paying a private visit to Germany. Later, in Waldorf's study Philip Lothian and Dr Jones continued the discussion, with Lothian warning Ribbentrop that any agreement entered into by England would also have to ensure the peaceful revision of the treaty with Austria. Blandly Ribbentrop agreed.

The next morning Ribbentrop left Rest Harrow and the following afternoon his secretary, von Wussow, met Dr Jones at the Pilgrim Trust office where they devised a secret code for communication purposes between England and Germany. Then Dr Jones and von Wussow arranged a meeting between Geoffrey Dawson and Ribbentrop.

Cockburn would have argued that the 'plot had thickened' and so it had in a way. The main fault of the Cliveden group, and the reason it could have been said to have earned the title 'Set' was that it was elitist, powerful and had access to the 'back door' of power. But to say the group was pro-Nazi is absurd. In fact they were very naive and over-optimistic. For intellectual and non-violent people they were conspicuous in their ability to blind themselves to Hitler's violence – and in their hopeless attempts to make honourable arrangements with him.

The public charge against the Set was that it acted subversively to introduce a pro-German policy that the country did not want. This is highly exaggerated for the Set simply supported the views of the government. In fact the group were publicly formulating government policy because many of its members were *in* the government. There was no need for subversion – their lobbying tools were quite legitimate and included the editorial and correspondence columns of both *The Times* and the *Observer*, lectures at Chatham House and their own speeches. Although their views were confidentially passed on to members of the Cabinet who were not members of the group, there was nothing secret in their conveyance – or acceptance. They supported a policy of appeasement in a largely appeasing parliament whose members included Chamberlain, Butler and Halifax. The most obvious dissenters were Churchill, Duff Cooper, Anthony Eden and Lord Salisbury. The popular press also supported appeasement – at least until it was clear that appeasing Hitler was like giving sweets to a mindless and greedy child. Then they turned on those at Cliveden with all the fury of the guilty.

A typical Cliveden weekend during this pre-war period would mean thirty to table and politics day and night. The more familiar faces were often supplemented by such figures as Nevile Henderson, Sir Alex Cadogan, Lord Curzon's daughters, Lady Alexandra Metcalfe and Lady Ravensdale, as well as most members of the Cabinet.

Dr Jones was also a regular visitor and on 24 October 1937 he noticed that Eden was particularly concerned over the weakness of the Cabinet and the fact that the rearmament programme was well behind schedule. But Jones noticed that Eden also argued that no business could be done with Hitler until Britain was fully armed.

Philip Lothian was as optimistic as any of the Cliveden group and he met Hitler twice, in February 1935 and May 1937. He wrote to Nancy: 'I hope the British government will go and have a real talk in Germany as to how Europe is to be pacified. Hitler is a prophet – not a politician or an intriguer. Quite straight, full of queer ideas, but quite honestly wanting no war.' But in August 1936 he wrote to Nancy rather more uneasily: 'The trouble is that it is all done by compulsion from outside. They are not taught to think for themselves ... As you know, I don't think Hitler means war. I think he means the recovery of Germany's position in the world without it. But if Hitler goes, or through the follies of others there is another war, Germany will go into it better prepared, better disciplined and more formidable than ever.'

On 7 November 1937 Nancy wrote to Philip Lothian in India. This letter clearly indicates she was a believer in appeasement but not necessarily a sinister manipulator:

'Edward Halifax came to luncheon the day after he returned from Germany. He liked everyone he met in Berlin and particularly Goebbels. What struck him most was the attitude towards the League of Nations and anything like Collective Security. He said he felt that he was speaking a completely different mental language, but he realized that it was absolutely necessary for us to get on with them. However, by the time this reaches you, you will know more about it all than I can tell you. Tom Inskip says that those against it are working violently and subtly, for Vansittart has changed his tone, and people are beginning to realize that France is no use either in munitions or men. Apparently Neville sees the situation very clearly and is very firm about it. He does not use T.J. but Horace Wilson.'

On 12 December 1937 Nancy wrote to Philip Lothian mentioning for the first time the Cliveden Set: 'Neville Chamberlain is lunching with me on Thursday, and I hope Edward Halifax and Tom Inskip. A letter from Rebecca West will be coming to you from Waldorf. Apparently the Communist rag has been full of the Halifax-Lothian-Astor plot at Cliveden, and then *Time and Tide* has taken it up; people really seem to believe it.'

Time and Tide, Lady Rhondda's weekly, was a pro-Churchill paper. A strong warning was given to all readers concerning the dangerous views that were held by certain important figures. They were said to be fascinated 'by the surface tidiness of the Fascist regimes in central Europe, stand for a rapprochement with Germany. To some of them, Hitler, the dreamer, the visionary of the mystic face, a non-smoker, a non-drinker, the anti-Bolshevik, is becoming almost a fuehrer, almost, we should say, the fuehrer.' There was no question of coming to a settlement with Germany, *Time and Tide* decreed. A letter from Nancy appeared in the next issue, part of which read: 'I have desired to restore a sense of security in Europe by treating Germany as an equal. I have worked for the reversal of the policy of goading her people and rulers into restlessness by trying to keep them in a state of inferiority.'

But this spirited defence had little effect on the growth of the myth about the Cliveden Set. Throughout the spring of 1937, whilst Hitler increased his army and air-force, Nancy opposed Churchill's recommended Anglo-Russian Alliance and hoped to control Hitler's activities through the League of Nations. By the end of the year the Cliveden Set was an established threat and by February 1938 one Labour MP was telling a mass meeting in Hyde Park that the country had now arrived at a position where 'we must have society ladies determining our foreign policy. The foreign policy of this country is no longer settled by the Cabinet in Downing Street but at the country home of Lady Astor at Cliveden.'

Some sections of the press then began a concentrated campaign against a bewildered and increasingly fearful Nancy. *Reynolds News* burst into print, declaring that the entire country was ruled from Cliveden, and it was the Set who had forced Eden's resignation and forced Chamberlain to wreck the League of Nations. All this sensational copy came under the headline BRITAIN'S SECRET RULERS. Harold Nicolson added intellectual weight to the campaign by alleging on 12 March 1938 in *Newsletter* that Nancy 'fought bravely for Hitler and Mussolini.' Meanwhile Low's cartoons continued to appear in the *Evening Standard*, the Shiver Sisters making a third appearance on 23 March 1938. The cartoon showed Nancy taking the salute from the Cliveden porch as some of her associates goose-stepped their way past her, whilst Shaw, wearing a bonnet, is seen crawling along in front of them. The caption read 'To mark our leader's recent successes, a party was thrown at the Cliveden nest. Nancy took the salute from the troops who were ably officered by Ladies Lothian and Grigg. Old Mother Shaw was most amusing, and Nancy's two editors, Frau Garvin and Frau Dawson, obliged with a spirited rendering of the "Horst Wessel" song.'

By March 1938 Hitler had invaded Austria and was turning his sights towards Czechoslovakia. In America, horrified at what was happening, the novelist Upton Sinclair wrote an article headed WE HAVE TRAITORS IN OUR MIDST. This was the first time that the word traitor had been applied to Nancy and she found her position growing more and more untenable.

At the end of March Stafford Cripps also attacked the Cliveden Set. He said: 'They are the people who got Viscount Halifax to go to Germany behind Eden's back. They are the people who have been entertaining Ribbentrop and making friends with many other Nazis. They are the people who are running the policy behind Chamberlain and they are the people who would like to see Britain a Fascist state as well. Chamberlain must go.'

Nancy's divorce from Robert Shaw was given an airing when the *Tribune* savagely attacked the Astors in an article entitled 'Who's Who in the Cliveden Baronage' and reporters gathered both at St James's Square and Cliveden. Continuously, Nancy denied any hint of pro-Fascist leanings and one of her many public statements, given this time on a visit to America in early 1938, read: 'I abhor Hitler and Hitlerism. I have no friendship whatever for the Nazis. I deplore the whispering campaign against me, which has now started in America.'

Philip Lothian tried to negate the rumours and was successful over a short-term period. Whilst talking in Glasgow to the Scottish Liberals in April 1938, Lothian stated:

'May I refer briefly to a widespread story about the intrigues of the so-called Cliveden Set, said to be pro-Fascist, to exercise malign and sinister influence over the Foreign Secretary and the Prime Minister. The whole thing is a mare's nest originally invented by the communist editor of the *Daily Worker* and spread in pamphlets issued by the Communist party. There is no such Set. There has to the best of my knowledge never been a meeting of the supposed principals to discuss foreign policy. On the very date meetings are alleged to have been held at Cliveden, I was in India and Lord and Lady Astor in the United States.'

Philip Lothian continued his speech by reaffirming his principles of appeasement, saying 'We cannot hope to stand up to their unreasonable demands till we have rectified their reasonable grievances.'

Both Nancy and Waldorf backed up Philip Lothian's defence by sending letters to *The Times* and the *Daily Herald*, trying to justify their belief in appeasement and denying once again any pro-Fascist or pro-Hitler sympathies. As a result of Philip Lothian's and the Astors' efforts, rumours surrounding the so-called Cliveden Set died away, only re-circulating a few months later with the Munich crisis.

In September 1938 Chamberlain returned optimistically after his famous meeting with the superficially reassuring Führer. Nancy and Waldorf shared Chamberlain's optimism and temporarily believed that their policy of appeasement had been right and all their recent suffering tenable. In the Commons, a few days later, Churchill challenged Chamberlain's reliance on Hitler's word. He started his speech by saying 'If I do not begin this afternoon by paying the almost invariable tributes to the Prime Minister for his handling of this crisis it is certainly not from any lack of personal regard.' Later he attacked: 'I will therefore begin by saying the most unpopular and the most unwelcome thing. I will begin by saying what everybody would like to ignore or forget but which must nevertheless be stated, namely that we have sustained a total and unmitigated defeat, and that France has suffered even more than we have.'

At this point Nancy very unwisely interrupted Churchill with a cry of 'nonsense'. Immediately this made Churchill's speech seem directed towards the Cliveden Set rather than to the complacency and naivety of the whole country – as it was intended to be. Churchill replied:

'When the noble lady cries "Nonsense" she could not have heard the Chancellor of the Exchequer admit in his illuminating and comprehensive speech just now that Herr Hitler had gained, in this particular leap forward, in substance all he set out to gain. The utmost my Right Honourable friend the Prime Minister has been able to secure by all his immense exertions, by all the great efforts and the mobilisation which took place in this country, and by all the anguish and strain through which we have passed in this country – the utmost he has been able to gain – '

And at this point Nancy interrupted again, drawing even more fatal attention towards herself. She shouted out, 'Is Peace.'

But Churchill was quite unruffled and calmly continued, 'I thought that I might be able to make that point in its due place when I propose to deal with it. The utmost that has been able to be gained from Czechoslovakia, and in the matters which were in dispute, has been that the German dictator instead of snatching his victuals from the table has been content to have them served to him course by course.' He went on to discuss Chamberlain's negotiations with Hitler saying that of the three occasions: '£1 was demanded at the pistol's point. When it was given £2 were demanded at the pistol's point. Finally the dictator consented to take £1.17s.6d. and the rest in promise of goodwill for the future.' Later, of Czechoslovakia, Churchill said in the full drama of his oratory: 'All is over. Silent, mournful, abandoned, broken Czechoslovakia recedes into the darkness. She has suffered in every respect by her association with the Western democracies and the League of Nations of which she has always been an obedient servant.'

Once again there was an interruption from Nancy and later on there was a further confrontation. Churchill had been saying: 'We are talking of countries which are a long way off and of which, as the Prime Minister might say, we know nothing.' Nancy then childishly shouted: 'Don't be rude about the Prime Minister.' Churchill continued: 'The noble lady says that that very harmless allusion is – ', and once again Nancy interrupted, 'Rude.' Nothing, however, and certainly not a petulant Nancy, could now put Churchill off his eloquent stride and he went on to say:

'She must very recently have been receiving her finishing course in manners. (Shouts from the Labour benches that the finishing course had come from Von Ribbentrop.) What will be the position, I want to know, of France and England next year and the year afterwards? If the Nazi dictator should choose to look westward, as he may, bitterly will France and England regret the loss of that fine army of ancient Bohemia which was estimated last week to require not fewer than thirty German divisions for its destruction.'

Nancy made no further interruption and was silent. But the damage was done and, well before Hitler had broken his Munich promises, the rumours began all over again. This time they centred on Nancy's relationship with Lindbergh, who had stayed at Cliveden following his famous solo flight across the Atlantic. In the summer of 1938 Colonel Lindbergh had accepted invitations both to Russia and to Germany. He had effectively seen through Russian propaganda – but not German. He accepted a decoration from Hitler and returned to England, declaring how much mightier was the German air-force than the RAF. Lindbergh went on to tell the press that no European combination of air-forces could possibly stand up to Hitler's air attack. Once again the press attacks descended mercilessly on Nancy's head and the chill smear of traitor swept over her and her friends again. The Cliveden Set was alive once more, and very difficult to kill.

Perversely Nancy did nothing to moderate her already unsympathetic public image. During question time, on 9 October 1938, Harold Macmillan was asked to assure the House that the refugees from the over-run Sudetenland of Czechoslovakia and, in particular, the Social Democrat Germans, were being treated well. R. A. Butler was to answer the question but Nancy leapt up first. She claimed that the Sudeten German refugees might well be Communists and should therefore be sent to Russia. Amongst cries of 'Insult' Butler replied to Macmillan's question, totally ignoring Nancy. Impetuously Nancy rose up again, demanding an answer to her question. She then went on to say that, 'Communists should be sent to a Communist country. I do not see any insult. The Communist countries would not take capitalist refugees from this country.' But Butler evaded the issue and a few days later Macmillan wrote a reprimanding letter to Nancy.

'You said in the House of Commons last week that the

Sudeten German refugees were Communists and shd. be sent
to Russia. I do not of course know the views of all the 350 for
whom the British Government had granted visas & of which
I think less than half have (I think) yet arrived.

'But we have about twelve of them here. Dorothy has just
motored 6 of them to East Grinstead to the Roman Catholic
Church; I have taken 1 to the English Parish Church; the rest
I think are cooking & cleaning.'

Macmillan went on to point out that most of the refugees
were middle class and intelligent. Indeed, one of them had been
Mayor of Aussig until a few weeks ago and another was a
leading barrister. He emphasised their quietness and cultivation
and the fact that they were bewildered and overwhelmed by
their plight. Macmillan concluded his report by grimly pointing
out that he did not see why they should be insulted in our
parliament as well.

The renewed anti-Astor campaign was now pursued vigor-
ously in England and America, climaxing in the American
Liberty magazine. Frederick L. Collins published an article
associating Lindbergh with the Cliveden Set and accrediting
them with pro-Nazi views. In desperation Nancy turned to
Shaw, asking his advice as to whether they should defend themselves – or ignore the new campaign. Gallantly, Shaw came to
Nancy's rescue on New Year's Day 1939. He wrote an answer
to Collins' article which did a good deal to take the immediate
heat out of the allegations, although, in the long term, many
people in America and England continued to believe in the
existence of the Cliveden Set. *Liberty* ran a photograph of
Nancy and Waldorf dressed in sinister and conspiratorial black.
This attempt at prejudice was blatant and there was no hint in
the caption that the reason for the Astors' sombre attire and
expression was that they were attending the funeral of Rudyard
Kipling in 1936. Part of Shaw's article read:

'Cliveden is like no other country house on earth. Mr Collins'
list of noble conspirators is authentic; but you meet these
aristocrats at Cliveden because you meet everybody worth
meeting, rich or poor, at Cliveden. You meet the Duchess of
Atholl; but then you meet also Ellen Wilkinson, the Leftest
member of the Labour Party in Parliament. You meet Colonel

Lindbergh, the friend of Herr Hitler's Chief of Staff; but you meet also Mr Charles Chaplin, whose dislike of the Nazi rule is outspoken to a degree which most seriously threatens his interests in Germany. You meet the Marquess of Londonderry, descendant of Castlereagh and so far to the Right that he was too much for even the existing "Nationalist" Cabinet, with his famous majestically beautiful wife; but then you meet also ME, an implacable and vociferous Marxist Communist of nearly sixty years' standing, with MY beautiful wife. By simply suppressing Mr Collins' list and extending my own, I can prove that Cliveden is a nest of Bolshevism, or indeed of any other bee in the world's bonnet.'

Of Nancy, Shaw said: 'She has no political philosophy and dashes at any piece of kindly social work that presents itself, whether it is an instalment of socialism or a relic of feudalism. In the House of Commons she is the most vital member and was certainly the most disorderly until her disorder became a national institution.'

Shaw concludes: 'As for deep and Machiavellian plots for the subjection of the human race, with Virginian Protestant Nancy conspiring with Hitler, I should find it far easier to suspect Roosevelt of conspiring to revoke the Declaration of Independence. I hope I have now succeeded in substituting credible portraits for the phantasms of the Cliveden legend. Never has a more senseless fable got into the headlines.'

On 15 March 1939 German troops marched into Prague, Czechoslovakia ceased to exist as an independent state and the Munich agreement was broken. Miserably, Nancy rose at question time to ask: 'Will the Prime Minister lose no time in letting the German Government know with what horror this country regards Germany's action?' But another Conservative MP Vyvyan Adams interrupted, saying 'You caused it yourself!'

In April 1939 Nancy defended herself in *Forum*. Here she openly states that her foreign policy views may well have been wrong. She continues: 'But it was right to try to the uttermost for peace . . . But who, standing in his place, would not have tried, as Chamberlain tried, to hold the wolves of war in leash?'

The appeasement policy had now been clearly wrong and Nancy bore a great deal of responsibility here. But the only

alternative to appeasement would have been immediate confrontation and Britain would not have been militarily equipped
for this at the time. Indeed the previous disarmament policy
ensured that Britain was in no position to confront anyone. At
least the policy of appeasement did give the country a vital
breathing space, even if it did mean that Czechoslovakia had
to be sacrificed in the process. But this was not what motivated
the Cliveden Set in their appeasement policy.

Public criticism deeply hurt Nancy and eventually brought
about her political eclipse. But it must be remembered that her
life was still pursued by tragedy throughout the entire period of
the allegations over the Cliveden Set. Nancy was still grieving
for Lawrence, she was still watching the grim deterioration of
Bobbie, and early in 1937 the son of her much loved sister,
Phyllis Brand, died by falling from a window in New York.
Suicide was suspected; Phyllis never recovered, and a few
months later she died from pneumonia. Nancy completely
broke down under the strain and Rose Harrison vividly describes her suffering:

'When Lady Astor heard the news she was almost out of her
mind with grief. Mr Blyth, Mrs Brand's butler, came rushing
to me and said, "Go to Lady Astor, she needs you." When I
arrived at her rooms she was screaming, crying and praying. I
took her in my arms and comforted her as best I could . . .
Somehow it worked, her sobbing quietened down and
whether it was that she had for the moment lost her inhibitions and could allow herself to give rein to other emotions
I don't know but she turned to me and kissed me. It was just
then that I knew she had affection as others had. It was just
that she thought it a weakness to show it, which of course
was nonsense; all feelings need an airing now and then.'

Nancy's last surviving brother, Buck Langhorne, also died in
1938 and this further depressed her. Jakie, her youngest son,
survived a serious motor accident in 1939 and this continuous
turmoil in her domestic life probably contributed to some of her
wilder and less calculated remarks in the Commons. But even so,
she was still at fault for completely underrating Hitler's devious-
ness. The Cliveden Set was not a pro-Nazi organization but it
was an elitist one. Figures such as Churchill had no influence at

Cliveden and it is definitely true to say that the Chamberlain government used Cliveden as a meeting place. Britain was not governed by the Cliveden group, but they did exert considerable influence. Indeed the Set were no more than the establishment itself, reflecting the mood of the country both accurately and powerfully.

Finally, it is very important to remember that much of the population of Great Britain and certainly not only the Cliveden Set, spent many of these pre-war years suffering from severe paranoia concerning the 'reds under the beds' scare. The general feeling was totally opposed to Communism in any shape or form and any Communist-opposed party, even the Nazi party, was preferable. With hindsight it is all too easy to look back on the limited but increasing hostility to the Cliveden establishment and Nancy's public débâcles with sardonic amazement that any group of people could be so obtuse as to try to trust and reconcile themselves with the policies and activities of the Führer. But the mitigating circumstances and public mood go a long way towards excusing the so-called pro-Fascist activities of Nancy Astor and her Cliveden group.

※❦❧❦※

Weakening Powers

The regular occurrence of tragedy in Nancy Astor's life, linked to the past scandals surrounding Cliveden, had thoroughly weakened Nancy's position. Had it not been for the arrival of the Second World War, she would undoubtedly have been forcibly retired from the Commons for she was now regarded as a liability in the Conservative Party. The five war years were again personally traumatic for Nancy.

Yet in many ways the war acted as a necessary distraction to her. On 23 August 1939 Philip Lothian was appointed British Ambassador in Washington. Shortly before the outbreak of war he wrote enthusiastically from the *Aquitania* to Nancy about a possible new dawn for Christian Science:

'We land tomorrow morning early. The news, as we get it by radio, seems worse & worse. At least everybody is clearly preparing for war. But I still hope that at the last moment the clouds will clear as they did last year. But you can never tell. The Bible certainly seems to prove that there will seem to be some pretty livid happenings before dawn. But we can know that none of this is going on in the Own Mind and that (if) in preparation we can purify ourselves sufficiently to reflect that Mind, "this world" will lose its power to influence & control us. Anyhow I am sure that Scientists are working far more intelligently about world affairs than they ever have before & that whatever the commotion may be through which we have to go, in reality good is coming through. We may get Union now in a new & better form.'

When war was declared Bobbie enlisted with the Scots Greys, discovered they were to abandon their horses and was transferred to a barrage balloon squadron; David took a commission in the Royal Marines; Bill went as an Intelligence Officer to the Middle East Command; Michael became an officer in the Berkshire Yeomanry and Jakie joined the Life Guards. Nancy and Waldorf again offered Cliveden as a hospital, and the Canadian Red Cross, with Astor financial backing, built a 480-bed hospital and research unit there. The Cliveden estate was also put to good purpose as an evacuee centre.

Nancy became more positive in the House of Commons after the end of the phoney war when Hitler invaded Norway. Confidence was now declining in Chamberlain's ability to lead and Nancy realised that he had to go. He was almost seventy-two now, in poor health – and Churchill was waiting in the wings. With typical forthrightness, Nancy said in the House on 11 April 1940: 'People are beginning to feel that Mr Chamberlain is not the wisest selector of men. Duds must be got rid of, even if they are one's dearest friends. And if there is a sweep, it should be a clean sweep and not musical chairs.' On 8 May 1940 the Labour Party expressed a vote of no-confidence in the Prime Minister and this was supported by 33 Conservatives including Nancy. Six Conservatives abstained. Two days later Chamberlain resigned and Churchill, whom Nancy now considered the right man for the job, took his place at the head of a Coalition government.

Meanwhile, Philip Lothian was overworking in America. He was obviously seriously ill now, but refused to recognise the symptoms. Churchill, never an admirer of Lothian, met him at Ronald and Nancy Tree's house at Ditchley near Blenheim. He found him much changed. Churchill wrote:

'Ditchley is only four or five miles away from Blenheim. In these agreeable surroundings I received the Ambassador. Lothian seemed to me a changed man. In all the years I had known him he had given me the impression of high intellectual and aristocratic detachment from vulgar affairs. Airy, viewy, aloof, dignified, censorious, yet in a light and gay manner, he had always been good company. Now, under the same hammer that smote upon us all, I found an earnest, deeply stirred man. He was primed with every aspect and detail of the American attitude. He had won nothing but goodwill and confidence in Washington by his handling of the Destroyers-cum-Bases negotiations. He was fresh from intimate contact with the President, with whom he had established a warm personal friendship. His mind was now set upon the Dollar Problem; this was grim indeed.'

Lothian wrote his last letter to Nancy on his return to the States on the 16 April. In it he said 'I am sorry to leave England. It is an inspiring place. But I know I have a job to do in USA this next year. Stick to your Science & it will see you through – with perfection as a reality in the background of your thinking. Thank you for all your help. I greatly value it.'

Nancy greatly valued Philip Lothian too. On Thursday 12 December, Philip was too ill to read a powerful address he had written and so his second-in-command, Nevile Butler, read it instead. That night Philip Lothian died from a kidney disease. He refused all medical help to the last, sticking firmly to his Christian Science beliefs. The news of his death, another in the long, relentless line of tragedies that surrounded Nancy, affected her the hardest. She never recovered from it. Her spiritual counsellor and best friend had gone. Now life was very barren and she began to rely on Shaw for counselling and help, but he was not a Scientist and was unable to fulfil Philip Lothian's spiritual role.

Stanley Baldwin realised how much Philip Lothian had meant to Nancy and wrote perceptively : 'My dear Lady Nancy. This needs no acknowledgement but I think I know what this means to you and I just want to grasp your hand for a moment. With affection and regard, S.B.' Baldwin was currently suffering a total political eclipse and so his letter, setting aside his own misery, was all the more praiseworthy.

As Mayoress of Plymouth, Nancy rightly committed herself to spending much of her time inspiring the population and the city, particularly when the German air-force began to devastate the area in March 1941. By 20 March Plymouth had undergone 37 raids with German aircraft dumping their excess bombs on the city whilst returning from Bristol or Liverpool. These, then, were indirect raids. But on that day, just after a visit from the King and Queen, the city centre of Plymouth was flattened by one of the worst air-raids on any English city during the entire course of the war. Rose Harrison remembers the raid vividly :

'The bombs and incendiaries started raining down, though fortunately not on us. Her ladyship was nowhere to be seen. Foolishly and fearlessly she and Mr Robertson (a visiting American journalist) were standing outside in the street watching it all happen – I don't know whether it was my voice that summoned him, but after a while an air raid warden came along and ordered them both into the house. It was just as well he did because as they came into the hall a stick of bombs fell nearby and blew the glass of the front door out. Both Mr Robertson and my lady had the good sense to throw themselves on the floor as they heard them coming down. I helped my lady up and we went to the shelter in the basement, with Mr Robertson sensibly following. As we were going down she was reciting the 23rd Psalm "The Lord is my shepherd : therefore can I lack nothing . . ." and when we were in the shelter she began on the 40th Psalm, "God is our hope and strength : a very present help in trouble . . ." She seemed serene and quite without fear.'

Later they put out a fire in the roof of Elliot Terrace with buckets of sand and water. The next day Nancy was suffering from delayed shock. Next morning another raid damaged the house further whilst Nancy was out visiting the ruins with Robert Menzies, the Australian Prime Minister. Rose Harrison writes that a house at the back of No. 1 Elliot Terrace had been destroyed and much of the street was in ruins. Rose began to clear up the damage in the Astor house. Then a distraught Nancy arrived :

'Just as I got to the foot of the stairs her ladyship came rushing in, she looked frantic. "Rose," she screamed, "thank God you're safe." And she flung her arms round me. "I'll never leave you again," she sobbed. My tears started to flow too though I was astonished at her outburst. It later transpired that as she approached the house she saw the shells of the buildings at the back of us and thought that we had been hit too. It was an astonishing show of emotion, particularly from my lady, but they were emotional hours when we were all on the brink of eternity.'

Nancy's reliance on Rose was increasing and Ben Robertson remembers her making this clear whilst they sat in the cellar during the air raid. He wrote: 'The air raid warden ordered Lady Astor to the basement. There she talked about Virginia and her childhood and the tobacco fields and about Rose Harrison, her maid, saying that Rose was the only woman in the world who would put up with her, and that she was the only woman in the world who would put up with Rose.'

During the raids, Nancy continued to go from shelter to shelter giving encouragement and her own brand of humour. The press reported on her activities favourably: 'Lady Astor escaped injury last night, although she worked much of it in the shelters. The townspeople call her marvellous in the way she went from shelter to shelter throughout the attack, giving encouragement and help.' She always liked to make people laugh. Seeing a man taking courage from a bottle, she said: 'You see that man standing there? Well, he can drink a couple of bottles while another man is looking for the corkscrew.'

Nancy was now sixty-two. She was dividing her time between Plymouth, the House of Commons and the Canadian hospital at Cliveden. Nancy was also obsessed by regrets over her original naivety regarding Hitler and her blind support of the appeasement policy. In a speech in Cheltenham in 1942 she said: 'When the admirals and generals and those who have been round the world warned this country not to disarm, politicians did not take their advice. This was not one person's fault. After the last war we were all striving after peace. The trouble was that we didn't understand Europe or the world as the admirals and generals did. I am afraid that I was one who was against those who didn't want us to disarm.' Nancy went on to say that she had learnt from her mistakes, but was still not prepared to believe or trust the Russians. She firmly pointed out that they were not fighting for the Allies but merely defending themselves, and that the Allies should be as wary of the Russians as they were of the Germans.

The gradual drifting apart of Nancy and Waldorf was a sad but somehow inevitable factor. He had borne so many of Nancy's friendships, but now so many of them were dead, Nancy had only Waldorf to fall back on. Whilst Philip Lothian was alive she had a spiritual guide and soul-mate. But with Philip dead all she had was a sounding board – Waldorf – and she found this extremely difficult to live with. Admittedly there was Shaw but he was a very old man and much too involved in public affairs to act as Nancy's sole confidante.

Nancy's changed attitude to Waldorf is typified by one particular and horrendous incident which started over a childish triviality. Nancy had a very sweet tooth and was passionately fond of chocolates and sweets. Having no other addictive vices this was her one outlet. Naturally war-time supplies of these goodies were rationed and an overpowering temptation was presented to her when a large parcel of chocolates arrived at Elliot Terrace from America. The idea was that they should be distributed to the people of Plymouth – an idea that Nancy tried to thwart. In the middle of a lunch party Nancy demanded some of the chocolates but Waldorf refused to accede. Nancy, careless of her embarrassed guests, flew into a rage, refusing point-blank to accompany Waldorf down to Rock, a small village in Cornwall. Here Waldorf and Nancy had been intending to stay at the home of a friend for a few days' rest. As a result of Nancy's rage, Waldorf hurriedly left the room whilst Nancy, still furious, told one of the maids to unpack her suitcase. Eventually Rose Harrison was told to do this. Whilst she was engaged in this task she was urgently called up to Waldorf's office. There she found him having a minor but painful heart attack. The rest of the account belongs to Rose's inimitable style:

' "Rose," he said, "Lady Astor has upset me badly. She now refuses to go to Rock. She must go and I need your help to see that she does." I was moved by what he said and very worried at his condition.

' "Very well, my lord, I'll see to it." I waited for the guests to leave then went into the drawing room. "I hear from Florrie, my lady, that you're not going to Rock."

' "No, I'm not," she said, rushed out of the room and up the stairs. I was ready for her and caught her on the landing. I got hold of her by the shoulders and shook her.

' "Listen to me," I said, "I don't know what you've done to his lordship, but he's now very ill indeed. You'll go with him to Rock and if you don't I'll write to all the boys and tell them that his condition is your fault because you were greedy and selfish over a few miserable sweets." Then I threw her away from me in anger and waited for the storm to burst over me. To my astonishment she looked at me meek and ashamed.

' "All right, Rose, I'll go," she said. At that moment it was hard to believe that this sorry-looking person was my heroine of a few hours before and would be again a couple of days later.'

Under Rose's duress, Nancy went to Rock with Waldorf. Without compassion, she returned the next day, leaving Rose to nurse Waldorf throughout the next six weeks. He recovered but with little thanks to Nancy. Naturally he saw no doctors, relying entirely on his faith in Christian Science to see him through.

Nancy Astor was now losing her grip and becoming a public embarrassment. For instance, in 1942, during a debate on broadcasting held by the House of Commons supply committee, she calmly warned everybody about the dangers of Catholic influence. The Foreign Office, Nancy stated, was riddled with Catholics and there were far too many of these sinister zealots in active communication with Nazi-dominated Europe. Amongst Nancy's ill-favoured Catholics were Robert Bruce Lockhart, Director of the Psychological War Executive, Ivan Kirkpatrick, Controller of the BBC's European Radio Services and his second-in-command, Harman Grisewood. But her speech of 17 February 1942 was incoherent and rambling and as a result she was dismissed by the House as a conspiracy scaremonger – which is ironic considering how badly she had suffered herself from the Cliveden Set rumours.

Waldorf fell out with Garvin on an issue concerning Churchill's suitability as Prime Minister combined with Minister of Defence (Waldorf against and Garvin for) and eventually Garvin resigned after a tribunal had been called. This tribunal had the power, under the *Observer* constitution, to arbitrate when there were irreconcilable differences between Proprietor and Editor. The tribunal found against Garvin and he decamped to the *Sunday Express*, part of the Beaverbrook empire and a newspaper sympathetic to Churchill's centralisation of power. Perhaps because of the strain of the dispute or as a result of his heart attack and slow recovery in Rock, Waldorf was now as critical of Nancy as she was impatient of him. He no longer felt so tolerant about 'managing' her faults and Waldorf watched Nancy's political disintegration with a dyspeptic eye. Although she still showed some of the old flair at winning-over audiences, she was now capable of making the most enormous gaffes as she did at a League of Nations rally later in the year. Her sentiments were abhorred by all intelligent politicians and the speech was yet another nail in Nancy's political coffin. She said : 'I am grateful to the Russians but they are not fighting for us. They are fighting for themselves. In the Battle of Britain it was America who came to our aid. The Russians were allies of Germany. It is only now that they are facing German invasion that they have come into the fight. To hear people talk, you would think they came to us in our own dire need. Nothing of the kind. It was the United States of America, and don't you forget it!'

Nancy's correspondence with Shaw continued. Charlotte was dying of a bone disease and Shaw was heartbroken. Yet he maintained an air of bravado and optimism in his letters, such as the letter he wrote to Nancy on 25 May 1942 : 'The times are changing with a vengeance,' Shaw thundered. 'Cripps, the Leader of the House, makes speeches which might be made by Stalin; and *The Times* leaders on the next day approve of every word of them. The Archbishop of Canterbury comes out with a Penguin volume advocating a full Socialist programme. Nobody expresses the least surprise.'

But Nancy, in her political and marital decline, was still deeply caring for her friends. In the summer of 1942 she invited the Shaws to Cliveden so that Charlotte could rest. Just before they came, Charlotte wrote her last letter to Nancy. It expresses well Charlotte's gratitude for Nancy's reliable and resilient kindness: Charlotte wrote: 'Nancy – dear darling I do love you. No one but you could possibly have done all this so beautifully and *happily* – I am so looking forward to getting to Cliveden and you.' She went on to talk of her own anxiety about her illness and how she was hoping that her nurse would give her courage. The letter was affectionate and touchingly humble for she concluded by pointing out that Whitehall Court (the Shaws' London home) was always available if Nancy grew tired of her ailing visitor.

In parliament, Nancy continued her trail of disaster. On 18

March 1943 in a Commons debate on proposed Foreign Office reforms, Nancy returned to a muted version of her attack on Catholics. This time she broadened the issue a little: 'The Foreign Office,' she announced, 'has been dominated by the Latin point of view. This is why the policy is dominated by France. Since the last war France has been a shell-shocked nation and everyone knows it but the Foreign Office. The Latin point of view is dangerous. What is wanted is the British point of view.'

Harold Nicolson later wrote: 'She has one of these minds that work from association to association, and therefore spreads sideways with extreme rapidity . . . It was like playing squash with a dish of scrambled eggs.'

In 1943 Nancy was involved in a black-market scandal, which, surprisingly, the press did not capitalise on. A few years before they would definitely have taken her to task but she was becoming accepted as an eccentric rather than a political force. With typical disregard for the law, Nancy asked the American Red Cross emissary to bring her in some black-market clothes from America. The letter was opened by the censor, and Nancy was summoned to appear before the Bow Street Court. She was fined £50 with £10 costs and the magistrate condemned her by saying that she had shown 'a depth of ignorance and degree of carelessness which was startling'.

The year drew to a close with the death of Charlotte Shaw and the prostration of Shaw himself. Nancy spent a great deal of time with him and helped to bolster Shaw's strong will to face up to this appalling loss. There was another heavy air raid on Plymouth and Cliveden remained full of guests. Shaw found, like Lawrence, that he was eventually unable to take the conviviality, and in reply to an invitation from Nancy, he wrote on 8 May 1944:

'Why should I come to Cliveden? I am quite well and contented here where the spring is beautiful and I can bore nobody with my old stories and general obsolescence. At Cliveden I should see Waldorf occasionally for five minutes at breakfast and you precariously for a few words later in the day when you were not away in London or Plymouth. All the rest of the time I shall be either trying to get through my

work and business out of reach of my papers and books of
reference, or trying to entertain a fearfully miscellaneous
crowd of nobodies whom your ridiculous Virginian hospitality tolerates. Now that the old round table South African
group of Curtis, Dawson, Elliot and Phil is gone I have to act
as the Cliveden Set. Do you want to kill me? But perhaps that
would be the kindest thing.'

Although Nancy was always tolerant of Shaw, she was, as
usual, religiously intolerant and when Jakie became engaged to
the daughter of the Ambassador for the Argentine Republic,
Nancy refused to acknowledge her because she was a Catholic.
She even persuaded Waldorf to stay away from the wedding,
which considerably embittered their youngest son.

To underline the by now rapid decline of Nancy's political
career, this memoir of Harold Nicolson's is particularly sadden-
ing. He recorded these comments in his diary after Nancy had
given a rambling and discordant speech at a press lunch.

'For once she had got some notes in her hand, but each note
suggested an idea and each idea some other idea, and then
that reminded her of a story her nurse had once told her in
Virginia and how little, now she came to think of it, the
British Press knew about Virginia although Sir Walter Raleigh
had colonised it and how odd that Raleigh was less well
known in England than in the United States although we
knew all about Philip Sidney not the VC of course such a nice
young man and the best type of Conservative although she
herself was not a Conservative although her husband was and
nor was Winston really since he had been a Liberal once and
oh yes she must tell them about Winston she had asked him
why he was so cold to her when she first entered the House
and he had said because I feel you have come into my bathroom and I have only a sponge with which to defend myself
not that she had not forgiven Winston we had all forgiven
Winston but it was really the Merchant Navy which had done
the great deeds where should we be without the Merchant
Navy now in Plymouth . . .

'At this stage Waldorf, who was sitting beside her, gave a

slight tug to her dress. "Now, where was I?" she said looking at her notes. "Oh yes . . ." and then she started again. This was perhaps the last speech she would make while still in the House of Commons and she had a favour to ask Winston (who had preceded her as a speaker), would he please make her a peer, as she would wake up the House of Lords as she had woken up the House of Commons, and Philip Lothian always used to say . . . At which came another tug from Waldorf, so strong that Nancy sat down suddenly with an expression of pained surprise. I suppose her rambling is amusing, but it rather saddens me, as I like her, and I wish that she would not make quite such an idiot of herself in public.'

At the end of 1944, Nancy and Waldorf were both aged 65 and this seemed an appropriate moment for retirement. Waldorf did not stand again as Lord Mayor of Plymouth, but it was Nancy who suffered the worse fate. The government announced that as soon as the fighting was over in Europe the Coalition would be disbanded and there would be a general election. Nancy was well prepared to stand again and she was completely blind to the fact that she was now regarded both nationally and locally as a liability. Waldorf realised this and in November told her that both he and the family strongly recommended that she should not stand again. Indeed he went further – should she attempt to stand he would refuse to support her. The blow to Nancy was enormous and indeed it was as deep a blow as the deaths of her parents and closest friends.

At the same time, Waldorf's decision widened the gulf between him and Nancy even more. Nancy threw herself on Shaw's sympathies but found that he was not realistically minded enough to grasp all the implications of her retirement. Eventually Shaw advised her to ask Churchill to make her a peeress but he refused to co-operate.

On Nancy's last day in Westminster she was told by a fellow member that she would be missed. She replied: 'I will miss the House; the House won't miss me. It never misses anybody. I have seen 'em all go – Lloyd George, Asquith, Baldwin, Snowden, MacDonald – and not one of them missed. The House is like a sea. MPs are like little ships that sail across it, and disappear over the horizon. Some of 'em carry a light. Others don't. That's the only difference.' But Nancy did not merely carry a light. She carried a blazing torch.

II

❀❀❀

An Extinct Volcano

Gradually, Nancy Astor had lost everything worthwhile in her life and the years between the end of the war and her death were only notable for brief revivals of her old verve – and a series of tantrums, scenes and self-indulgent remarks which nobody but Rose would tolerate.

On 7 January 1946 Nancy and Waldorf, accompanied by Rose, sailed for New York on a small freighter named the *Eros*. The waiting list for berths on the liners was considerable after the war and the *Eros* was the only expedient method of travel. But stormy seas extended the original crossing schedule of eight days to a fortnight. On her arrival Nancy told reporters that she was an 'extinct volcano'. She was later asked if she was going to become the first woman member of the House of Lords and she replied 'Winston might have done it for me, but I've no hope since this Labour Government got in.' When told that Churchill was also in the United States and asked if she was going to meet him Nancy replied : 'No, it would be a busman's holiday for both of us. He hasn't come to America to meet me.'

Nancy went on to make a number of appearances in Virginia but she received a poor press as a result of her usual mixture of spiky humour and illogical passion. The *New York Herald Tribune* sternly wrote: 'Perhaps she demonstrated, in spite of the coruscations, that her initial statement was valid, and that she, like so much else of the '20s and '30s is "extinct".'

After a visit to Lynchburg, the Astors went on to Miami, so that Waldorf could take advantage of the sun and recover from his now frequently recurring rheumatism and asthma. Even here Nancy could not avoid being tactless and when asked by the press what she thought of Savannah she abruptly replied: 'The city is very beautiful, as everybody knows it is. It's one of the most beautiful cities of America. But the way y'keep it. It's revoltin'. Never seen anything so revoltin' in m'life. Litter. Wherever y'go, there's litter. I'll tell you what I think of Savannah. I think it's a beautiful woman with a dirty face. One of the loveliest women in th'world who's forgotten to wash.'

Nancy then went on to Mirador and basked in nostalgia. But this period of introspection added nothing to her perception and at the end of April she made a speech about the colour problem which underlined Nancy's own problem – that of being completely out of touch, out of date and certainly a very extinct volcano. Addressing the Dunbar High School, which was exclusively black, Nancy told the pupils how she had come to admire the negro population through the 'Uncles' and 'Aunts' of Mirador – particularly 'Aunt Liza'. She went on to criticise the Harlem style of black life, and stated that 'no race can develop beyond its moral character.' The same problem, she pointed out, affected the white population. Finally, Nancy suggested that the problem could be solved by a return to the feudal values of years before – in other words the 'Uncle' and 'Aunt' system. Naturally, this grotesque suggestion and all that it implied was resented by pupils and black press alike. To be classified as 'Uncle Toms' and 'Aunt Lizas' in 1946 was quite ludicrous.

Meanwhile, the gulf between Nancy and Waldorf was still widening. She was bitterly angry over her forced retirement and Waldorf's refusal to support her. Waldorf still loved Nancy as much as ever but Nancy found his presence and company distasteful. In her mind he had sabotaged not just her career but her real reason for living. Her frenetic and sometimes absurd antics on this American tour, for instance, simply masked the hollowness inside her. Nancy desperately strove for as much activity as possible so that she could hide from herself the grim fact that she had no political future.

In September 1945 Shaw wrote: 'You are very puzzling about W. Have you separated? You write as if you have no latchkey of Cliveden nor he of Rest Harrow. I hope not. You will neither of you do better. But of course you should both have Sunday spouses to keep you young.'

The same year Waldorf sold 4 St James's Square to the Arts Council and bought a house at 35 Hill Street for Nancy. Waldorf now spent much of his time at Cliveden whilst Nancy remained at Rest Harrow. They now met only for public occasions and these were difficult. Nancy was lonely, depressed and lacking a spiritual confessor. She would have liked Shaw to have filled that role and tried to blackmail him into it by claiming that Charlotte had asked her to 'look after him'. Shaw however was determined that he was not going to become a counsellor and he had written, in 1945, saying 'I want you to forget and drop me because I am an old and dying man (actually I am dead and considerably decomposed) and you must find a Sunday husband young enough to last your time.'

For a brief period Nancy saw her brother-in-law, Bob Brand, as a counsellor and indeed he took a room at 35 Hill Street. But he saw her as completely prejudiced and found her views on the Catholics and the Jews quite unbearable. He also regarded Christian Science as a sham. To assuage her loneliness Nancy revisited New York in May 1947 alone and in style. She arrived on the *Queen Elizabeth* and opened her statement to the press with 'The last time I saw you disreputable fellows, I called myself an extinct volcano. That's not right. I'm not an extinct volcano, I'm a politically suppressed one.' But this tour was not as public as the first and Nancy spent most of her time at Mirador.

The years of isolation continued with Nancy doing as much as she could to fill them. She visited Germany, revisited America, and continued to search unavailingly for a counsellor. Her antipathy against Waldorf became milder but they did not become closer and Nancy's bitterness remained. Waldorf made considerable attempts to ameliorate this. For instance, he wrote to Nancy in an attempt to see if she could take an objective view of herself. Waldorf said : 'Think of the historian. Whatever you may feel about it you cannot avoid being a historic personage, and having played a historic part. This historian is now and in the future to write about you. Please please do nothing – say nothing – which may mar the historian's account.' Waldorf also tried to involve her with the political careers of their sons – Michael was Conservative MP for Surrey's Eastern division, Bill for Buckinghamshire's Wycombe division and Jakie for Nancy's old stamping ground – Plymouth Sutton division. Michael Astor writes: 'During the 1950 general election my father had asked my brothers, Bill and Jakie, and me, who were all standing as candidates, if we would each give my mother one big meeting in our constituencies. He made the point that it would comfort her to feel that she was helping her sons and at the same time give her the satisfaction of playing some part in the battle about which she felt so strongly. Also, with a certain sense of general-ship, he probably felt that a few diversionary attacks on the flanks would relieve the pressure on his own front. He was at the time held responsible by her not only for her being out of politics but also for the neutralist policy which the *Observer* was adopting towards the struggle.'

Michael agreed and went round to see Nancy in Hill Street, hoping that he could persuade her to be moderate. At first he was not reassured as Nancy stated that she was going to make a speech either rousing the women of England or alternatively denouncing the humbug of the Labour Party. Then she said :

'You've given me a good idea. I'm going to make a speech about *you*. I'll pay you out, Michael, I'll tell the meeting that politics bore you stiff, and that all you really like is paint-ing . . . or I might tell them how *privileged* they are to have the opportunity of voting for my distinguished son, how *privileged* they are to be addressed by his distinguished mother. That wouldn't rouse them; that would put 'em to sleep. Now get on with you. I must work on this. Oh dear, oh dear, I never knew that I could ever miss anything as much as the House of Commons.'

Nancy arrived at the meeting in Purley, Surrey, sitting in the back of her car reading the ninety-first psalm. Her speech turned out to be non-controversial and as her son says 'a *tour de force*, most of it improvised once she got into her stride'. He adds, 'It was enjoyable at Purley of all places – this respectable com-munity full of local intrigues and jealousies – to hear her ramming home the point that Our Lord preferred a harlot, any day, to a hypocrite. And being applauded for it.'

Nancy enjoyed this brief moment of glory. The joy of political speech-making went to her head like the wine that she had never tasted. But when it was over, the flatness of her life seemed intolerable. She returned to chivvying Shaw although he had already, in May 1949, told her firmly that she was wasting her time. On 8 May Shaw wrote saying,

'You must positively not come on the 13th. If you will not let me manage my work and my household in my own way you must not come at all. I have arranged with Mrs Laden that there are to be no visits for the next three weeks; and no visits there shall be.

'All this nonsense about my having to be looked after, and the job bequeathed to you by Charlotte, is a worn-out joke which you are beginning to believe in yourself. Let me hear no more of it. You need looking after more than I do: and nobody knew this better than Charlotte, except perhaps your unfortunate secretaries. You must upset your own household, not mine.'

At the end of September 1950 Shaw had a bad fall in his garden, breaking his leg at the thigh. In hospital it was discovered that his kidney and his bladder were damaged. He was taken back to Ayot St Lawrence to die and now Nancy could at last seize her opportunity to care for him. As far as she could Nancy organised his return from hospital, but, to her credit, she decided against seeing Shaw unless he asked for her. At last he rather testily told his nurses 'Let her come if she wants.' She did, and Shaw seemed pleased to see her. He talked a good deal to her of Charlotte and Nancy was with him to the end. On 11 November Nancy told the press: 'He gave me such a lovely smile, but he is very, very tired. I bent down and spoke to him. He said "Oh Nancy, I want to sleep, sleep." I sat beside him just gently rubbing his head to help him to sleep.' Shaw died the next morning.

At seventy-one, Nancy was now even more alone. The rift between her and Waldorf remained, her last and closest old friend was dead and she became extremely unhappy. Waldorf had also recently suffered another heart attack and he was now very much of an invalid. Nancy went to him at Cliveden where he was living on the ground floor and although he tried to persuade her to live with him there permanently, she was too restless to do so. Nevertheless, as Waldorf began to decline, their relationship became easier and less tense. To distract herself

Nancy travelled in America and Canada, although her beloved Mirador had now been sold. Nevertheless she still found a certain sense of security in America. Nancy was asked to write her autobiography and although she began the work with enthusiasm, she soon found she was unable to go beyond a draft. She asked Jakie what to call the book and he replied: 'That's easy. Call it Guilty but Insane.'

These distractions, however, were not enough, and Nancy was faced with her own bitterness and Bobbie's continuing disintegration. One of her friends, Ernesta Barlow, wrote this moving portrait of Nancy's misery in 1951:

> 'Her husband, an ill man, was unable any longer to face the flame of her vitality. He moved alone into a wing of Cliveden. On a Monday morning after a weekend at Cliveden I saw for the first time the spring of her gaiety run dry. Her eyes were red and troubled when she said goodbye to me. "Bobbie and I have been sayin' what we think of each other," she said. "I don't think it did either of us much good. But I'm not goin' to drive up to town with you after all. Waldorf may ask to see me. Sometimes he likes to have me read to him. I never know."
>
> 'I left her standing in the front door, waving her hand; after a crowded, tempestuous life, a lonely woman.'

In October 1951, Bill and Jakie were both successful in the General Election which was a Conservative victory. Winston Churchill was once again Prime Minister with a small working majority. Nancy roved restlessly from public engagement to public engagement, haunting the House of Commons, covering her all too frequent appearances with the excuse that she was visiting her sons.

Waldorf, meanwhile, was deteriorating fast and was now confined to a wheelchair. Michael Astor writes: '... his mind reverted to his earlier interests; to his horses, to forestry, and the business of running his estate. The sternness which as a child I had found disconcerting had evaporated. Instead, his innate gentleness and his consideration for other people made him a delightful man to meet.'

On 30 September 1952 Waldorf died and was buried at Cliveden. Their son, William, became Viscount and went to live there. Despite their rift, Nancy was profoundly shocked and she wrote, with considerable honesty, to Thomas Jones: 'We had 40 happy years together. No two people ever worked harder than we did – These last 7 years have been heart-breaking – but thank God he was like his old self the last ten days and oh how it makes me grieve of the years wasted!' Nancy's desolation was partially eased by Mrs Judy Musters, Shaw's cousin. Mrs Musters had helped Shaw secretarially and she began to correspond with Nancy after Shaw's death. She was sympathetic to Christian Science, rigidly opposed to Catholicism and therefore an ideal spiritual companion for Nancy.

When not communing with Mrs Musters, Nancy travelled to America, to Africa and back to America again. Then, in 1954, Richard Aldington's critical biography of Lawrence appeared in Paris. This attack on Lawrence was a severe blow to Nancy and she began a campaign in association with Basil Liddell Hart to prevent the book's publication in England. In the book's introductory letter to Alister Kershaw, Aldington wrote:

'Gradually as I went more closely into the material available I came to the conclusion that this Egypt affair is not a regrettable exception. On the contrary it is one more example of a systematic falsification and over-valuing of himself and his achievements which Lawrence practised from an early date. In other words the national hero turned out at least half a fraud ... As I investigated the strange and tortuous psychology of this extraordinary man, I felt more and more convinced that some time in his early life he had been dealt a terrific blow by Fate, some humiliating and painful wound which he was always trying to compensate. In spite of the newspapers, he was something of a mystery man, there was a secret somewhere. You will recollect that a friend of ours hinted strongly to us of a family scandal, and that I refused at first to believe it. Further investigations showed that these hints were well-founded, and the secret which oppressed Lawrence's life was the fact of his birth.'

It is true that Lawrence was illegitimate, but it was basically homosexuality and masochism that oppressed him. Nevertheless Nancy was determined not to allow the book's publication in England, basing her case on the fact that Lawrence's mother was still alive and that the potential English publishers would be subject to libel proceedings. Unfortunately Thomas Jones had already revealed Lawrence's illegitimacy in his *Diary with Letters*, although he had not known Mrs Lawrence to be still alive. In 1955 the book was published in England by Collins and no libel proceedings took place.

Frustrated by the demythologising of Lawrence, Nancy continued her restless travelling, mainly to America. She sold Hill Street and moved into a flat at 100 Eaton Square, with Bob Brand taking some of the rooms. Nancy regularly visited Cliveden and Maurice Collis, who was about to become her biographer, has some vivid memories of her there. At one dinner party he remembers 'Old Lady Astor sat at the far end, with the King on her right and Lord Hailey on her left. We had soup, lobster, grouse, an iced sweet, a savoury, fruit, coffee. Sherry, sauterne, port and kummel were offered. Lady Astor, as was her wont, tended to monopolise conversation. She found it hard, apparently, to forget that she had been for so many years Cliveden's famous hostess.' Strangely, Nancy now relaxed her prohibition views and took a little Dubonnet from time to time. This partially shocked and partially amused the family.

Writing in his diaries, Collis remembers Nancy's habit of reminiscence :

'Lady Astor, having the King and Lord Hailey by her, exerted herself to amuse. She told of her famous visit to Moscow with Bernard Shaw. The things she said straight out to Stalin were staggering. "Your regime is no different from the Czars." "Why?" "Because you dispose of your opponents without trial." Stalin laughed. "Of course." She also spoke of Bernard Shaw's last illness. "I went to see him the day before he died. I sat by him stroking his head. He was quite clear." '

Nancy went on to tell them an anecdote Shaw had told her before he died. Then she turned to King Gustav of Sweden and told him it was time for him to go to bed. How typical of Nancy is Collis's description. At seventy-nine she was still outrageous, still exaggerating yet still truthful about her friends.

On 19 May 1959 Nancy was eighty. She was made a Freeman of the City of Plymouth which delighted her and for a while she was happier. In 1960 she saw Terence Rattigan's sympathetic portrait of Lawrence in his play *Ross* and felt that Lawrence's reputation had been regilded a little. By 1963, Nancy's memory began to fail and although she eventually found out about the Profumo affair, which the family had been carefully keeping from her, she was too muddled to relate properly to it – which everyone found a thankful relief.

In the summer of 1963 Bob Brand died – his death severing her last link with the Kindergarten. The next spring Bobbie tried to commit suicide. Nancy, who was staying in the South of France with Wissie at the time, was told that he had had a stroke. Nancy returned to England and went to see Bobbie in hospital. She must have guessed that the stroke was only a cover story and she returned home defeated and deeply shocked.

A few weeks later, Nancy suffered a stroke herself. Shortly afterwards it was clear that she was dying.

Michael Astor wrote in his diary on 21 April: 'I could see her quietly, gently, uncertainly dying: going at no particular pace, but dying in the same way as she (particularly as a young woman) must have done much of her living, unevenly, at different paces. Dying, gliding, reviving, trying, submitting. What a relief to see her not struggling.'

Christian Science helped her to the end and Waldorf was much in her thoughts. She woke crying his name and obviously her mind was far back in the former solidarity of their relationship. On 30 April 1964, Michael Astor read his mother the 23rd Psalm and he later recalled: 'Mother seemed to be living already on another plane, and the practical and mundane observations of her nurse seemed out of place in the room. I had the feeling that she was free of relationships. At last . . . She seemed to be searching for an essence, not a person. Or was this my imagination? She gave me the feeling of someone who was moving or attuned to very simple values and to a belief in spiritual existence.'

Later she asked Jakie 'Am I dying or is this my birthday?' He replied 'A bit of both.' Then on the afternoon of 1 May 1964 she uttered her last word, 'Waldorf'. Rose Harrison was with her as she lapsed into her final coma. In the early morning of Saturday 2 May, the invincible Nancy Astor died. She was buried at Cliveden in the same grave as Waldorf and on 13 May there was a memorial service held for her in Westminster

Abbey. There was a distinguished gathering including Sir Alec Douglas Home, Harold Macmillan and representatives of the Royal Family. Nancy would have been further delighted by the presence of the Speaker of the House of Commons, symbolising the place where she had her achievements, her disasters and where all her ambitions lay. The House of Commons had been her real spiritual home – a home that she had sadly missed for so many years.

Postscript

Nancy made little impact in her political career and she only technically advanced the feminist cause by the fact of being the very first woman MP. Her fight against social injustice could have been more decisive if only she had not been so immersed in trying to bring prohibition to England. Even Nancy realised that this was more of an ideal than a practicality but her insistence on driving on with minor but time-consuming anti-drink legislation still bogged her down.

She used Christian Science to suit her own needs and to boost her own inadequacies. Nevertheless she still kept strongly to the faith that she had contrived and by anyone's lights was definitely both pious and deeply spiritual. Nancy's life was one of spiritual search and, as we have seen, Michael Astor believes that towards the end of her life she may have found peace. But it was peace with essence, not people. Nancy could never be at peace with people. Nevertheless, her relationships were the most important part of her life. With Philip Lothian she had a deep and consistent platonic love which was reciprocated. He made no sexual demands on her, and because of this Nancy felt safe. With Billy and Julian Grenfell, T. E. Lawrence and Bernard Shaw she had the same, safe platonic love affairs. They were on a more superficial level than Lothian but still very consuming in their intensity. Nancy treated these friends extremely well and her loyalty could be relied on in any hour of need. To them all she represented a power house of verve, courage and energy which is why she attracted their friendship. The Astor influence also played its part in the case of Shaw and, to a lesser extent, the socially conscious Lawrence.

Nancy may well have been a loyal friend but she could also be very possessive. Lord Revelstoke and Angus McDonnell were the highest on her list of victims and McDonnell suffered twice over from Nancy's quite unreasonable bullying. Waldorf also suffered at the hands of Nancy but more from neglect. He was undemanding and the only man with whom Nancy was not frightened to have sexual intercourse. On this basis, Waldorf had no reason to be jealous of other men as lovers but he had every reason to be disturbed by the intense friendships from which he was excluded. At the same time he had to stage-manage Nancy's political career which was rather like trying to steer an unnavigable sailing dinghy in a typhoon. Eventually Waldorf also had to forcibly close that political career and face the inevitable consequences of Nancy's bitterness. Yet she did love him in her own way and at least she made him happy for much of his life. She also made his children happy and she was not possessive with them. One child, of course, she could never make happy : Bobbie spent much of his life in deep depression, pursuing a course of self-destruction. He was the Achilles heel to Nancy's fortress of energy and was capable of wounding his mother far more than anyone else could.

The last few years of Nancy Astor's life were spent miserably alone. She was without influence and her friends and husband were dead. In British political life Nancy had been an outside force, a unique and erratic wind storm that was entirely memorable. Now she was spent. Overlaying all her aspirations and idiosyncrasies had been her search for the 'Secret Way'. As she wrote to Philip Lothian :

> You and I have found the secret way,
> No one shall hinder us or say us nay.
> All the world may stare and never know
> You and I are twined together so.

But it was not with Philip Lothian that Nancy was to find the secret way. It was through her own tangled and often tragic life. Harold Nicolson said of her, 'There is something about her, a flame somewhere.' This exactly describes the effect that Nancy had on herself and others. She burnt herself up as she burnt up those closest to her. The flame was erratic, unpredictable and never controlled. Had it been so, then Nancy could have been a brilliant politician of lasting value. But instead, whim, caprice and ineffective idealism destroyed this potential.

Waldorf's dying words to his son William were 'Look after your mother.' But this was a very daunting task, for Nancy was not the kind of person who could easily be 'looked after'. In fact the only person who could do this effectively was the devoted Rose, who was with Nancy to the end. This account by Rose of Nancy's behaviour is consistent with her entire life:

> 'Let me not though become too introspective on her behalf. She still had plenty of spirit and fun in her and she remained a formidable lady to serve. She and I continued to battle on together. She didn't give up trying to outdo and better me till the end. I have a letter she wrote me only three years before her death in which, after giving me a bit of praise and urging me to return before the end of my holiday, she went on to say, "There's one thing I feel I must ask you Rose, and that is not to interrupt me before I've finished speaking. It's a very bad habit of yours, you know." That after thirty-two years of my doing it!'

It was Rose who most intimately witnessed her 'lady's' growing isolation and misery. Nancy's faith was considerably tested by her loneliness. In a letter to Douglas Pitt she wrote bitterly, 'Oh, how I miss my Waldorf, my Phyllis, and my whole family who have gone. . . . Where do we go? No one knows – and no one has come back.' One of her friends, Ella Smith, writes with irony, 'Nanny was a devout Christian Scientist, but not a good one. She kept confusing herself with God. She didn't know when to step aside and give God a chance.'

On her death-bed Nancy Astor may well have found what she had been searching for. Like Michael Astor, I would like to think she did.

Select Bibliography

ADLINGTON, RICHARD, *Lawrence of Arabia*, London 1955

ASQUITH, LADY CYNTHIA, *Diaries 1915–1918*, London 1968

ASTOR, MICHAEL, *Tribal Feeling*, London 1963

BIRKENHEAD, LORD, *Halifax*, London 1965

BROOKES, PAMELA, *Women in Westminster*, London 1956

BULLOCK, ALAN, *Hitler: A Study in Tyranny*, London 1962

BUTLER, SIR JAMES, *Life of Lord Lothian*, London 1960

COCKBURN, CLAUD, *Crossing the Line*, London 1958

COLLIS, LOUISE (ED.), *Maurice Collis. Diaries 1949–1969*, London 1977

COLLIS, MAURICE, *Nancy Astor: An Informal Biography*, London 1960

COLVIN, IAN, *The Chamberlain Cabinet*, London 1971

ERVINE, SIR JOHN, *George Bernard Shaw, His Life, Work and Friends*, London 1956

GARNETT, DAVID, *T. E. Lawrence*, London 1938

GILBERT, MARTIN, *The Roots of Appeasement*, London 1966

GILBERT, MARTIN, *Winston S. Churchill Vol V 1922–1939*, London 1976

GOLLIN, ALFRED M., *The Observer and J. L. Garvin 1908–1914*, London 1960

GREEN, MARTIN, *Children of the Sun*, London 1977

HARRISON, ROSINA, *Rose: My Life in Service*, London 1975

HENNESSY, JAMES POPE, *Queen Mary*, London 1959

HOLROYD, MICHAEL, *Lytton Strachey*, London 1967

JONES, DR THOMAS, *Diary with Letters 1931–1950*, London 1954

JONES, DR THOMAS, *Whitehall Diary Vol II 1926–1930* (edited by Keith Middlemass), London 1969

KAVALER, LUCY, *The Astors: A Family Chronicle*, London 1966

KNIGHTLEY, PHILIP and SIMPSON, COLIN, *The Secret Lives of Lawrence of Arabia*, London 1969

LANGHORNE, ELIZABETH, *Nancy Astor and her Friends*, New York 1974

LAWRENCE, A. W. (ED), *T. E. Lawrence by his Friends*, London 1937

LEHR, ELIZABETH DREXEL, *King Lehr and the Gilded Age*, London 1935

LESLIE, ANITA, *Edwardians in Love*, London 1972

LLOYD GEORGE, DAVID, *The Truth About the Peace Treaty*, London 1938

MACK, JOHN E., *A Prince of our Disorder*, London 1976

MARGETSON, STELLA, *The Long Party*, London 1974

MARTIN, RALPH G., *Lady Randolph Churchill Vol I 1854–1895*, London 1969

MARTIN, RALPH G., *Lady Randolph Churchill Vol II 1895–1921*, London 1969

NICOLSON, HAROLD, *Diaries and Letters 1939–1945*, London 1967

NIMOCKS, PROFESSOR WALTER, *Milner's Young Men*, New York 1968

OWEN, FRANK, *Tempestuous Journey*, London 1954

ROBERTSON-SCOTT, J. W., *Life and Death of a Newspaper*, London 1952

SPEAIGHT, ROBERT, *The Life of Hilaire Belloc*, London 1957

STEWART, DESMOND, *T. E. Lawrence*, London 1977

SYKES, CHRISTOPHER, *Troubled Loyalty*, London 1969

SYKES, CHRISTOPHER, *Nancy: The Life of Lady Astor*, London 1972

WAUGH, EVELYN, *Ronald Knox*, London 1959

INDEX

'N.' stands for Nancy Astor.